c. 3

McCarthyism and New York's Hearst Press

A Study of Roles in the Witch Hunt

Jim Tuck

D1264695

University Press of America, Inc.
Lanham • New York • London

Copyright © 1995 by
University Press of America,® Inc.
4720 Boston Way
Lanham, Maryland 20706

3 Henrietta Street
London, WC2E 8LU England

Library of Congress Cataloging-in-Publication Data

Tuck, Jim.
McCarthyism and New York's Hearst press: a study of roles in the
witch hunt / Jim Tuck
p.   cm.
Includes bibliographical references and index.
1. Anti-Communist movements--United States. 2. McCarthy, Joseph,
1908 -1957. 3. Press and politics--New York (N.Y.)--History--20th
century.   I. Title.
E743.5.T83   1995   071',471--dc20   95-3171
CIP

ISBN 0-8191-9877-3 (cloth: alk. paper)
ISBN 0-8191-9878-1 (pbk: alk. paper)

To Jim Compton and the late Jim Blessing
The "Tucson Two"
Who Confronted McCarthyism in the Trenches

"Let me tell you of two teachers,
Comp and Blessing were their names,
They stood up to the fearmakers
And refused to play their games.
Two men who valued freedom,
Oh, they knew what to do,
And we'll fight McCarthy's witch hunt
As we back the Tucson Two."

From "The Ballad of the Tucson Two"

Contents

Preface

If Senator Joe McCarthy was the best-known individual representative of the post-World War II heresy hunt, its leading media representative was the Hearst publishing empire. My focus in this study is on the segment of that empire which operated in New York between 1942-57, from the beginning of the Second World War to the death of Joe McCarthy. There the local Hearst papers were the flagship *Journal-American* and the tabloid *Mirror,* which served as main base for the dreaded Walter Winchell.

For Hearst's anti-communist crusaders, New York was a headquarters and political nerve center during this decade and a half. The massive files of J. B. Matthews, Red fronter turned Red hunter, were stored in the Hearst Building on Eighth Avenue. The city also harbored an elite of hardline anti-communist intellectuals and activists. For strategy sessions they would meet in Matthews's London Terrace penthouse. On more relaxed occasions some convened at the Stork Club, where they were frequently joined by such influential allies as Joe McCarthy, J. Edgar Hoover, and Roy Cohn.

Though my newspaper source material derives almost exclusively from the *Journal-American* and *Mirror,* I have not ignored the broader implications of the Hearst-McCarthy relationship. An important theme in this work is the alliance between McCarthy and the Hearst organization that began shortly after his February 1950 speech at Wheeling, West Virginia, and ended with McCarthy's censure in December 1954. The progress of this alliance can be charted by concentrating on the New York papers alone. The best-known *Journal-American* and *Mirror* columns were replicated throughout the Hearst chain and William Randolph Hearst Jr.'s "dispersal of power" policy, announced in 1951, applied almost exclusively to coverage of local news.

Today, many who recall the McCarthy era somehow assume that McCarthy and the Hearst press marched in lockstep against their enemies.

Such a view is misguided. If there was a dominant characteristic of the Hearst-McCarthy relationship, it was its uneven and dysfunctional nature. In one of his earliest political pronouncements, McCarthy attacked Republican presidential candidate Alfred M. Landon as "William Randolph Hearst's puppet." In 1946, when the Hearst press was denouncing Soviet expansionism, McCarthy was praising Stalin's disarmament plan. In 1955, when a trio of top Hearst executives paid a friendly visit to Moscow, McCarthy was branding even Republican rightists as soft on communism.

I begin with an assessment of William Randolph Hearst's role as pioneer of the Cold War. That role dates back to the beginning of World War II. At a time when generals and industrialists vied with each other in lauding the Russian military effort, the Hearst press viewed our Soviet ally with the most jaundiced eye. Particular attention is directed to the writings of Benjamin De Casseres and Westbrook Pegler, and to why they can rightly be considered as point men of the Cold War.

The next focus is on the 1946-49 period of "pre-McCarthy McCarthyism," when leading exponents of hard-line anti-communism were Parnell Thomas, Rankin of Mississippi, Richard Nixon, and J. Edgar Hoover. During this period the Hearst press played a strong activist role in the Red hunt while McCarthy's anti-communism was opportunistic, perfunctory, and related mainly to his own concerns. He virtually ignored controversies as burning as the Hiss case and the trial of Cardinal Mindszenty – causes célèbres in the Hearst press – and concentrated all his energies on minor issues that had little to do with communism as a global threat.

Then came McCarthy's celebrated February 9, 1950 speech in Wheeling, West Virginia, when he announced that he had the names of 205 Communists who were still working and shaping policy in the State Department. This was the prelude to a three-year Hearst-McCarthy honeymoon, as McCarthy completely embraced the Hearstian agenda on communism and was rewarded by unqualified editorial and column support in the Hearst papers.

In 1953 some of the *Journal-American* columnists broke ranks and began to criticize McCarthy. This defection was by no means unanimous: Westbrook Pegler and E. F. Tompkins defended him to the end while William Randolph Hearst Jr. occasionally chided him in signed editorials and Frank Conniff moved from strong support to outright opposition. Nineteen fifty-four witnessed a further disintegration of the Hearst-McCarthy entente, as former supporters among Hearst writers were repelled by his humiliation of General Ralph Zwicker and his conduct during the Army-McCarthy hearings.

The final phase begins with McCarthy's censure in December 1954 and ends with his death in 1957. The Hearst press was then cautiously edging toward the Republican mainstream, to the point of advocating coexistence with the Soviets after a trip to Moscow by Hearst Jr. and two top aides. McCarthy, by contrast, had become so reckless and alcoholically irrational that his accusations of "communist appeasement" extended even to Republican right-wingers. By the time of McCarthy's death, both the *Journal-American* and *Mirror* were fully committed to the prevailing policy of subjecting the Wisconsin senator to a press "brownout," in which his utterances and actions received minimal attention.

Scrutiny of this strange alliance discloses an interesting irony: that the Hearst press was both *more* and *less* "McCarthyish" than McCarthy himself: more so in the pre-Wheeling period; less so in the last years between McCarthy's censure and death.

An epilogue examines McCarthy as redbaiter and seeks to define the precise nature of his anti-communism. The conclusion is that it was volatile, changeable, and strongly tinged with ethnic prejudice – a prejudice directed far more against privileged WASPs than against minorities. A mind-set of this nature explains such anomalies as McCarthy's courtesy to black witnesses with clearly defined pro-communist backgrounds while he savaged such strongly anti-communist Ivy League WASPs as Dean Acheson and Reed Harris.

This work seeks to engage not only scholars but also thoughtful laypersons who, with the advent of films like *Guilty by Suspicion* and *Citizen Cohn,* are increasingly curious about the McCarthy era and the Hearst press's role during this disquieting period in our history.

In many ways, this project was a researcher's dream. I estimate that 70 to 75 percent of my source material derived from microfilmed back copies of the *Journal-American* and *Mirror,* these stored in the Annex of the New York Public Library till 1991, at which time the collection was moved to the Main Building. Aided by the efficient and courteous staff at both facilities, I was able, in the course of two extended research trips, to take over thirty thousand words of notes.

As heavily as I relied on newspaper material, completion of this work would not have been possible without the help of several leading academic specialists on the McCarthy era. I particularly wish to thank Professor David M. Oshinsky of the History Department at Rutgers

University. Dave has been unfailingly generous with his time and sage in his advice. I have also benefited from correspondence with Professors Richard M. Fried, Michael O'Brien, and Thomas C. Reeves. All have written authoritative works on the life and career of Joe McCarthy. In New York I am indebted to Ronald Radosh, David Evanier of the Anti-Defamation League, and Thomas A. Bolan, conservative activist and former law partner of Roy Cohn. Mr. Evanier was kind enough to make available vital material from ADL's files and Mr. Bolan, from his unique vantage point, furnished me with a wealth of useful insights.

Locally, my work was made easier through the cooperation of María Elena Saucedo, Director of the Benjamin Franklin Library in Guadalajara, Mexico. It was through this United States Information Service-sponsored facility that I obtained transcripts of testimony before McCarthy's committee by Reed Harris, William Marx Mandell, Langston Hughes, and Eslanda Robeson.

As publishing moves inexorably into the electronic age, many typewriter generation authors are increasingly finding themselves left at the post. Thanks to the industry and camera-ready expertise of Carol Wheeler Esparza, I have been spared this unenviable fate.

Finally, for her patience, moral support, and contributions to furnishing an environment friendly to the creative process, a heartfelt expression of gratitude goes to my wife.

1. The Cold War Within the Hot War: Hearst as Pioneer

When William Randolph Hearst died at the advanced age of eighty-eight, he was regarded by many Americans as a grotesquely dinosauric figure – part sinister and part comic. His flamboyantly extravagant lifestyle, his extreme-right politics, his espousal of public morality while living openly with his mistress – all these combined to make him, in the eyes of progressives, an odious symbol of everything that America could profitably do without.

Hearst was consistent only in that he was always capable of making enemies. There consistency ended. The enemies of Hearst's youth were a far different breed from those of his old age. Where antagonists of the 1930s and 1940s damned Hearst as an isolationist, reactionary, and red-baiter, turn-of-the-century foes condemned him with equal fervor as an internationalist, radical, and socialist.

They did so with good reason. Though born to wealth, Hearst in his youth was a populist *enfant terrible.* In 1887, at the age of twenty-four, he took over his father's money-losing paper, the *San Francisco Examiner.* The young publisher immediately launched crusades against two local corporate Goliaths, the Spring Valley Water Company and the Southern Pacific Railroad. The former, a private monopoly, was accused of bribing city supervisors to keep San Francisco's water rates unreasonably high. Hearst's campaign was so successful that Spring Valley finally knuckled under and agreed to a 16 percent reduction.[1]

In the fight against Southern Pacific, Hearst enlisted the acid pen of Ambrose Bierce. Like Spring Valley, Southern Pacific charged its users exorbitant rates. In return, it furnished wretched service – service characterized by multiple safety violations, shoddy equipment, and chronic tardiness. This gave Bierce the ammunition he needed. In his diatribes against the railroad, Bierce's prime targets were SP's miserly CEO, Collis P. Huntington, and his partner, Leland Stanford, who was then serving a term in the U.S. Senate. (The other California senator was Hearst's father.) "Let £eland $tanford (as Bierce always wrote his name) remove his dull face from the United States Senate and exert some of his boasted 'executive ability' disentangling the complexities in which his frankly brainless subordinates have involved the movements of his trains."[2]

Hearst did not confine his crusading zeal to attacks on corporate malefactors. A Democrat, he scored his own party for being unresponsive to the people's needs. As far back as 1884, he favored union labor and came out for such radical proposals as the eight-hour day, the graduated income tax, and popular election of United States senators. As W. A. Swanberg comments: "The San Francisco upper crust eyed him with suspicion and began to fasten on him what was then a dirty word: Socialist."[3]

Even Hearst's imperialism and jingoism had a radical tinge. In 1897 the Dreyfus case was at its height. Infuriated with the French government for its treatment of the unjustly accused officer, Hearst considered a plan to rescue Dreyfus from Devil's Island.[4]

In the same year, Hearst was putting maximum pressure on the newly-elected President William McKinley to go to war with Spain over Cuba. The Hearst chain had expanded and one of its properties was the *New York Journal*. The *Journal* saw war with Spain as a class issue – something demanded by the justice-loving masses and opposed only by "bloated Wall Streeters who feared that war would upset the market."[5]

Hearst was elected to Congress in 1902. By then he legally resided in New York and was a member of the state's delegation. In Congress Hearst did nothing to detract from his wild man image. He reiterated his support for the eight-hour day, the graduated income tax, and popular election of United States senators, explaining that this would make them more responsive to the people and less "subservient to big business."[6] Hearst's ultraconservative foes had long accused him of leaning toward socialism. But the epithet, as they used it, could cover advocacy of the most mildly liberal legislation. Now Hearst, as if to confirm their wildest fears, actually took a plunge into socialism. He called for government ownership of railroads and telegraphs and even suggested that nationalization of mines be considered.[7]

Hearst saw his House seat as a springboard to the White House. At the

1904 Democratic convention he was bested by Judge Alton B. Parker, a conservative supporter of the gold standard. In 1905 he ran for mayor of New York against George B. McClellan Jr., son of the Civil War general and protegé of Tammany boss Charles F. Murphy. Attesting to Hearst's radicalism was a *New York Times* cartoon bearing the caption "Under Which Flag Do You Vote?" McClellan's likeness appeared under Old Glory and Hearst's under a red banner.[8] In an election marked by the use of Tammany "repeaters" and attacks on Hearst election watchers, McClellan squeaked through by a narrow margin.[9]

During the First World War Hearst was unjustly accused of being pro-German. His opposition to America's entry into the conflict stemmed not from any love of Kaiserism but from a populist animus against big bankers, particularly the Morgan interests. Hearst felt the bankers were trying to drag America into the war to protect the huge loans they had made to the Allies.[10] To his credit, Hearst also tried to combat the anti-German hysteria that was sweeping the country – hysteria that caused people to insult fellow Americans with German names, to kick dachshunds, and to call sauerkraut "liberty cabbage."

Hearst's move to the right was no overnight conversion. It was, rather, a prolonged, tortuous, two-steps-right-and-one-step-left process that consumed almost two decades.

In 1919 Hearst opposed the Boston police strike and the unionization of editorial workers. By 1923 he had reversed himself on the graduated income tax and come out for a sales tax.[11] But much of his liberalism remained. During the 1924 election he made what amounted to a plague-on-all-three of your houses statement. Calvin Coolidge and John W. Davis, the Republican and Democratic candidates, were "too conservative" while the Progressive candidate, Robert M. La Follette, was a "little too radical."[12]

In 1926 Hearst backed wealthy Ogden Mills in his gubernatorial race against Al Smith. Too much should not be made of this. Hearst and Smith hated each other, and, as W. A. Swanberg wryly observed, Hearst "doubtless would have backed W. C. Fields if he was running against Smith."[13]

The last hurrah of Hearst's liberalism came in 1932, when he swung the California delegation behind Franklin Roosevelt. Personal feelings may have had something to do with this. Hearst detested Herbert Hoover, FDR's 1932 opponent, and described him in a letter to movie mogul Louis B. Mayer as "selfish and stupid" and one who will "handicap the whole conservative movement, and strengthen the hand of the radicals."[14]

Hearst supported Alfred M. Landon against Roosevelt in 1936. He backed Franco during the Spanish Civil War, opposed Upton Sinclair's bid for the California governorship, fought the Newspaper Guild and the San Francisco longshoremen's strike, and viewed the rise of fascism, if not with approval, at least with equanimity. His particular *bêtes noires* were communism (Communists were strong in the Newspaper Guild) and what he described as "confiscatory" taxation.[15]

By 1937 he was the most hated man in America along a spectrum ranging from liberal to extreme left. The Hearst-Metrotone newsreel was hissed in movie theaters, boycotts were urged against the Hearst papers, and organizations that condemned the publisher included the American Federation of Teachers, the Farmer-Labor Party of Minnesota, the United Automobile Workers, and the Communist-dominated American League Against War and Fascism.[16]

Hearst's move to the right was not a pure exercise in ideology. In the late 1930s his empire was on the brink of collapse. Driven to the wall by "confiscatory" taxes and his own extravagance, he was "shorn of financial control, bankrupted out of Hollywood... and auctioneers were putting his treasures under the hammer." At one point the seventy-five-year-old man was reduced to soliciting a million dollar loan from his mistress, Marion Davies, whose financial acumen was sharper than his own.[17]

The publisher survived disaster due, ironically, to the war he had so vociferously opposed. The wartime boom and a dramatic rise in circulation and advertising turned the tide. Though the Hearst holdings had been reduced by 40 percent, the rump organization that survived was lean, mean, and efficient. By 1942, America's first year at war, Hearst was back in the black.[18]

Hearst's close brush with calamity fortified his already existing prejudice against ideological systems dedicated to his impoverishment. The New Deal was one; Soviet Communism was another. It was with this monomania that William Randolph Hearst contemplated Soviet-American relations as the United States entered the Second World War.

When we ponder the world-wide triumph of de-Stalinization, it is difficult to imagine the outpouring of good will that Americans lavished on Stalin's Russia in the early days of World War II.

Everywhere the paranoid dictator was affectionately referred to as "Uncle Joe" or "Good Old Joe." This misplaced esteem was by no means limited to the left or even the center. Also vociferous in praise of Stalin were such traditional-conservative figures as generals, industrialists, and members of the DAR. In January 1942, from his stronghold on Bataan, General Douglas MacArthur issued a communique stating that "the hopes of civilization rest on the worthy banners of the courageous Russian Army."[19]

Equally mesmerized was the Luce publishing empire. In 1942 *Time* named Stalin Man of the Year. Throughout 1942 and 1943 Luce publications "described a valiant and suffering people. The political and economic characteristics of the Soviet Union were ignored. So was the ruthlessness of her leader, Joseph Stalin... The famines and the purges of the 1930s, even the Nazi-Russian pact was explained away."[20]

Even such an implacable foe of communism as New York Archbishop (later Cardinal) Francis Spellman accommodated himself to the climate of the times. In September 1943, following a meeting with Roosevelt, Spellman sent a two-page memorandum to the Vatican. In it he tacitly urged papal acceptance of an international order controlled by the Big Four (with smaller nations virtually powerless) and a Russian-dominated regime in Austria.[21] In November, during the Tehran conference, Spellman arranged a secret meeting with Andrei Smirnov, Soviet ambassador to Iran. "Implicit was the possibility of a relaxation in Vatican-Soviet relations."[22]

These conservatives' wartime benevolence toward the Soviet regime had nothing to do with pro-communism. Far from going over to Stalin, many of them mistakenly thought that he was going over to them. Approvingly they noted Stalin's use of nationalist slogans, the relaxation of restrictions against the Orthodox Church, and the introduction of Guards divisions into the Red Army. In 1943 *Time* optimistically discerned "signs that the Russians were abandoning their support for revolution abroad while encouraging political liberties at home."[23]

Of these high-level Russophiles, even the most slavish apologist for the Soviet system rejected communism as a solution to America's problems. Joseph E. Davies, American ambassador to the Soviet Union between 1936-38, wrote a book about his experiences called *Mission to Moscow*. In this naive and damaging work, published in 1941, Davies rhapsodized over Stalin, defended the Moscow Trials, and made the astounding assertion that "the Christian religion could be imposed upon Russian Communism" because both precepts are based on "the brotherhood of man."[24] Yet even Davies affirmed that "the essentially religious character of our people" made impossible "the spread of communism over here."[25]

And what of the minority who rejected Soviet-American amity in those early war years? A lonely and unpopular band, they could not even be called premature anti-communists. Equally anti-communist were the press lords, generals, and big business executives who innocently believed they were winning Stalin over to American values. A better term would be premature cold warriors, people who discerned the Soviet menace even as we were allied with the Soviet government. The premature cold warriors had a voice in what was then known as the Hearst-Patterson-McCormick press. A loose, interlocking, hydra-headed entity, its four leading figures were a brother and a sister, their first cousin, and Hearst. Hearst was connected through original ownership of two Washington papers that were leased, then bought and combined, by the sister, Eleanor Medill ("Cissy") Patterson. The brother was Joseph Medill Patterson, publisher of the *New York Daily News,* and the cousin was Robert R. ("Bertie") McCormick, publisher of the *Chicago Tribune.*

McCormick alone was a consistent reactionary. Joe Patterson had been a Socialist, campaign manager for Eugene Debs, and Cissy supported the New Deal in three elections. With Hearst's antecedents we are familiar. As in Hearst's case, Cissy and Joe's anti-Soviet fervor was intensified by disillusionment with the left.

Of the four, Hearst was unquestionably *primus inter pares.* Though diminished, his empire dwarfed the Patterson-McCormick holdings. The tone of Hearst's wartime relations with the Soviets was set by this acrimonious exchange in October 1942. Smarting from Hearst press attacks, *Pravda* accused the Hearst papers of "spilling poisoned ink to wreck the great cause of the anti-Hitler coalition." *Pravda* concluded that Hearst was "Hitler's best friend in America."

Hearst counterpunched effectively. "Marshal Stalin, in his controlled press, calls me a gangster journalist and a friend of Hitler. These accusations have their amusing sides, coming from the gentleman who is head of the Communist press – the only gangster press I know." Hearst also pointed out that "the estimable Marshal Stalin" was "until recently Hitler's best friend and buddy... his partner in the plunder of Poland."[26]

During the war years Hearst's chief political columnists were George Rothwell Brown, Benjamin De Casseres, Paul Mallon, and Westbrook Pegler. Brown and Mallon, conservative in style as well as politics, expressed Hearstian views on Russia and communism in tones that were relatively restrained. Besides, their columns – Brown's "The Political Parade" and Mallon's "News Behind the News" – dealt mostly with domestic issues. The shock troops were De Casseres and Pegler.

Since Pegler didn't begin writing for Hearst till the war's final year, America's chief purveyor of impassioned anti-Soviet rhetoric for almost three years was De Casseres. True, there were other journalists – notably

John O'Donnell of the *New York Daily News* – who were as fiercely Russophobic as De Casseres. But the latter, through Hearst syndication, reached a wider audience. If William Randolph Hearst was the pioneer anti-Soviet cold warrior, Benjamin De Casseres and Westbrook Pegler were his point men.

Benjamin De Casseres

Though his name today is virtually unknown, the Parnell Thomas and McCarthy movements owed much to Benjamin De Casseres. Partly accounting for his obscurity is that he had the ill fortune to die in December of 1945 – on the eve of the era he did so much to bring about. De Casseres's loathing for the Soviet regime was matched only by his fanatic intolerance against those he perceived as domestic subversives. Thomas, McCarthy, and their followers would surely have agreed with De Casseres's view that "the Bill of Rights should apply to "LOYAL AMERICANS ONLY!"[27]

Because of his Gallic-sounding name, there were those who believed De Casseres to be some sort of arrogant French or French-descended aristo, possibly of clerical and *pétainiste* tendency. Reality is otherwise. The product of an old Sephardic Jewish family, De Casseres was born in Philadelphia in 1873. On his father's side he was a collateral descendant of Spinoza.

Starting work at the age of thirteen, De Casseres began his career as office boy to Charles Emory Smith, editor-in-chief of the *Philadelphia Press*. He was soon writing editorials and, from this springboard, blossomed as a poet, drama critic, biographer, editor, and political columnist. His collected works include fifteen books and a long prose poem. Among his books are biographies of James Gibbons Huneker and of his ancestor, Spinoza.

De Casseres once articulated his political philosophy as follows: "My core passion is liberty. I am a militant, radical individualist. I hate Communism, Fascism, Socialism, and any system that suppresses the individual and enlarges the power of the state."[28]

One must view this declaration with skepticism. Though De Casseres was certainly passionate in desiring liberty for himself, he could be cheeseparing in dispensing that commodity to those whose opinions he disliked. A more accurate exercise in self-analysis would be this later statement: "I never think logically. I believe logic to be one of the lowest forms of mental activity and imagination the highest... Creators should spurn Reason as an eagle would spurn a ladder."[29]

Brendan Gill once described John O'Hara, another prickly customer, as "the master of the fancied slight."[30] De Casseres was the master of the unprovoked attack. It was his periodic custom to launch, suddenly and without warning, a volley of abuse at an unsuspecting target and in an area completely extraneous to his normal concerns.

It was one such outburst that ended De Casseres's long friendship with Eugene O'Neill. De Casseres and O'Neill were so close that O'Neill broke his longstanding rule about never writing forewords to the works of other authors. In a preface to "Anathema!," De Casseres's prose poem, O'Neill wrote that it was "a unique and inspiring poem. It is the torment and ecstasy of a mystic's questioning of life... Benjamin De Casseres is the poet who affirms the chaos in the soul of man."[31]

Another bond between them was O'Neill's mystical Irish belief in the divinatory powers of Bio Terrill, De Casseres's wife. Mrs. De Casseres had once read O'Neill's palm and correctly predicted a favorable turn in the playwright's chaotic love life.[32]

De Casseres's fury was brought on by O'Neill's 1934 play, *Days Without End,* whose theme was reconciliation with the Catholic Church. For some obscure reason, possibly because the play offended his free-thinking sensibilities, De Casseres was rabid with anger. Dashing off a clumsy but venomous lampoon, which he titled *Drivel Without End,* he submitted it to Isaac Goldberg, editor of *Panorama.* Though Goldberg had published many contributions by De Casseres, this time he refused: he was a friend of O'Neill. De Casseres then had the parody printed privately and distributed to critics and mutual friends in the literary community.

A bewildered O'Neill waited for an explanation of De Casseres's bizarre behavior. None was forthcoming and the two men never spoke again. De Casseres only relented two weeks before his death. "I'm sorry I wrote that about O'Neill," he said to his wife.[33] A final irony is that O'Neill never did return to the Catholic Church.

De Casseres's association with Hearst began in 1933. He wrote editorials, literary criticism, and a column called "March of Events." The column served as a vehicle for De Casseres's wartime political commentaries, appearing in the *Journal-American* till December 1943 and in the *Mirror* till November 1945, a month before his death. MOE also appeared in the *Los Angeles Examiner* and other Hearst papers.

In those early wartime days, respectables who supported Allied unity viewed De Casseres with the distaste one reserves for a skunk at a garden party. This was particularly true in 1942. The Russians had stopped the *Wehrmacht* at the gates of Moscow, suffered a terrible bloodletting that summer, and were heroically contesting every inch of Stalingrad – and here was this man speculating on the possibility of a future Soviet-American war.[34]

The rankest heresy during the Russo-American love feast of the early war years was any suggestion that an Allied power might seek a separate peace with Hitler. The topic was not off limits to De Casseres. "If Russia made a separate peace with Germany and joined Hitler's 'New Order,'" he wrote in MOE, "the Reds here would quickly reveal their allegiance to Moscow."[35] That entry appeared on January 15, 1942, when Americans of all political persuasions were cheering on the Soviet winter offensive before Moscow.

Nine days later De Casseres's target was Joseph E. Davies. The Stalin-admiring former ambassador was then at the peak of his prestige and his book was being made into a movie by Warner Brothers.

Responding to Davies's observation that Stalin was "kindly" and "sincerely modest," De Casseres wrote that "when meeting diplomatists Nero, Caligula, Genghis Khan, Napoleon, Hitler, and Mussolini were cozily charming" and that Davies's book had left him "with a desire for a bath with a large bar of medicated soap."[36]

The February 6 MOE demonstrated that De Casseres was as unsympathetic to totalitarianism of the right as he was to communism. Declaring the present time an "age of Satan," he doubted if "there were gathered together as rulers... such incarnate forces of pure deviltry as Hitler, Goering, Goebbels, Streicher... Lenin... Stalin... Mussolini, Quisling, and Hirohito."[37]

This attitude was also reflected in the February 14 MOE, in which De Casseres warned that "almost as great a calamity for the human race as the triumph of Hitler would be the triumph of Bolshevism in Europe."[38]

In two subsequent columns De Casseres focused on his domestic foes. On February 18 he wrote that "it is ABSOLUTELY NECESSARY to exterminate Communism in this country if we are at war with totalitarian ideas."[39] The March 3 MOE urged that "the House of America be cleaned of bureaucratic parasites... Reds, fellow travelers – all 5th Columnists of varying degrees."[40]

A March 16 editorial echoed the same theme. Under the heading BOONDOGGLING AS MACARTHUR FIGHTS, it charged that the major boondogglers were "the left wing of the New Deal, including a thousand or more Communists or near Communists who are using the war as an instrument of revolution."[41]

From the style, it is probable that De Casseres wrote the April 1 editorial headed AN OLD TRICK. Here, displaying uncharacteristic fairness, he warned readers against blanket condemnation of persons lending their names to Communist-front organizations. Rather, they should distinguish between "Marxist sympathizers" like Dorothy Parker, Lillian Hellman, and Corliss Lamont and those who "scribbled their names or shouted OK over the telephone without knowing what they were doing." In the latter category De Casseres placed William Rose Benet, Walter Damrosch, and Dolores del Rio.[42]

Two days later De Casseres returned to the international arena. "Fascist Germany and Fascist Japan must be annihilated, but if on the ruins there arises an ology just as ruthless – Communism – then that means World War III."[43]

This grim warning was followed by one of De Casseres's inexplicable tangents into private vendetta. This time his target was Marcel Proust. The English poet Alfred Noyes had written that the underlying cause of France's 1940 defeat was the moral decay exemplified by such writers as Proust. Denying Noyes's charges, De Casseres, in his April 15 column, exempted the French from any stigma of moral decay. Absolution did not extend to the chronicler of things past. With characteristic brio, De Casseres denounced Proust as a "nut," a "queer," the author of "long-winded and boresome books," and a "nuisance who rang people up at 4 a.m."[44]

The euphoria induced by Russia's winter offensive evaporated in late spring of 1942. In May Marshal Timoshenko's offensive was stopped before Kharkov. In June-July the *Wehrmacht* drove a huge gap between the Soviet Central and South-West fronts. By August 5 the Germans were at the outskirts of Stalingrad, almost four hundred miles east of their winter defensive line.

As the Russians fought desperately to survive, American sympathy and good will escalated accordingly. But not in the Hearst papers. Swanberg comments that "the Hearst press was not overly concerned about the Russian plight at Stalingrad."[45] That indifference was reflected in this July 23 headline: NAZIS MENACE ROSTOV AS REDS RETREAT. In the same issue De Casseres approvingly quoted Ambrose Bierce's definition of a Russian as a "person with a Caucasian body and a Mongolian soul."[46]

On September 19, while the Stalingrad battle was raging, De Casseres responded to charges of isolationism that had been leveled against the Hearst press. "The 'isolationist' versus the 'internationalist' has always been a false issue... the (real) issue has always been COMMUNOFASCISM v. Americanism."[7]

In early 1943 De Casseres attempted to drive a wedge between the

Russians and the American Communists, objects of his special loathing. The February 4 MOE contained one of its few favorable references to the Soviet war effort. In an open letter to "Joseph Stalin, Moscow," De Casseres called on the dictator to "call off the Communists in the USA who are trying to high pressure us into a third front. (De Casseres considered the landing in North Africa a second front.) It is prejudicing millions of Communist-hating Americans against Russia's brave efforts to free herself from the German hordes."[48]

Wartime breeds a climate hostile to civil liberties. In 1942 a New York book publisher urged a ban on all works critical of the Soviet Union.[49] De Casseres was aware of the outrage caused by his writings and of views that they bordered on sedition. Half-humorously, he confronted the issue in the July 16, 1943 MOE: "I have several times hinted that it is the United States that is smashing Germany on the Russian front. (De Casseres had pointed out that Russian victories would have been impossible without American supplies.) But I didn't dare say it out too loud for fear of being accused of being in the pay of Hitler or the Jap sun goddess."[50]

By fall of 1943 the film version of *Mission to Moscow* had been released. De Casseres's view of this propagandist work shows him at his most prescient. Articulating conclusions that today we know to be true, De Casseres wrote in the November 2 MOE that "if there is a muddled mind in these USA, it is the mind of Joseph E. Davies, who gave us that masterpiece of film propaganda, *Submission to Moscow*."[51] With that latter reference, De Casseres coined the nickname that would plague Davies the rest of his life. The sobriquet was appropriated, and used with numbing regularity, by a later Hearst columnist with a special antipathy toward Davies.

By 1944 De Casseres had switched to the *Mirror*. On June 22, while American troops were fighting their way off the Normandy beachhead, De Casseres trained his guns on Britain's Socialist planner, Professor Harold Laski. Scoring Laski's "ant-heap philosophy," De Casseres expressed surprise "that this apostle of a planned economy isn't living in Moscow."[52] As a precursor of McCarthyism, De Casseres deliberately obfuscates the line between democratic socialism and totalitarian communism. In 1953 Joe McCarthy would attack another British Laborite, the anti-communist Prime Minister Clement Attlee, as "Comrade Attlee."[53]

In the same column De Casseres noted that Earl Browder's Communist Political Association was backing FDR at the Democratic convention. Recalling Roosevelt's 1936 statement that "I reject the support of any advocate of communism," De Casseres commented that "it would be nice if our President would repeat his words of 1936, wouldn't it?"[54]

There was in fact a vast difference between the Communist party of 1936 and the Communist Political Association of 1944. In May 1942 FDR commuted Communist leader Earl Browder's conviction for passport fraud. On release from prison, a grateful Browder dissolved the Communist party and replaced it with the Communist Political Association, which he said would be little more than a discussion group. To keep supplies moving to Russia, the Communists adopted a no-strike pledge. When the United Mine Workers struck, *Daily Worker* editor Louis Budenz organized a back-to-work movement. Browder even offered to shake J.P. Morgan's hand if the financier would support Soviet-American unity. Told he would fit in nicely with the far-right National Association of Manufacturers, Browder said, "I'm awfully glad to hear that."[55]

But Browderism – as the tendency came to be known – aroused antagonism among Communist hard-liners. One of them, the apostate millionaire Frederick Vanderbilt Field, sneered that Browder was "too impressed with the ability... he found in the camp of the class enemy," a reference to Browder's admiration for FDR.[56] In early 1946 Browder was ousted as Communist leader and replaced by the militant William Z. Foster. De Casseres, in his rush to judgment, completely ignored the strange anomaly of "Browderism."

Predictable was the columnist's reaction to Roosevelt's reelection in 1944. "Are we on the road to becoming Germanized and Russianized?" he inquired in the November 9 MOE. The same column contained a favorable allusion to that free enterprise bible, Friedrich von Hayek's *The Road to Serfdom.*[57]

By the end of 1944 it was no longer unfashionable to criticize the Russians. The Luce publications, in a retreat from their 1942-43 position, began publishing anti-Soviet material. The September 4 issue of *Life* carried an article by another ambassador to the USSR, William C. Bullitt. Bullitt warned that Stalin would soon replace Hitler as the great threat to Europe.[58]

On November 17, in a portent of things to come, *Time* Foreign News Editor Whittaker Chambers delivered an outspoken attack on American correspondents in China. Denouncing their pro-Mao reporting as "agitprop," Chambers rejected the view that the Chinese Communists were "agrarian liberals." Instead, he insisted, they were "Marxists in close alliance with the Soviets" whose purpose was "the spread of totalitarianism in China."[59]

This trend seems to have had the effect of toning down De Casseres's rhetoric. Though as anti-communist as ever, he was no longer the strident

Cassandra of 1942-43. Increasingly, humor began to replace invective as the columnist's weapon.

Age and health factors may have contributed to producing a kinder and gentler De Casseres. From February 1945 to his death on December 6 the columnist was seriously ill. Yet he courageously soldiered on.

The "new" De Casseres made his appearance during the Yalta Conference, from February 3-11, 1945. In the February 8 MOE De Casseres derisively observed that "Joe Stalin, the celebrated pipe smoker, is blowing kinnikinick in your eyes, Uncle Sam." Kinnikinick, the columnist explained, was a mixture of roots, manure, and other ingredients designed by Native Americans to befuddle the white man.[60]

The next target of De Casseres's jibes was Henry A. Wallace, the ascetic former vice-president and future candidate of the Communist-infiltrated Progressive Party. De Casseres, a *bon vivant* who enjoyed scotch and good cigars, saw nothing praiseworthy about Wallace's puritan lifestyle. "He does not smoke, drink, or dance (the do-goody wowser type)... He serves the totalitarian wave of the future and is riding on it like an Iowa Neptune."[61]

That entry was in March and there is no other till August. A logical explanation is the declining state of the columnist's health. Hearst's loyalty to trusted old employees and De Casseres's workaholic nature combine to rule out other possibilities.

In the August 22 MOE De Casseres reviewed *One Who Survived,* the memoir of Soviet defector Alexander Barmine. Unlike some ideologues of the McCarthy era, De Casseres was not an uncritical admirer of turncoats. "I am a little skeptical of 'converts.' How can a man support a regime for years (like Barmine, Max Eastman, and Eugene Lyons) and suddenly get sick to his stomach and begin to yip!, yip!, yip! for the other side."[62]

Sardonic humor also dominates the September 28 MOE: "How lucky are Communists in capitalistic countries! No Siberia!... No concentration camps! No torture chambers! Just a Bill of Rights and fat government jobs!"[63]

The October 24 column saw De Casseres at his most mellow. In a charming and sentimental reminiscence, he recalled a Lillian Russell opening in Philadelphia and his own role as a youthful stage door johnnie.[64]

The last flash of his old fire came a week later. This was the column in which he advocated limiting Bill of Rights protection to loyal Americans.

De Casseres's final column, on November 2, was something of an anticlimax. In it he praised candy bar manufacturer Milton Hershey for attempting to keep the CIO from organizing his workers.[65]

Thirty-four days later De Casseres was dead. His obituary and picture appeared in the *New York Times* and the *Mirror's* final tribute referred to him as the "beloved" author and columnist.[66]

Given his temperament and ideological baggage, there is little doubt that De Casseres would have found the McCarthy era a paradise on earth. The disdain he suffered for his wartime anti-Soviet diatribes and attacks on American Communists would have turned to hosannas for his clear vision. The tragedy of Benjamin De Casseres is not only one of a prophet crying in the wilderness. It is also the tragedy of a prophet who died when the Promised Land was just over the next hill.

Westbrook Pegler

Though Benjamin De Casseres may have been a beloved figure within the Hearst organization, the same cannot be said for Westbrook Pegler. Shortly before he began writing his column in the *Journal-American,* Pegler was invited to the great family estate at San Simeon, California, to be presented to "the Chief," as Hearst was known throughout his empire. The old man disliked his new columnist intensely.[67]

Hearst's personal aversion to Pegler made no difference in his career. If Joseph E. Davies was a useful naif for Stalin, Westbrook Pegler was a useful character assassin for Hearst. Besides, Pegler got on well with Richard E. Berlin, the hands-on executive who served as president of the Hearst Corporation.[68]

Like many ardent rightists, Pegler had once been an ardent leftist. In 1935 he gave an interview to the *Daily Worker* in which he supported the Communist program for a farmer-labor movement.[69] Once he changed sides, his most pronounced hatreds were for labor unions and the Roosevelt family. Pegler advocated hanging pickets and habitually referred to the presidential couple as "Old Moose Jaw" and "La Boca Grande."

Though Pegler had a Jewish wife (to whom he was devoted), he strongly disliked Jews. In print he had to be careful. Yet he was successful in getting in the occasional snide dig. Two of his enemies were film star Melvyn Douglas and State Department official David Niles. Pegler rarely referred to Douglas and Niles without letting his readers know that their original surnames were Hesselberg and Nihus.

On other occasions he was apt to be more... direct. One night, screaming anti-Semitic obscenities, a drunken Pegler was forcibly ejected from the Stork Club.[70]

Pegler had started out as a sports writer. His career as a political commentator was launched in 1933, on the Scripps-Howard *New York World-Telegram.* He concentrated mainly on crooked labor unions and scored some noteworthy exposés. In 1941 he won the Pulitzer Prize for a series of articles on corruption in organized labor. The year before, Pegler had attacked Hearst as a "never-to-be-adequately-damned demagogue" and his employees as "high-principled poor men (who will) sell their principles for a few dirty dimes."[71]

By 1944 relations had become strained between Pegler and Roy Howard, publisher of the *World-Telegram*. Though Howard was a conservative Republican, he disliked Pegler's ad hominem attacks on Roosevelt and members of his family.

The final straw came in June 1944, just before the Democratic convention. Despite health problems, Roosevelt was an announced candidate for the nomination. Though FDR looked gaunt and ill, there was a gentleman's agreement in those days that forbade mention of the president's appearance.

Only Pegler violated the code. "To judge by reports and photos," he wrote, "President Roosevelt might not be able to serve out a fourth term. His reelection would serve only to inflict Henry A. Wallace on the country as president."[72]

This was too much for Howard. He was appalled by Pegler's callous speculation over the life expectancy of a public official. Speculation now turned to the life expectancy of Pegler's column, with a consensus that it would be brief.[73]

But Pegler had a safety net. He had been dickering with Hearst and was now invited to make the jump. The only problem was that Pegler's contract with Howard did not expire till November. This obstacle was overcome when Howard agreed to accept token columns up to November – columns he had no intention of using.[74]

Pegler made his debut as a Hearst columnist on September 18, 1944. His column appeared in the *Journal-American*, with wider circulation arranged through Hearst's gigantic King Features syndicate. The column also changed its name. In the *World-Telegram* it had been called "Fair Enough"; the new title was "As Pegler Sees It."

In comparing Pegler to De Casseres, it is incorrect to speak of a high road and a low road. Both were vitriolic, De Casseres intermittently and Pegler consistently, but Pegler's vitriol was far more personal than his fellow columnist's. De Casseres's strongest abuse was usually reserved for foreign tyrants; Pegler, on the other hand, routinely savaged other journalists, labor leaders, members of the Roosevelt family, and entertainers whose politics displeased him.

De Casseres's most bitter personal attacks were those on Eugene

O'Neill and Marcel Proust. But the object of De Casseres's vituperation was O'Neill's play, not his private life, and Proust had been dead twenty years when De Casseres excoriated him. Pegler was bound by no such constraints. One of his targets was the dancer Paul Draper, accused of performing for left-wing groups. That Pegler did not limit his commentary to Draper's political sins is shown from these excerpts: "Affecting skin-tight pants... (he) puts his hands daintily on his hips, tosses his head, makes a saucy mouth, and whirls and flounces madly."[75] On another occasion he referred to Draper as a "mincing twirp" with "twittering toes."[76] So the high road-low road analogy is inappropriate. De Casseres took a low road but Pegler took a much lower one.

This may have been what Hearst intended all along. De Casseres was over seventy and in poor health. Now a younger and stronger voice was needed to spread the Hearstian doctrine of distrust for Russia and militant anti-communism and anti-New Dealism at home. When Pegler signed on with Hearst, there was a clause in his contract stipulating that the employer would assume financial responsibility in event of libel suits.[77] This provision removed any inhibition that Pegler might have had about giving the freest rein to his talent and passion for invective.

One of Pegler's most interesting columns came out on November 1. Beginning routinely enough, he observed that "there are among the Roosevelt political following some thorough Americans who support him though they know that thereby they put themselves in alliance with the Communists." This was pretty standard fare: loyal Americans getting into bed with Roosevelt and finding themselves in bed with Communists.

Then came an intriguing deviation. Not only was Roosevelt not a Communist but his love of power and official privilege were the "identifying attributes of the Fascist." Supporters of FDR forget that "Fascism or National Socialism has been happening throughout the Roosevelt reign and the Communist program calls for Fascism first and Communism later."[78]

Once he got hold of an idea, Pegler was loath to let it go. On November 10, after Roosevelt's reelection, he remarked that FDR's victory "was aided by the Fascistic phase of unionism" represented by Sidney Hillman's PAC. Since Pegler's most devoted readers were not conspicuously intellectual, he felt called upon to explain his position. "It may seem inconsistent of me to say that the PAC is dominated by Commies and then say that the immediate effect of this program is Fascist. The explanation is that Communism and Fascism are alike in all important elements and that the Communists... are willing to go through Fascism to arrive at Communism."[79]

Pegler was never truly at home in the area of abstract political discourse. His specialties were innuendo, personal invective, wounding ridicule, and knee-in-the-groin adversarial reporting. The January 26, 1945 column found him back on familiar ground as he mocked Roosevelt's accent. "What is this Roosevelt Choctaw, anyway?" Alluding to FDR's pronunciation of "again," Pegler concluded that it wasn't even "real Harvardese or Bahstonese or Grotonese."[80]

To help implement Hearst's grand design of an anti-Soviet foreign policy and an anti-communist, anti-New Deal domestic policy, Pegler stepped up his attacks on FDR in the period immediately following the Yalta Conference. In his February 14 column he opposed a labor draft, piously protesting that such a move would curtail civil liberties. He then got around to the real reason for his opposition. "A labor draft would increase the authority of Roosevelt, who already has more power than any President and many of the powers exercised by Adolf Hitler and Joseph Stalin."[81]

Franklin Roosevelt died on April 12. The Hearst press, realistically bowing to the national mood, adopted a reverent attitude in editorials and news stories. Significantly, Pegler's column did not run for the next ten days. One can only guess as to what took place behind the scenes. Possibly some Hearst executives tried to prevail on the columnist to demonstrate a routine token of courtesy toward the man he had attacked so viciously and for so long. If so, their efforts were unsuccessful.

By April 22 Pegler's bosses had apparently decided that the grace period had expired. That day he returned to print. In one of his most mean-spirited entries, he wrote that "the Roosevelt government gave aid and comfort to… (pro-Soviet) revolutionaries and maintained for all the years of the New Deal many of their sympathizers in offices in Washington."[82]

Pegler's words were prophetic as well as an expression of *schadenfreude*. His theme – coddling of subversives by a Democratic administration – would become a trademark of the Parnell Thomas and McCarthy years.

The columnist now escalated his attack. On May 10 he wrote that "many in office in the National Government and many in the powerful unions of the CIO would then turn against the United States in any conflict… with Russia."[83]

This was strong stuff. Germany had surrendered two days before but fighting still raged on Okinawa. The atomic bomb had not yet been tested and the prospect of a costly invasion of the Japanese main islands loomed ahead. Pro-Russian feeling continued to be strong and the American government was doing everything possible to get the Soviets into the war with Japan. Against this background, Pegler openly considered the possibility of World War III and speculated on which Americans would betray their country when that war broke out.

Though Westbrook Pegler came late to Hearst, he nevertheless played an important part in the Hearst press's cold war within a hot war. Taking the reins from an ailing De Casseres, Pegler succeeded in infecting millions of Americans with his bile.

Stalin and the Cold War

In breaking up the Soviet-American honeymoon and bringing on the Cold War, the Hearst press had a valuable ally in Josef Stalin. The reservoir of American good will toward the Russians was depleted no less by the Hearsts, the Pattersons, and McCormicks than by the Soviet dictator's rapaciousness. That quality began to manifest itself even before Roosevelt's death. Pegler and other enemies had long portrayed Roosevelt as at best a woolly-minded appeaser and, at worst, a secret sympathizer with communism. Hearst-Patterson-McCormick attacks on Roosevelt were so virulent that in December 1942 the president was goaded into sending a Nazi Iron Cross to John O'Donnell, Joe Patterson's hatchet man at the *News*.

There was one man who would come to shed all doubts about FDR's anti-communism: Josef Stalin. In violation of the Yalta agreement, the Russians were ruthlessly communizing Poland. Shocked by this act of bad faith, Roosevelt sent Stalin a telegram of protest. The response was an angry accusation that Roosevelt and Churchill were negotiating to sign a separate peace with the Germans on the Western Front. After heatedly denying Stalin's charges, Roosevelt sent Churchill a telegram on April 6, six days before his death. "We must not permit anybody to entertain a false impression that we are afraid," he wrote. "Our Armies will in a very few days be in a position that will permit us to become tougher than has been heretofore advantageous to the war effort."[85]

Stalin's behavior also made an unbeliever out of Harry Truman. The new president had come to the Potsdam Conference determined to establish an amicable relationship with "Uncle Joe." He left a disillusioned man. According to Margaret Truman, daughter and biographer, the president was particularly angry over Stalin's rude dismissal of his inland waterways proposal and evasiveness when asked about the fate of fifteen thousand Polish officers who had been captured and later murdered in Poland's Katyn Forest.[86]

This set Truman on the road to becoming a cold warrior. When Winston Churchill made his "Iron Curtain" speech at Fulton, Missouri, in

March 1946, HST applauded him from the audience. In September, he yielded to Secretary of State James F. Byrnes's demand that Henry Wallace be fired from the cabinet after making a pro-Soviet speech in Madison Square Garden. In March 1947 Truman asked Congress for $400 million in aid to Greece and Turkey. The measure, passed in May, became known as the Truman Doctrine and symbolized America's will to defend countries threatened by Soviet expansionism.

Yet the Hearst-Patterson-McCormick forces continued to snipe at Truman for being soft on Stalin. Truman undoubtedly played into their hands by retaining, for an unreasonably long time, a sneaking personal affection for the Soviet dictator. At Potsdam, when not in conference, the two had got on well, discussing crops and exchanging toasts at banquets. Though Truman was firm in his opposition to Russian territorial ambitions, he mistakenly continued to believe that the Politburo, not Stalin, was in charge. As late as 1948, during the presidential campaign, he declared that he liked "old Joe" but that Joe was a prisoner of the Politburo.[87]

Truman's assessment was not accepted by the American public, who saw Stalin in a clearer and colder light. His violation of the Yalta agreements, the move into northern Iran, the Czech coup, the Berlin blockade, the show trial of Cardinal Mindszenty – as one enormity followed another, it was almost as if Stalin was doing Hearst's work for him.

The Cold War and the Witch Hunt

All witch hunters were cold warriors but not all cold warriors were witch hunters. There were many who faced up to the reality of Soviet power without succumbing to domestic hysteria. Pegler called Undersecretary of the Army Robert P. Patterson a "renegade Republican who turned New Deal bureaucrat with a strong sympathy for the Communist treachery."[88] Senator William Jenner, a McCarthy stalwart, denounced General George C. Marshall as "a front man for traitors."[89] Joe McCarthy charged that Communists in government were protected by "Truman's iron curtain of secrecy."[90] Patterson, Truman, and Marshall were, of course, standup cold warriors, men who were attacked as regularly in *Pravda* as they were by Pegler, Jenner, and McCarthy.

Why, then, did these impeccable anti-communists come under attack from Hearst and his allies? Though one may wonder about the unbalanced Pegler, surely Hearst and his top executives were intelligent and sophisticated enough to know that men like Truman, Marshall, and Patterson were not treasonable coddlers of Communists. A logical explanation is that these victims of the late 1940s and early 1950s were members of the establishment – an establishment which, in the eyes of Hearst et al, had been criminally slow in grasping the true nature of Soviet Communism. Richard Rovere quotes Peter Viereck's definition of McCarthyism as "the revenge of noses that for twenty years... were pressed against the window pane."[91] The Hearst-Patterson-McCormick forces had endured establishment ridicule and ostracism for their fervent anti-Sovietism during the early war years.

Now was the time for revenge – and no niceties or fine distinctions were drawn as they dragged down their erstwhile detractors. So William Randolph Hearst and Joe Patterson gave free rein to the Peglers and O'Donnells. Hearst and his allies had pioneered the Cold War and they were damned if they were going to see it hijacked by impure men who were praising "Marshal Stalin" and "our great Russian allies" while they were keeping alive the anti-Soviet flame.

There are historians who say that the witch hunt began with Truman's Loyalty Order on March 1947, when 2,200,000 federal employees were required to swear that they had never been affiliated with any group on the Attorney General's list of subversive organizations.

Others challenge this view, arguing that Truman's loyalty-security program was a necessary safeguard against Communist infiltration of government. The witch hunt, they insist, began only when representatives of the paranoid right got into the act and started to make a mockery of legitimate investigative procedures. For purposes of this study, the term witch hunter will be confined to those whose credentials are beyond doubt – William Randolph Hearst and Parnell Thomas in the 1940s, the Hearst heirs and McCarthy in the 1950s, and Westbrook Pegler and J. Edgar Hoover throughout.

Autumn of 1946 was a happy one for the patriarch. Though the eighty-three-year-old Hearst would suffer a disabling heart attack the following spring, that fall he was still in full control of his revitalized empire. The Republicans had captured both houses of Congress and, thanks to Stalin's actions, distrust for the Russians was steadily mounting. Mainstream liberals, now fed up with Soviet intransigence, were about to organize the anti-communist Americans for Democratic Action (ADA), whose founders were Eleanor Roosevelt, Walter Reuther, and Hubert Humphrey. The liberal community in America would soon be rent by a bitter internecine war, with ADA denouncing a rival left-of-center group, the Henry Wallace-led Progressive Citizens of America, for being insufficiently anti-communist. J. Edgar Hoover, then America's most respected public official, warned of "Red Fascism" that threatened "unions, newspapers, magazines, book publishing, radio, movies, churches, schools, fraternal orders, and government itself."[92] Anti-communism was the national mood and gone were the unhappy early war years when Hearst, the Pattersons, and Bertie McCormick were viewed as a hyena chorus of discord.

As Hearst contemplated the Republican congressional victory, he focused particular attention on the House Un-American Activities Committee, the country's leading watchdog against subversion. With satisfaction he noted that HUAC now had a new chairman, an aggressive fifty-three-year-old New Jersey Republican named J. Parnell Thomas.

2. Pre-McCarthy McCarthyism: The Hearst Press and Parnell Thomas

The Hearst press's benevolence toward Parnell Thomas pre-dated the 1946 congressional elections. In September of that year five American airmen were killed when their plane was shot down over Yugoslavia. Marshal Tito's Communist government was then closely allied with the Soviets. When Thomas added his voice to the chorus of outrage that swept the country, his action was noted favorably in a *Journal-American* editorial: "Representative Thomas deals squarely with the moral issue involved when he insists that the Yugoslavian murderers of five Americans... be held accountable for their crimes."[1]

Parnell Thomas was born in Jersey City in 1895. After attending public schools in Allendale and Ridgewood, he graduated from the University of Pennsylvania in 1916. He entered the Army in 1917 and served overseas during the First World War. Thomas then embarked on a career in which politics and business seemed to be interchangeable.

From 1926 to 1931 he was mayor of Allendale. Between 1935 and 1937 he served in the state legislature and in the latter year was elected to Congress. There he remained till his resignation in 1949. Yet he maintained links with the investment securities field between 1920 and 1938, as a bond salesman and later manager of a bond department.[2]

Thomas had none of the *bonhomie* and self-mocking charm that many were later to discern in Joe McCarthy. An irritable terrier of a man, he not only bullied and intimidated witnesses but was loath to allow them and their counsel even the simplest courtesies. "When the Communist party leader Jacob A. Stachel appeared as a witness... his lawyer made a... request:

Mr. Brodsky: May I move my chair closer to Mr. Stachel, so I can advise with him?

Mr. Thomas: No."[3]

This was exactly the sort of spirit that appealed to the Hearst high command. No New Deal pussyfooting here – this was a man who would treat Communists with the blunt contempt they deserved. Not that there was cause for complaint about Thomas's predecessor, John S. Wood of Georgia. A Dixie racist and supporter of the Ku Klux Klan, Wood's credentials as a hard-line anti-communist were unimpeachable.[4]

At the same time, people like Wood and his committee colleague, John E. Rankin of Mississippi, posed something of a problem. Not only was Rankin a more virulent racist than Wood but an anti-Semite to boot.

This did not sit well with the Hearst directorate. Though the Hearst papers were not noted for flaming advocacy of civil rights, Hearst executives (some of whom were Jewish) wanted to focus single-mindedly on the Red hunt and not have it sidetracked into a Red-and-black hunt, or, even worse, a Red-and-black hunt with anti-Semitic overtones.

Wood was reasonably tractable but Rankin kept causing embarrassment. To the part-Jewish William C. Bullitt, a friendly witness, Rankin inquired if it was true that 75 percent of American Communists were Jews.[5] Annoyed by such gaffes, Thomas and his colleagues left Rankin off the subcommittee investigating subversion in Hollywood. A piqued Rankin responded by dispensing the information that Edward G. Robinson's original surname was Goldenberg and Eddie Cantor's Iskowitz.[6] (As if "Cantor" were an anglicization.)

Of the eight men on the committee, the Hearst press singled out two for special favorable treatment. These stars were Thomas and a poised, incisive freshman congressman from California named Richard M. Nixon.

Nixon was hailed as a comer as early as his maiden congressional speech on February 18, 1947. In it he presented a resolution to cite accused Communist functionary Gerhardt Eisler for contempt, following Eisler's defiance of the committee on February 6. Though Nixon made the unsubstantiated charge that Eisler was connected with the Canadian atomic espionage ring, his coolness and no-nonsense manner set him apart from the bumblers and ranters on the committee.[7]

In March the committee held hearings on two bills to outlaw the Communist Party. One of them, drafted by Rankin, called for ten years imprisonment and a $10,000 fine for teaching courses in any school, college, or university that would "convey the impression of sympathy with, or approval of, Communism or Communist ideology...."[8] The irrepressible Rankin also called on the president to issue an executive order designed to curtail the "pernicious activities" of the Anti-Defamation League.[9]

Antics like these contributed to the committee's decision, by a five-to-three vote, against reporting any bill to outlaw the Communist party. Spurred by Nixon, the legislators were now inclining toward a bill that would allow the CP to remain legal but require compulsory registration of Communists.[10]

The committee's main event in 1947 was the Hollywood investigation. Though the Washington hearings didn't begin till October, there had been a preview in May, at the Biltmore Hotel in Los Angeles. Accompanied by Representative John McDowell of Pennsylvania, a fellow committee member, and Robert Stripling, the committee's chief investigator, Thomas came west and heard testimony from Robert Taylor, Adolphe Menjou, and Mrs. Lila Rogers, Ginger Rogers's mother. The hearings were closed but, with the news coverage, they might as well have been open. After every session, Thomas and Stripling gave the press a complete briefing.

On May 15, the *Journal-American* reported that "Representative Thomas, committee chairman, charged that... the screen star (Robert Taylor) was kept from joining the Navy until he had completed the picture." The picture in question was *Song of Russia*, a blatantly pro-Soviet film released in 1943. Thomas added that this pressure came from Lowell Mellett, an Office of War Information official who had once been Franklin Roosevelt's secretary.[11]

Mrs. Rogers testified that her daughter refused to speak the line, "share and share alike – that's democracy," in the film *Tender Comrade*. *Tender Comrade* was written by Dalton Trumbo, who would later go to prison for his defiance of the committee. As for Menjou, the fashion plate actor assured Thomas & Co. that "Hollywood is one of the main centers of Communist activity in America" and that the Screen Writers Guild was "lousy with Communists."[12]

On the same day, the *Journal-American's* headline read HOUSE QUIZ LINKS WALLACE TO RED FRONT. The committee had issued a statement citing former vice-president Henry A. Wallace's membership on the advisory board of the Southern Conference for Human Welfare. The article described SCHW as an organization that "has displayed constant anti-American and pro-Soviet bias." Also identified as affiliated with

SCHW were Joseph E. Davies, Paul Robeson, and Melvyn Douglas. The same issue contained a briefer article noting that Thomas had received a letter from Davies denying that Roosevelt ordered Hollywood to film *Mission to Moscow.*[13]

In parallel coverage, the *Mirror* quoted Thomas's description of Adolphe Menjou's testimony as "very enlightening" and of the actor as "one of our best witnesses."[14]

Walter Winchell and J. Edgar Hoover

Walter Winchell had been writing a column for the *Mirror* since 1929. On May 19 he approvingly quoted film critic Jack Moffitt's observation that "Movietown's record (for resisting Communist infiltration) is cleaner than Broadway's." The columnist added that "most Commie propaganda comes to Hollywood via the Broadway stage and books."[15] Winchell had a strong motive for endorsing Moffitt's views. In 1947 he was just starting his career as one of the country's premier Red hunters. Winchell's territory was New York and, while no stranger to Hollywood (he made two movies), his strongest emotional ties were always to the city of his birth. It was therefore to his interest to have Broadway, rather than distant Hollywood, as the most dangerous nest of subversion.

Winchell's case was special. Unlike most Hearst writers, who were isolationist and anti-New Deal, Winchell had been a strong Roosevelt partisan and anti-Nazi interventionist. So uncritical was his adoration of the late president that in one column he gushingly recommended "the Nobel Prize for FDR'S smile."[16]

These views drew fire from the far right. *Today's World,* a fevered Coughlinite journal, denounced him as a Communist.[17] Rankin, with customary delicacy, characterized Winchell on the House floor as "a little slime-mongering kike" whose real name was Lipshitz. This smear had originated with German-American Bund leader Fritz Kuhn.[18]

Winchell had a tactile sense of major political shifts. By war's end, he saw that militant anti-communism was the wave of the future. At the same time, he was loath to abandon his pro-Roosevelt and anti-fascist sentiments. Hearst, who could be flexible about these things, gave Winchell special status as a sort of house liberal. He could continue to revere Roosevelt's memory, to attack Franco (a favorite target), and to hound Nazis, Fascists, and collaborators whom he felt had been insufficiently castigated – just as long as he showed himself to be sternly intolerant of Soviet Communism and domestic subversion.

Winchell accepted the arrangement and immediately began to beat the anti-Red tom-toms in his column. But he knew that a media campaign against communism was not enough. To truly legitimize the Red hunt, the support of a towering national public figure was needed. In early 1947 Thomas was just getting started and McCarthy was an unknown freshman senator. What Winchell wanted was a high profile – a profile such as that cast by J. Edgar Hoover.

Winchell's friendship with Hoover dated back to the early 1930s, when the columnist glorified Hoover's campaign against such malefactors as John Dillinger, "Ma" Barker, "Creepy" Karpis, and "Machine Gun" Kelly. Another link between the gossip and the G-man was a shared admiration for Franklin Roosevelt. Though Hoover would become a symbol of reaction to 1960s militants and civil rights activists, the New Deal years were among his happiest. FDR liked Hoover (despite Hoover's distaste for Eleanor Roosevelt) and admired his skill at setting up a domestic intelligence apparatus which the president felt was needed "as part of (his) covert preparation against the possibility of war."[19]

With FDR's death, Winchell seemed to be looking for a new hero. By the beginning of 1947, he had found him. In a January 5 entry that combined redbaiting with adulation, he wrote that "the frightened scummunist voice (the *Daily Worker*) doesn't want J. Edgar Hoover considered as a presidential threat... The best reason why he should be."[20] Winchell had always been a Hoover partisan but with this declaration he now saw the FBI chief as presidential timber.

The Hearst directorate looked benignly on the Winchell-Hoover entente. Nothing but good could come from the friendly association of their star columnist with America's star law enforcement officer.

Hoover was in Winchell's debt not only for reams of publicity but because, at Hoover's request, he had sat for twenty-four hours on what would have been the greatest scoop of his career. This was the FBI's capture of Bruno Richard Hauptmann, the German carpenter who would be convicted of kidnaping the infant son of Charles A. Lindbergh.[21]

Hoover appeared before the Thomas Committee on March 26, 1947. He had first declined, but changed his mind because he was dissatisfied with Truman's loyalty program.[22] Hoover was treated by committee members like a deity descended from Olympus. The tone of the hearing was set by Thomas's obsequious statement that this would be "a grand opportunity" for Hoover to "say anything he wanted to say."[23]

Hoover, using all his public relations skills, painted the weak and unpopular American Communist Party as a menacing Goliath. Taking a dubious example from history, he pointed out that in 1917 there was only one Communist for every 2,777 persons in Russia while in 1947 America the proportion was 1-1,814. Lost on many Americans – including members of the committee – was the vast difference between the disorganized, war-torn Russia of 1917 and the strong, victorious America of 1947. At the same time, Hoover counseled against outlawing the Communist Party. The best weapons against communism, he insisted, were constant vigilance and "prescriptive publicity."[24] These ex-cathedra pronouncements, no less than Rankin's extremism, convinced the committee that it would be a tactical error to outlaw the CP.

The FBI director's appearance before the committee sealed the Hoover-Hearst-HUAC alliance, with Winchell serving as liaison between the Hearst organization and Hoover. Another bond between Winchell and Hoover was a shared antagonism against Harry Truman. Both were Roosevelt loyalists who had no use for his successor.

Winchell's animus against the new president was personal. In late 1945 the columnist was invited to the White House for a face-to-face meeting. Winchell's longtime assistant, Herman Klurfeld, described the encounter as "more a collision than a meeting."[25] Winchell told Klurfeld that Truman's speech was laced with profanity and that he was crude and petty compared to the patrician Roosevelt. In attacks on press critics, he allegedly referred to the *New York Post's* Dorothy Schiff as "that damn Jew publisher."[26] According to another biographer, Bob Thomas, Winchell claimed that Truman had been cordial during the interview. Winchell left, then noticed that he had forgotten his hat. When he returned to retrieve it, he heard Truman say: "I guess we pulled the wool over that son of a bitch's eyes."[27]

Thomas also cites another version, attributing it to Defense Secretary James Forrestal. During the meeting Winchell advanced a plan for a secret Truman-Stalin conference. When the Missourian seemed unimpressed with the idea, Winchell excitedly began to pound the presidential desk. Forrestal, seeking to avoid further friction, "ended the conference as quickly and deftly as he could."[28]

Whatever happened, Winchell never relented in the savagery of his attacks against Truman. In vilifying the president, both the "conservative" and "liberal" Winchell got into the act. While the former denounced Truman as a coddler of Communists in government, the latter branded him an anti-Semite and former member of the Ku Klux Klan.[29]

Where Winchell's disenchantment with Truman was personal, Hoover's was ideological and bureaucratic. On March 22, 1947, Truman issued his Loyalty Program under Executive Order 9835. Hoover objected to provisions of the program that "limited FBI investigation to incumbent employees... handed the investigation of new employees... to the Civil Service Commission... and gave departments discretion on whether to call on the FBI for its services."[30] In curtailing the FBI's authority and forcing the agency to share its responsibility with the less qualified Civil Service Commission, Truman was, in Hoover's opinion, "weakening national security" and "defending evil."[31] Confident that the Republicans would win the presidency in 1948, Hoover jumped ship and entered into a de facto alliance with the Republican-dominated HUAC and the Hearst-led anti-administration media.

Enter Doc Matthews

Some of the data received by HUAC came from the FBI. Another important segment derived directly from the Hearst organization. Adela Rogers St. Johns, a writer who served as political troubleshooter for the Hearst directorate and MGM's Louis B. Mayer, contributes this insight: "Hearst had spent millions of his own money before Congress moved in with that committee (HUAC). Everyone in Congress got all their material from us. We had two floors of the Hearst magazine building on Eighth Avenue in New York devoted entirely to the investigative answers we had gotten... out of this, of course, came the Hiss case and the breakup of the group in the State Department."[32]

Supplier and custodian of much of this material was an unusual man named Joseph Brown Matthews. Born in Hopkinsville, Kentucky, in 1894, Matthews was ordained a Methodist minister at the age of twenty. Then followed a stint as a missionary in Java. Back in the United States, Matthews lost his faith and became a socialist. Though he never joined the Communist party, Matthews took perverse pride in admitting that he had been a staunch fellow traveler and member of twenty-eight Communist-front organizations. In 1935, at a Friends of the Soviet Union meeting, he denounced the reactionary foreign policy of William Randolph Hearst.[33]

In 1938 Matthews broke dramatically with the left. HUAC was then under the leadership of right-wing Texas Democrat Martin Dies. Matthews, after informing on hundreds of his friends in a star witness performance, signed on with the committee as Chief Researcher.

The title was well merited. Matthews had a phenomenal memory and a genius for amassing and organizing files. Over the years his vast collection would provide a mother lode of information for congressional inquisitors. Joe McCarthy, as his career was taking off, was moved to attribute "whatever I have done" to "J. B.'s encyclopedic knowledge."[34] Though Matthews, British-style, signed with initials only, he was known to friends and admirers as "Doc." The honorific stemmed from a theology degree Matthews had earned at Kentucky's Wilmore College.[35]

A disillusioned Dies left Congress in 1944 and the following year Matthews took himself and his files over to Hearst. From his London Terrace penthouse Matthews became ideological godfather to the "New York crowd," a Manhattan-based elite of hard-line Red fighters that included Winchell, Hearst Corporation president Richard E. Berlin, *Journal-American* columnist George Sokolsky, and, later, Roy Cohn. Matthews's titles were "assistant to the publisher of the *Journal-American* (William Randolph Hearst Jr.) and 'consultant' on matters relating to subversive activities." His material included the famed "Appendix 9," a listing of 100,000 individuals allegedly associated with Communist fronts, and a minutely cross-indexed file of over 500,000 names. These had been collected from letterheads and programs of supposed Communist-front groups.[36]

As Parnell Thomas and his colleagues prepared for the Hollywood investigation, they had reason to be pleased with the Hearst organization. Thanks to that connection, they now had two potent weapons: Winchell, whose voice and column reached millions, and Matthews, master of the files who knew where all the names were buried.

Hollywood on Trial

The Hollywood hearings began on October 20. HUAC was represented by a subcommittee consisting of Thomas and two other Republicans, McDowell and Richard B. Vail of Illinois. Site of the hearings was the Caucus Room of the Old Office Building, chosen mainly for its size. At the hearings were over a hundred newsmen and a large delegation of middle-aged women who had come principally to get a look at Robert Taylor. There were floodlights, movie cameras, and – that rarity in 1947 – a TV camera.[37]

Winchell, grinding a private ax, commented that the "wisest thing the Thomas investigating group has done yet is shove Rankin (allegedly electioneering at home) into the background."[38] Thomas undoubtedly agreed. Walter Goodman has commented that Hollywood was New Deal territory to Thomas but Semitic territory to Rankin.[39] Several of the key friendly witnesses were Jewish. Thomas wished to keep the focus on Hollywood Reds and the last thing he wanted was Rankin blotting his copybook with references to Hollywood Jews.

The first witnesses were two studio heads, Jack L. Warner and Louis B. Mayer, and an independent producer-director named Sam Wood. All expressed the view that the CP should be outlawed and Warner denounced as "un-American" the film writers Dalton Trumbo, Donald Ogden Stewart, and John Howard Lawson.[40]

Of the three witnesses, only Warner was on the spot. Mayer was a lifelong Republican and Wood in 1944 had organized a group called the Motion Picture Alliance for the Preservation of American Ideals, a rightist coalition designed to combat the spread of communism in Hollywood.

By contrast, Warner Brothers had gained a wartime reputation as the most liberal studio in Hollywood. Its pictures included that kiss of death, *Mission to Moscow,* and *Action in the North Atlantic,* a film in which an American seaman sees a Soviet plane and cries out, "It's ours!"[41] The screenplay was written by John Howard Lawson, head of the Hollywood branch of the Communist Party.[42]

The nervous Warner, in a cringing and apologetic performance, named scores of suspects and boasted of having fired several subversive writers, including Clifford Odets and Irwin Shaw. (Odets and Shaw, it turned out, had not been fired at all.)[43] Whether Warner honestly erred or padded his total to propitiate the inquisitors is not known.

Warner continued his efforts at ingratiation by offering to set up a fund to deport to Russia people who didn't like the American way of life. Sitting in that day with the subcommittee was Richard Nixon. He had been coldly listening to Warner and now asked him how many anti-communist films he had produced. Warner sheepishly admitted that the total to date was zero. But, he eagerly assured the subcommittee, he was working on one now.[44]

Unlike Warner, Sam Wood had no suspect pictures to atone for. A true believer, his October 20 testimony drew a SAYS REDS AIM TO RULE FILMS headline in the *Mirror.* Wood, director of the 1940 hit *Kitty Foyle,* said that four directors of his acquaintance had "attempted to scare us into the Red line," the most "dangerous advocates of Communism are writers."[45]

By 1947 Frank Conniff's "East Side, West Side" column was running regularly in the *Journal-American.* Like Winchell, Conniff was a species of house liberal. A Democrat, he had written speeches for Harry Truman. During the war he struck up a friendship with William Randolph Hearst Jr., while both were serving as correspondents. As the younger Hearst relates it, Conniff taught him that "the Democratic party was not full of evil-doers" and "the ADA (Americans for Democratic Action) was not a Communist front."[46]

Conniff's liberalism had its limits. An Irish Catholic, he fiercely detested communism and strongly favored investigation and exposure of those he saw as domestic subversives. His October 22 column was largely given over to criticism of Paul V. McNutt, counsel for the Motion Picture Producers Association. McNutt, charged Conniff, was out of line for his "attack on the Committee's methods and purposes." Conniff also pointed out that McNutt's views "clashed sharply with statements given earlier by a couple of up-and-coming producers named Louis B. Mayer and Jack Warner."[47]

On the same day the *Mirror* headline read SWEARS FILM AGENT WAS SPY FOR REDS. The accused spy was one John Weber and his accuser was Jack Moffitt, the film critic who had been quoted favorably by Winchell when he declared that Broadway was redder than Hollywood.[48]

Such liberal groups as Americans for Democratic Action consistently opposed HUAC. Not only did they consider the whole concept ridiculous (who ever heard of a Committee on Un-British Activities?), but they were outraged by Thomas's high-handed conduct.

When Sam Wood was testifying, an attorney for some people named by his group as Communists requested the privilege of cross-examination. Thomas ordered the lawyer ejected from the Caucus Room.[49] Rising to defend Thomas was the sober George Rothwell Brown. In the October 24 "Political Parade" Brown commented that "any attempt to deceive the people into believing that the Thomas Committee is conducting the hearings under self-made arbitrary rules of procedure may be set down to deliberate falsehood and complete ignorance of historic Congressional methods."[50]

The hearings were occasionally enlivened by comic relief. Two unwitting humorists were Mrs. Lela Rogers and superstar Gary Cooper. The former told investigators that she had prevented Ginger from appearing in *None But the Lonely Heart* and *Sister Carrie* because the pictures presented capitalism in a negative light. Mrs. Rogers also testified that she knew Clifford Odets was a Communist. How did she know? Because she had read it in a magazine and never come across a denial. As for Cooper, the taciturn Western hero, in his best "yup" manner, allowed as he didn't like Communism "because it isn't on the level."[51]

Silliness was not confined to Hollywood witnesses. On October 27, Louella Parsons discussed the coming film version of the Broadway musical *Call Me Mister*. She was pleased because "the pink tinge that so many people thought was indicated in this Broadway hit musical, will be absent in the movie."[52]

The "pink tinge" that so exercised Parsons was a skit about the "Red Ball Express," a segregated black trucking outfit that had performed prodigies in delivering supplies to the front line during World War II.

That Parsons column was consistent with a policy that would become standard throughout the Hearst organization during the witch hunt years. It can be defined as a belief that redbaiting was too important to be left to professional redbaiters alone. Not only would political writers tackle the Red Menace but also commentators on society, radio/TV, films, and the theater. Most of the latter were politically unsophisticated and a few almost as ungrammatical as Parsons. Had they not been in a position to destroy careers, their efforts would have caused more mirth than fear.

On October 27 part-time columnist Upton Close approvingly noted Thomas's comment that "we want to find out once and for all whether or not Communists actually control scenarios, film labor, and some movie stars."[53] If Conniff and Winchell were house liberals, Close was as near as the Hearst directorate ever came to nurturing a house fascist.

A writer, lecturer, and radio broadcaster, Close had been sponsored by the National Economic Council, an extreme right group whose director, Merwin K. Hart, advocated replacing democracy with a Falange-style political system.[54] Though Close denied being anti-Semitic and offered a $1,000 war bond to anyone who could prove that he was, John Roy Carlson was probably correct in stating that Close "reserved to himself the right to serve as judge and jury."[55] After the war, Close attempted to steer ex-servicemen into the exclusionary Christian Veterans of America.[56] In 1950 Close persuaded Joe McCarthy to insert one of his articles into the Congressional Record. Wisconsin Jewish groups objected and McCarthy expunged the article. In fairness, the ideologically untutored McCarthy had probably never heard of Close and knew nothing of his links to neo-fascist groups. By the time the Hearst-McCarthy alliance had been forged, Close's column had disappeared from the Hearst papers.

On the same day, a *Journal-American* editorial attacked Senator Claude Pepper of Florida for denouncing the Thomas Committee and urging nineteen witnesses to refuse to answer questions.[58] These included twelve writers, five directors, one producer, and one actor. Of the nineteen, ten declined to answer on grounds of the First, rather than the Fifth, Amendment. What dictated this choice? Years later, witness Dalton Trumbo said that it wasn't till 1950, in the Blau case, that the Supreme Court ruled that a witness could avoid contempt charges "by invoking the Fifth Amendment on the question of Communist Party membership."[59] Besides, it made witnesses look nobler to use the First (incursions against free speech) rather than the Fifth (protection against self-incrimination). Trumbo also said that the Fifth was barely mentioned at the time and that the witnesses contended that they were answering the questions, but "in their own way."[60]

That "way" turned out to be a strategy of openly defying the committee and challenging its legitimacy. Thomas was overbearing and arbitrary but the Hollywood Ten (also known as the Unfriendly Ten) were not an iota less boorish. Witness Albert Maltz called investigator Robert Stripling "Mr. Quisling" and witness John Howard Lawson haughtily announced that "rational people don't argue with dirt."[61]

Frank Conniff was particularly incensed with liberals who uncritically supported the defiant writers. "If the self-styled 'liberals' who are participating in the unparalleled smear attack on the Thomas Committee possessed the humility to question their own righteousness, I think they would be appalled at the implications of their recent activities." The columnist also denounced the witnesses' practice of bringing charges of anti-Semitism against their accusers.[62]

Here Conniff was on firm ground. Several of the writers deliberately muddied the waters, making charges of religious prejudice where none existed. Secretly they must have yearned for Rankin, who would have obliged them. (Six of the Ten were Jewish.) In Rankin's absence, they did their best to make surrogate Rankins out of his duller colleagues. Lawson shouted that the committee was trying to invade the rights of Protestants, Jews, and Catholics after Thomas refused to let him read a prepared statement denouncing HUAC as a fascist tool.[63]

The writers continued on this tack even in the face of assurances that religion was not an issue. "Next you are going to ask me what my religious beliefs are," said Maltz to Thomas. Thomas denied any such intent but Maltz was not to be swerved from his course. "And you are going to insist... that since you do not like my religious beliefs, I should not work in the (film) industry."[64]

Considering how much the committee had on the writers, it would have been ridiculous to bring up such irrelevant issues as religious belief or ethnic background. Eight of the Ten were CP members and, thanks to the efforts of the FBI and J. B. Matthews, a committee staff investigator was even able to read into the record the numbers of their Party cards.[65]

When the hearings began, a group called the Committee for the First Amendment was formed. A lustrous aggregation, it included such high profile Hollywood figures as Humphrey Bogart, Lauren Bacall, Frank Sinatra, and Groucho Marx. Within two months all these celebrities had withdrawn their support for the unfriendly witnesses. Bogart even went to the extent of distributing a mimeographed letter. "I went to Washington because I thought fellow Americans were being deprived of their constitutional rights," the letter read in part. Bogart added that the "trip was ill-advised, even foolish, I am ready to admit." He also described himself as "a foolish and impetuous American" and insisted on his detestation of communism.[66]

In the *Mirror,* George Sokolsky patronizingly "forgave" the actor. But he placed a price tag on forgiveness. "For a very foolish bit of exhibitionism," he wrote, "you ought to go further (than admitting error). You might tell us who suggested that trip to Washington. Whose brain-child was it? Who projected you and your wife to take the lead?"

Unlike De Casseres, Sokolsky thought highly of turncoats. On October 6 he wrote that "I have among my friends and acquaintances literally dozens of men and women... so ashamed of Soviet cynicism that from ardent Communists they have become ardent anti-Communists." Then he added a personal plug. "Such a man was Dr. J. B. Matthews, while never a Communist, was associated with that party as a fellow traveler."[68] Sokolsky could have included himself in that assembly of saved souls. A friend of Trotsky during the Russian Revolution, he was described in a July 17, 1930 FBI file as "a Mongoloid-Jew, an American citizen with Communist sympathies, and it is alleged he has been very active in Communist work for a number of years."[69]

What caused this change of opinion about the Hollywood Ten? Undoubtedly, a major factor was the behavior and political antecedents of the writers themselves. Their rudeness, their arrogance, their dishonesty and disingenuousness – these qualities combined to dispel any lingering notion that this was a gentle band of Thoreau-like spirits being persecuted for nonconformity alone.

Some of the writers were more Stalinist than others. Just how Stalinist is demonstrated by an incident that occurred in February 1946. Albert Maltz was disturbed because two of the future Ten, Edward Dmytryk and Adrian Scott, had been attacked by Communist writer John Wexley for removing some crassly unsubtle Party line propaganda from a film they were working on. The excised material had been inserted by Wexley himself. In a *New Masses* article Maltz challenged Wexley – though not too vigorously. But he did put forth the view that "art as a weapon is a strait jacket" and that "writers must be judged by their work and not by the committees they join." He also praised the anti-Stalinist writers John Steinbeck and James T. Farrell and pointed out that *Watch on the Rhine,* Lillian Hellman's anti-Nazi play, had been panned by the *New Masses* during the Hitler-Stalin pact and lauded after the Germans invaded Russia.[70]

Maltz could not have voiced his heresies at a worse time. It was in February 1946 that Earl Browder was removed from the CP leadership and replaced by the hard-lining William Z. Foster. Inspiration for the move came first from Paris rather than Moscow. "Jacques Duclos, the head of the French Communists, wrote a blistering article in *Cahiers de Communisme* which accused Browder of surrendering to the capitalists and called on the American Communists to repudiate the fatal political error."[71]

Taking their clue from Duclos and Foster, Maltz's Party colleagues jumped all over him. Maltz belonged to the same cell as two other of the Ten, Alvah Bessie and Herbert Biberman. They bashed Maltz at an all-night meeting, Bessie declaring that "we need writers who will joyfully impose upon themselves the discipline of understanding and acting upon working-class theory."[72]

What happened next was more characteristic of Moscow in the 1930s than New York in the 1940s. In a breast-beating *Daily Worker* article, Maltz recanted his "one-sided nondialectical treatment of complex issues" and "distorted view of the facts, history, and contribution of left-wing culture to American life."[73] This stench of the Stalin Purge did little to improve the image of the beleaguered writers.

The Ten, then, made an unfavorable impression. And many Americans were inclined, in the waning days of 1947, to believe the committee's allegations against them. This did not imply blanket approval of the committee. A November 1947 Gallup poll "indicated that as many people disapproved of the hearings as approved of them."[74] In addition, there was a wide gulf between judging the writers and judging their writings. What pictures actually contained Communist propaganda? Paul McNutt, a former governor of Indiana, pressed Thomas repeatedly on this point: his requests for information were never gratified. Even McDowell had to admit that he had seen little evidence of subversive content, except "that bankers were sometimes cast as villains."[75]

Nor were Thomas and his colleagues treated kindly by the press. Such establishment journals as the *New York Times,* the *Herald-Tribune,* the *Washington Post,* and the *Detroit Free Press* "roundly condemned the committee for airing unsubstantiated charges and denying accused persons basic means of defending themselves."[76]

But Hearst support never wavered. The hearings ended October 30 and Hearst writers, to counteract negative comment in the establishment press, outdid themselves in praising the committee. On November 3 author-lecturer Rupert Hughes began a strongly pro-Thomas series in the *Journal-American.* In the initial article, headlined HOW HOLLY-WOOD GOT THE SCARLET FEVER, Hughes asserted that "it is only natural that the Parnell Thomas Committee... should be vilified as an instrument of 'tyranny'... because it turns the national spotlight on crawling Red microbes whose purpose and practice is to be as un-American as they can be...."[77]

Two days later Pegler wrote that "the great work of the House Committee on Un-American Activities is slowly receiving recognition." He also noted that "the Thomas Committee is winning fights against the conspirators, victories over hecklers, and the respect of ethical newspapermen."[78]

About this time Pegler was winning some left-handed "respect" of his own. *The Daily Worker,* that humorless organ, was so agitated about his attacks that it made him the subject of one of its two comic strips. Protagonists of these features were Manichean polar opposites. The hero, interestingly named Pinky Rankin, was a bronzed, clean-cut industrial worker and model of Marxist virtue. His antithesis, a venal and reactionary journalist, was "Pestbrook Wiggler, Roving Reporter."

The same issue carried another installment by Hughes. Headed BENEDICT ARNOLD TO THE BAR, it identified enemies of the committee as "crypto-Communists and 'liberals' who cannot bear to hear Communism attacked." These enemies remain silent about Stalin's crimes while "shrieking to high heaven that Parnell Thomas is a fiend."[79]

To supplement the broadsides of Pegler and Hughes, the *Journal-American* printed one of its strongest anti-libertarian editorials on November 3. Fully indulging the Hearstian fondness for capitals and exclamation marks, the editorial thundered that "the need is for FEDERAL CENSORSHIP OF MOTION PICTURES! The Constitution PERMITS it! The law SANCTIONS it! The safety and welfare of Americans demand it!"[80]

That Thomas was able to gain partial victory in the hearings was due as much to the pusillanimity of the Hollywood moguls as to his allies in the press. At the end of November fifty top movie executives held a two-day meeting at the Waldorf-Astoria. The meeting ended with the announcement that the Ten would be fired and none rehired if he had not purged himself of contempt or been acquitted or sworn under oath that he was not a Communist. This decision, hailed by Thomas as "constructive," had been dictated by powerful New York financial interests that controlled the studios.[81] It was this action that launched the blacklist.

The decision was not unanimous. A minority, including the liberal Dore Schary and the individualistic Sam Goldwyn, opposed such drastic action against the writers. Even Jack Warner told Thomas at the hearings that he couldn't "figure where men could get together and try... to deprive a man of a livelihood because of his political beliefs." [82] But he ended up voting with the majority.

Equally equivocal was the role of Eric Johnston, president of the Motion Picture Association. Johnston, with a reputation as one of the business community's leading liberals, declared when the hearings opened that "as long as I live I will never be a party to anything as un-American as a blacklist." That life proved short. After the Waldorf meeting Johnston announced that the Ten would be suspended without pay and that "thereafter no Communists or other subversives would knowingly be employed in Hollywood."[83]

After that, it was a long downhill road for the Ten. On November 24, 1947 Congress cited them for contempt. Waiving a jury trial, eight were sentenced to a year in prison and two to six months. All were fined $1,000. Now their last hope was the Supreme Court. In an astounding stroke of ill fortune, two liberal justices, Frank Murphy and Wiley Rutledge, died in the summer of 1949. They were replaced by the conservatives Sherman Minton and Tom Clark. The Supreme Court refused to review the convictions and the writers went to jail in 1950.

On their release, they entered a world in which hysteria had become institutionalized. Totally blacklisted, some survived by going abroad and others by writing for pittances under assumed names. It wasn't till 1959 that "the Motion Picture Academy rescinded its by-law prohibiting awards to those who refused to cooperate with HUAC."[84]

In 1960 the blacklisted writer Dalton Trumbo received a credit under his own name for the first time since 1948. Trumbo wrote the screenplay for *Spartacus* in 1960 and for *Exodus* in 1962. Nineteen seventy-five was the year of maximum rehabilitation. Woody Allen starred in *The Front* (written, produced, and directed by blacklist victims), Lillian Hellman published the best-selling *Scoundrel Time* and the ordeal of Texas humorist John Henry Faulk was dramatized in a CBS-TV special called *Fear On Trial.* (In 1956 CBS-Radio had fired Faulk for alleged Communist sympathy.) Not only was the blacklist over but erstwhile villains were now being hailed as heroes.

The Fall of Parnell Thomas

In July 1948 the Atomic Energy Commission cleared Dr. Edward U. Condon, who headed the Bureau of Standards, of charges the committee had leveled against him. The charges were a mixture of innuendo and invention. A sinister connection with the Eastern Bloc was implied because Condon's wife was from Czechoslovakia. When he entertained some scientists who had pleaded the Fifth Amendment, he was accused – probably correctly – of being imprudent in his social relationships.

It was also charged that he was a member of the National Council of American-Soviet Friendship – a group to which he did not belong. With the support of the scientific community and the White House, Condon was given a clean bill of health.

Condon's exoneration was a bitter pill for Thomas to swallow. But it was also the dark prelude to a bright dawn. "Dawn" for the committee was the testimony of three witnesses – a woman at the end of July and two men in August. Thanks to this trio, the fame of Thomas and his colleagues rose to undreamed of heights. This "dawn" may in fact have saved the committee. So unsavory was its reputation that Truman aides had drafted a bill to abolish HUAC if the Democrats won the November election.[85]

The first witness's testimony was preceded by a piece of journalistic disinformation in Roy Howard's *World-Telegram* that dwarfed anything the Hearst papers had to offer that day. To titillate readers, the *Telegram* announced that a "beautiful blonde spy queen" was about to spill her secrets to the committee.[86] The spy queen turned out to be a frumpy, middle-aged brunette named Elizabeth Terrill Bentley. A Vassar graduate, she had shared an apartment in New York with Lee Fuhr, a health education student at Columbia Teachers College.[87] According to Bentley, it was Fuhr who led her into the Party.

Fuhr would later describe Bentley as a "love-starved nymphomaniac" and, indeed, Bentley seems to have rated the worth of male Party comrades in direct proportion to their willingness to gratify her sexually.[88] Her principal lover was a Soviet agent named Yakov Golos. He died in 1943 and two years later a saddened Bentley was telling all to the FBI.

Whatever her emotional difficulties, Bentley was a dynamite witness. As Communists she named Harry Dexter White, a former Assistant Secretary of the Treasury, Lauchlin Currie, assistant to President Roosevelt for six years, and William Remington, a Commerce Department official who had previously served on the War Production Board and Tennessee Valley Authority.

Bentley's was a tough act to follow. But followed it was – and then surpassed by the intense drama that accompanied the testimony of Whittaker Chambers and Alger Hiss. In the eighteen months between Chambers's accusation against Hiss and Hiss's conviction for perjury, America was split as deeply into ideological warring camps as France had been at the time of the Dreyfus case.

In early autumn of 1948 Parnell Thomas was riding high. His fall was so rapid that it can be compared to that of a surfer who is successfully riding a huge roller and suddenly loses his footing. Climax of the hearings was the dramatic August 25 public confrontation between Chambers and Hiss. On that day Thomas made the widely quoted statement to the principals that "certainly one of you will be tried for perjury."[89]

On September 17 a cocksure Thomas announced that the committee would soon reveal "a shocking chapter in Communist espionage in the atomic field."[90] This drew the salty riposte from Harry Truman that HUAC was "more un-American than the activities it is investigating."[91]

Ironically, the first major blow against Thomas was struck by a syndicated columnist who appeared in the *Daily Mirror*. Though Drew Pearson's syndicate was United Features rather than the Hearst-controlled King Features, his lively "Washington Merry-Go-Round" column was popular enough to be subscribed to by several right-wing papers. *The Mirror* achieved a measure of disassociation by placing this cautionary at the foot of every Pearson column: "The author of this column is given the widest latitude. His views do not necessarily reflect those of the *Mirror*."

In early October Pearson disclosed how "an affair between Thomas and a young secretary had irritated the less youthful spinster who ran the office and induced her to come to the column with evidence."[92] The evidence was of kickbacks to Thomas from his office staff.

On October 6 several papers ran a story that the FBI was checking the salaries of Thomas's staff. The story was carried in neither the *Journal-American* nor the *Mirror*.

Throughout October the Hearst high command did what it could to save Thomas. On the 23rd a front page news story appeared in the *Journal-American* under the headline THOMAS RAPS CLARK PROBE AS 'POLITICS.' The investigation had been initiated by Attorney General Tom Clark, a longtime enemy of Thomas. The article quoted Thomas's comment that the investigation was "despicable and revolting" and "cheap Pendergast politics." The congressman also accused Truman and Clark of "complete failure to prosecute the Fifth Column in the United States."[93]

The *Mirror's* story, on page 2, noted that the "inquiry (into Thomas's affairs) climaxed a longstanding feud between the brusk (sic) 53-year-old Thomas and U.S. Attorney General Tom Clark. Thomas' committee recently accused Clark of negligence in prosecuting persons suspected of Communist espionage."[94]

On October 27 a strongly pro-Thomas story ran in the *Journal-American*. The author, Washington correspondent David Sentner, declared that "the New Deal harassment of Representative J. Parnell Thomas... is similar to the experience suffered by former Representative Martin Dies, a Texas Democrat." Sentner also cited a Dies speech to the Southern Gas

convention, in which the congressman charged that a White House secretary who was also a Communist used his influence to thwart the Dies
Committee's objectives.[95] This was probably a reference to Lowell Mellett, who had been earlier accused of delaying Robert Taylor's entry into
the Navy so the actor could complete a pro-Soviet film.

Pegler did not join in the October campaign to save Thomas, being
then engaged in one of his name-correction crusades. On October 22 he
noted that a radio station owner named Samuel Novick had "after much
squirming" admitted that he gave money to the *New Masses.* Novick added
that he didn't know the *Masses* was a Communist publication. But Novick
was incidental; Pegler was really after two of his employees, the broad-
casters William Gailmor and Johannes Steel. With his usual conscien-
tiousness in these matters, Pegler informed readers that their original
surnames were Margolis and Stahl.[96]

Pearson, amply exercising his "widest latitude," charged on November
5 that Thomas had obtained four wartime deferments for his chief investigator and then procured his release after only nine months service.[97]

By this time the game was up for Thomas. The day before, he had
invoked the Fifth Amendment and refused to testify before a Grand Jury
on the charges against him. He was indicted on the 8th and this development
was noted by the *Journal-American* in a straight news story from which a
pro-Thomas slant was conspicuously absent. The headline read INDICT
THOMAS ON KICKBACKS.[98] The four-count indictment accused him
of thirty-four "overt acts" involving fraudulent salary claims for persons
he allegedly put on his office payroll.[99]

On November 30 Thomas pleaded *nolo contendere,* declaring that he
would not make a defense. The *Mirror's* December 1 headline read
THOMAS ADMITS GUILT IN KICKBACKS, ASKS MERCY.[100]

The next day Winchell wrote that "Drew Pearson deserves a Pulitzer
Prize for his public service via the Congressman J. Parnell Thomas
exposé."[101] This, as much as anything, signaled the Hearst directorate's
excommunication of Thomas.

On December 9, 1949 Thomas was found guilty and sentenced to 6-
18 months imprisonment by Federal District Judge Alexander Holtzoff.
He also received a $10,000 fine. At the Danbury Correctional Facility, his
place of detention, Thomas's fellow inmates were the Hollywood writers
Lester Cole and Ring Lardner Jr. In what seems a measure of poetic justice,
Thomas occupied a position in the hierarchy of desirable assignments far
lower than that of his former victims. Where Lardner worked in the office
and Cole tended the gardens, Thomas's duties included removing excreta

from the chicken coops. [102]

On release from prison, Thomas edited three weekly papers in New Jersey's Bergen County. In 1954 he attempted a return to Congress, billing himself "a fighter of the McCarthy type" and pledging "1,000-percent support" for McCarthy, "his objectives, and his methods."[103] Thomas's timing was poor. By 1954 McCarthy had become almost as much an irritant to the Republican establishment as he was to liberals and left-wingers. Thomas was defeated in the April 20 primary.

There was another reason why Thomas's comeback attempt was doomed to failure. McCarthy's staunchest supporters were militantly anti-communist Irish Catholics. Thomas himself was of that background, having been born John Patrick Feeney.[104] Then, living, working, and holding office in the suburban, predominantly Protestant Allendale-Ridgewood area, he changed his name and reinvented himself as a Republican, Episcopalian, and Mason. Thomas began his congressional career in the 1930s; by the 1950s his old district was increasingly populated by Irish Catholics who had made it into the suburbs. If these pugnacious Hibernians wanted a "fighter of the McCarthy type," they certainly didn't want one who had so opportunistically rejected his, and their, heritage. After this disappointment, Thomas moved to Florida. He died there on November 19, 1970.

An Assessment

How much help did the Hearst press give Parnell Thomas? Undoubtedly, a great deal. Establishment journals took a poor view of the Hollywood investigation and lined up solidly behind such figures as Edward U. Condon. But much of this influence was offset by the reckless élan with which the Hearst press was willing to buck the tide. The sneers of the sophisticated could not counter the cumulative effect on the public of glaring headlines, fevered cartoons, capitalized words, and forests of exclamation marks.

In supporting Thomas, Hearst executives and writers were not fair-weather friends. They backed him against the Hollywood "subversives," they backed him against Condon, and they even backed him in the initial stages of the Clark investigation. They only let go when revelations of Thomas's skullduggery made him unsalvageable.

Parnell Thomas once told the lawyer for an unfriendly witness that "the rights you have here are the rights given you by this committee. We will determine what rights you have and what rights you have not got...."[105] This hubristic assertion could serve as a slogan for the entire Parnell Thomas period. Under Thomas the committee outrageously favored friendly witnesses and arbitrarily silenced or ejected critics. In stigmatizing enemies, it freely resorted to exaggerated claims and downright falsehoods. Where Edward Condon was guilty of nothing more than indiscreet social relationships, Thomas leaked an article to Cissy Patterson's *Washington Times-Herald* in which he accused the physicist of "playing Stalin's game...."[106] Richard Nixon, without foundation, attempted to link Gerhardt Eisler to the Canadian atomic spy ring. John McDowell, in an even more imaginative departure from fact, charged that Albert Maltz was a colonel in the NKVD (later the KGB).[107]

If the Parnell Thomas Committee accomplished nothing else between 1946 and 1949, it amply demonstrated that McCarthyism did not begin with Joe McCarthy.

3. The Hiss Case and the Mindszenty Trial

In the late forties New York's Hearst papers faced communism as if they were preparing for Armageddon. Triumphalism was the watchword, and the containment policies of George F. Kennan and the Truman administration were viewed as irresolute and defeatist.

Given this total war mentality, one can understand the Hearst policy that redbaiting should not be limited to political columnists, editorialists, and news writers. In the years that spanned the Parnell Thomas and McCarthy eras, the leading political writers were Pegler, Sokolsky, Fulton Lewis, Howard Rushmore, E. F. Tompkins, and George Rothwell Brown at the *Journal-American* and labor columnist Victor Riesel at the *Mirror*. Of these, Rushmore was a former Communist and both Pegler and Sokolsky had antecedents on the far left. Sokolsky, the FBI'S "Mongoloid-Jew," would become a personal nemesis to the "millionaire Communist" Frederick Vanderbilt Field. Yet in 1934 he praised Field's book *Empire in the East* as "a brilliant discussion" that demonstrated "the inability of capitalism to survive without imperialism."[1]

Then there was the middle ground of general topics writers. These were columnists who wrote partially but not exclusively on political subjects. Some, like Frank Conniff ("East Side, West Side") were intensely political; others, like Bob Considine ("On the Line"), E. V. Durling ("Life With Salt on the Side"), Inez Robb ("Assignment America"), Henry McLemore ("In the Reviewing Stand"), and Elsie Robinson ("Listen, World"), less so. All the former were on the *Journal-American.*

The *Journal-American's* special feature writers included Louis Sobol (nightlife), Arthur ("Bugs") Baer (humor), Dorothy Kilgallen (Broadway/café society), Louella Parsons (Hollywood), Jack O'Brian (radio/TV), and an energetic but talentless prose poetaster named Harry H. Schlacht. This worthy was periodically trotted out to emote over events ranging from a Knights of Pythias anniversary to the triumphant return of Douglas MacArthur.

The *Mirror's* best-known columnists were Walter Winchell and Drew Pearson, whose relationship with the Hearst organization has been discussed. Victor Riesel began writing his "Inside Labor" column in 1949. His announced aim was to expose crooks and Communists in the labor movement. Of the two enemies, the former proved more dangerous: Riesel was acid-blinded by labor racketeers in 1956. Riesel also played an important part in Hollywood blacklisting in the fifties. In the manner of "O'Brien," Orwell's inquisitor in *1984,* he not only stalked unrepentant "subversives" but also went after actors like José Ferrer and Larry Parks, whose *mea culpas* Riesel castigated as "lukewarm and insincere...."[2] Riesel was such a hard-liner that he once imputed a flagging of anti-communist zeal to Senator Pat McCarran, chairman of the Senate Internal Security Subcommittee.

Next to Winchell, the *Mirror's* best-known special feature writers were Jacquin ("Jack") Lait, Lee Mortimer, and Nick Kenny. The latter's column, "Nick Kenny Speaking," was mainly devoted to radio/TV, Harry H. Schlacht-like poetry, and sycophantic references to Winchell. Lait and Mortimer were xenophobic, homophobic, and invincibly bigoted. Mortimer's field was entertainment while the elderly Lait, born in 1883, normally filled in for Winchell while he was on vacation. Lait was also one of Winchell's editors on the *Mirror.*

Lait and Mortimer's main contributions to stifling subversion were made independently of their affiliation with the Hearst organization. Together, they co-authored the four best-selling "Confidential" books, works that spotlighted aberrant political and sexual behavior in New York, Washington, Chicago, and the nation at large. Both were enthusiastic McCarthy backers. In *USA Confidential* Lait and Mortimer reported that "the University of Wisconsin, alma mater of so many Reds, is now lavender, where swishes... (get) up petitions against Joe McCarthy."[3] On another page, the authors assured their readers that "no college big-dome will approve this book. We are not 'advanced.'"[4] An evaluation, one is compelled to think, that inspired minimal dissent.

Among the nonpolitical writers, there were varying degrees of ideological commitment. Dorothy Kilgallen, far more interested in sensational trials, was at best a *pro forma* heresy hunter. While she would make dutiful anti-communist statements in her column ("Voice of Broadway") and radio program, she "avoided the red baiters at the *Journal-American*" and never attended their parties.[5] Kilgallen went so far as to write in VOB that a performer's inclusion in Red Channels did not "create the general inference that he is guilty of anything, including beating his wife or liking garlic."[6] (*Red Channels,* first published in 1950, was a 213-page directory that alphabetically listed 151 media and entertainment personalities, together with the politically suspect organizations they belonged to.) A close friend of Kilgallen, Robert Bach, recalls that "when it (the witch hunt) eased up in the late fifties, (Kilgallen) was... ready to say, 'Thank God it's over.'"[7]

The true believers were the political columnists, Frank Conniff (for a time), Winchell, Lait and Mortimer, Jack O'Brian, and – a special and unique case – the *Journal-American's* society editor, who wrote under the name of Cholly Knickerbocker.

Igor Alexandrovich Loiewski-Cassini was one of these exotic hybrids who exist in the rarefied world of emigré aristocracy. A naturalized American citizen, he was Russian by nationality, mostly Polish and Italian by ethnicity, and Orthodox by religion. Born in Sebastopol, he spent much of his youth in Italy and played on the Fascist tennis team in international competition. He came to America in the late thirties and, thanks to his mother's friendship with Cissy Patterson, became a society columnist on the *Washington Times-Herald.*

In June 1939 Cassini managed to get himself tarred and feathered. He was a house guest, in Warrenton, Virginia, of Major Austin McDonnell. Cassini was then courting the major's attractive daughter, Austine, known as "Bootsie." The punitive action was organized by a Virginia horse country blood named Alec Calvert. Calvert had a younger sister and was incensed by Cassini's candor in chronicling her amours in his column. In inflicting this antic chastisement, Calvert was assisted by two brothers named Montgomery.[8]

Cassini got the tar and feathers but he also got the girl. Bootsie married him and then took over his *Times-Herald* column when he was drafted during World War II. Following Army service, Cassini was moved up to the *Journal-American,* his first column appearing on September 4, 1945.[9]

As a fiercely partisan White Russian, the sincerity of Cassini's anti-communism was never in question. What puzzled many was its direction. Where colleagues hunted subversives in government, media, and the academy, Cassini tracked them through the pages of the *Social Register.* In his own words: "I had it in for celebrities who professed a sympathy for Stalin in total contrast to the way they lived."

Particular objects of his scorn were "the rich parlor pinks, traitors to their class...."[10] As early as 1947, Cassini's high society redbaiting caused the *New Republic* to describe him as "the most interesting economic theorist since Marie Antoinette."[11]

Of Cassini's adversaries, none fretted him more than former ambassador Joseph E. Davies. Davies appeared frequently in the Cholly Knickerbocker column, and never to his advantage. Cassini eagerly appropriated the nickname coined by Benjamin De Casseres and it was rare that Davies's name appeared in a form other than "Joe 'Submission to Moscow' Davies."

The crusading fervor of the *Journal-American* and *Mirror* in the late forties was fanned to fever pitch by the highly-publicized trials of two dissimilar men, Alger Hiss and Joszef Cardinal Mindszenty. Both were highly visible symbols: one of alleged pro-communist treachery by a "brightest-and-best" elitist; the other of militant anti-communist resistance by a peasant-born Prince of the Church. As the Hearst political writers and their nonpolitical but ideologically committed auxiliaries girded for battle, it is difficult to say which emotion was more dominant — sympathy for Mindszenty or loathing for Hiss.

The Hiss Case: August - December 1948

In the first stages of the Hiss case, there were many conservatives who could not bring themselves to believe the charges against the articulate, clean-cut former State Department official.

Reinforcing disbelief was the rumpled appearance and disreputable past of Hiss's accuser. John Rankin, the Dixie racist, made a point of shaking Hiss's hand after his August 5 testimony.[12] True, Rankin had a special ax to grind. Chambers was a senior editor of *Time,* a publication unswervingly critical of Rankin's anti-Semitism and Negrophobia. Deploring "the smear attacks... in *Time* magazine," Rankin declared that he was "not surprised at anything that comes out of anybody connected with it."[13]

Another handshaker was John McDowell, who had commissioned Albert Maltz a colonel in the NKVD. Two other right-wingers who reacted favorably to Hiss's testimony were Representative (later Senator) Karl Mundt of South Dakota and Louisiana Democrat F. Edward Hébert. Mundt feared that HUAC's reputation might become irreparably tarnished while Hébert's counsel was "let's wash our hands of the whole mess."[14]

Only Richard Nixon wanted to press on. His reasons were twofold. First, in 1946 he had read a confidential report prepared by Father John Cronin of the National Catholic Welfare Conference and submitted it to the American Catholic Bishops. Father Cronin had access to FBI files and his report, titled "The Problem of American Communism," identified Hiss as one of "certain Communists... in the State Department."[15] The second reason was personal. Nixon, that quintessential injustice collector, had discerned a snobbish and condescending attitude toward him on Hiss's part. So the suspicions of Hiss formed by Father Cronin's report were supplemented by strong personal antagonism.[16]

Though Hiss was far ahead in the personal opinion sweepstakes, the Hearst press was still predisposed against the debonair New Dealer. As early as August 4, the day after Chambers's opening testimony, the *Journal-American's* headline read WHITTAKER CHAMBERS' OWN STORY REVEALS HOW SPY RING OPERATED. The same issue carried an editorial headed TREASON TRIALS URGED. The editorial endorsed the recommendation of James F. O'Neill, National Commander of the American Legion, that "treason trials should be brought against every wartime federal official who fed military secrets to any Communist agent."[17] Though O'Neill referred to "wartime" and "military" secrets, it was hardly coincidence that his views should be so prominently publicized at a time when a peacetime federal official was accused of having fed government documents to a Communist agent.

The following day found the *Journal-American* on the defensive. With his cool and convincing performance, Alger Hiss had temporarily won the hearts of such as Rankin and McDowell. On the same day, Harry Truman responded affirmatively when a reporter asked him if "the Capitol Hill spy scare is a red herring to divert the public attention from inflation."[18] The *Journal-American's* tactic was to blanket the Hiss testimony and the Truman statement with a story headlined PROBER REVEALS US SENT A-BOMB SUPPLIES TO REDS.[19]

Returning to the attack on August 6, a *Mirror* editorial took aim at Truman's statement. It expressed outrage at hearing "the President of the United States defending the Communists with their own slimy weapon," that weapon being a tendency "to cloak themselves in a phony air of persecution" when under investigation.[20] Though the metaphor was cloudy, the challenge was clear.

Despite misgivings of other committee members, the persistent Nixon persuaded his colleagues to appoint him head of a three-man subcommittee that would hear additional testimony from Chambers. (The other members were Hébert and McDowell.) On August 7, in New York's Federal Courthouse, Chambers astonished the subcommittee members with his intimate knowledge of the Hisses' private lives. The ground covered nicknames (he was "Hilly," she was "Pross"), hobbies (ornithology), pets, and description of household furniture.[21] There were also discrepancies: Chambers said that Hiss at times called his wife "Dilly" and that Alger and Priscilla did not drink. The nickname was denied by the Hisses and friends. As for the accusation of teetotaling, the Hisses' abstention from spirits seems to have been limited to times spent with Whittaker Chambers.[22]

The case against Hiss gained ground when John Peurifoy, Assistant Secretary of State for security affairs, showed Mundt some file material damaging to the accused.[23] But it received a setback with the August 13 testimony – and death three days later – of Harry Dexter White, the Treasury Department official fingered by both Chambers and Elizabeth Bentley. "White's appearance had been gallant," wrote Whittaker Chambers, "he had skirmished brilliantly with the Committee. He had uttered the credo of a liberal... a statement of democratic faith so ringing, that *PM*, the New York leftist daily, had printed it verbatim...."[24] With White's death from a massive heart attack coming so soon after his testimony, Chambers's prestige skidded to an all-time low.

On August 17, the day after White's death, Hiss and Chambers confronted each other at a closed session in Room 1400 of New York's Commodore Hotel. Hiss believed that the meeting was part of a plan "to divert public sympathy from White by shifting attention to his own case."[25] During the tense confrontation, Hiss identified Chambers as "George Crosley," a deadbeat freelance writer he had known in Washington during the thirties.

If the New York Hearst papers were chastened by White's passing, the Commodore confrontation gave them an opportunity to get back in the hunt. The *Mirror's* headline that day read CHAMBERS NO STRANGER, HISS FINALLY ADMITS. The story, relatively brief, noted that Hiss "admitted that he had been acquainted with the ex-Communist courier under the name of George Crosley."[26]

On August 18 the *Journal-American's* headline read DISCLOSE HISS AND CHAMBERS SHARED HOME. Hiss had admitted to letting Chambers occupy his apartment at 2831 P Street during the early summer of 1935. Hiss claimed the arrangement was a sublet while Chambers maintained that Hiss had let him and his family live there free.[27]

Six days later a *Journal-American* editorial denounced Truman's "red herring" statement with the admonition that "it is not the Red Herring of American politics which is the concern of Congress... but the RED OC-TOPUS of international communism...."[28]

On August 25 Hiss and Chambers faced each other on Capitol Hill. Though television was still in its infancy, the hearing was considered important enough to warrant the presence of TV cameras. Just before it started, Hiss released a letter to Chairman Thomas that was a masterpiece of pejorative comparison and innocence by association. How could anybody believe the word of Chambers, a "self-confessed liar, spy, and traitor," over that of a man who had worked in government with such "living personages of recognized stature" as former Secretaries of State Cordell Hull, Edward Stettinius, and James F. Byrnes, Senators Tom Connally and Arthur Vandenberg, Dean Acheson, John Foster Dulles, Eleanor Roosevelt, and Chester Davis, Hiss's former superior at the Agricultural Adjustment Association?[29] Actually, some of these *prominenti* had grave reservations about Hiss. Byrnes had worked with J. Edgar Hoover to ease him out of the State Department, Davis believed he was associated with a group of Communist lawyers at AAA, and Dulles would end up by totally repudiating him.[30]

But nobody knew that on the morning of August 25. Thanks to the adroit timing of Hiss's letter, the public widely believed that the captains and kings were solidly in his corner. The *Journal-American,* making the best of a bad situation, carried the headline HISS IS LINKED AGAIN TO REDS. On the same page was a picture of Hiss with the ironic caption – "Giving His 'Best Recollection.'" Both headline and caption referred to Hiss's reiterated denials of Chambers's reiterated charges.[31]

The nine-and-a-half hour session went badly for Hiss. He claimed he had "thrown in" a 1929 Ford when he sublet the 29th Street apartment to Chambers but the committee produced records showing that he had sold the vehicle to the Cherner Motor Company in 1936. Worse, some of the committee members began to taunt Hiss. When he waffled about the Ford, Nixon caustically asked him how many cars he had given away in his life.[32] Hébert, the erstwhile handwasher, expressed astonishment at how a man of Hiss's intellect could give "to casual people his apartment, (toss in) an automobile" and lend "money to an individual just casually...."[33]

Frank Conniff praised Nixon's persistence in his August 26 column. Hiss was "home free" with his cool denial of Chambers's charges on August 5 and the committee was ready to buck "the case back to the Department of Justice and let it go at that. But not so Mr. Nixon. It was he who suggested that the contradictions were so flamboyant that either Hiss or Chambers had to be lying."[34]

The next day the committee issued an "interim report" which concluded that Hiss's testimony was "vague and evasive" while Chambers's
was "forthright and emphatic." Particularly damaging to Hiss were his
"unresponsive recollections" about the transfer of the 1929 Ford.[35]

That evening, appearing on the "Meet the Press" radio program,
Chambers responded to a challenge Hiss had issued him during their
August 17 confrontation. "I would like to invite Mr. Whittaker Chambers
to make these same statements (regarding Hiss's Communist affiliation)
out of the presence of this committee and without being privileged for suit
for libel. I challenge you to do it, and I hope you will do it damned
quickly."[36] In response to a direct question from Edward T. Folliard of the
Washington Post, Chambers said: "Alger Hiss was a Communist and may
still be one."[37]

The quickening tempo of events produced one spectacular development after another. On September 27 Hiss filed a $50,000 slander suit
against Chambers. Chambers responded that he welcomed "Mr. Hiss's
daring suit" but did not believe that Hiss could use "the means of justice
to defeat the ends of justice." This statement brought a second suit from
Hiss. Filed on October 8, it sought an additional $25,000 in damages. On
November 14 Chambers retrieved a dusty, document-filled envelope from
the Brooklyn home of his nephew's mother. The envelope contained
handwritten memos from Hiss, typed copies or summaries of confidential
State Department papers, two strips of developed microfilm, and a long
memo on yellow foolscap in the handwriting of Harry Dexter White.[38] On
December 2 Chambers handed over the famous "pumpkin papers" to
HUAC investigators William Wheeler and Donald Appell. These were
microfilms of State and Navy Department documents that had been se-
cured in a hollowed-out pumpkin on Chambers's farm in Westminster,
Maryland. Import of this material was that Hiss had engaged in espionage
and lied when he said he hadn't seen Chambers since 1936. On December
16 a Grand Jury indicted Hiss on two counts of perjury.

Following HUAC's damaging interim report, the *Journal-American*
and *Mirror* stepped up their attacks on the faltering Hiss. On August 28
Pegler ran a lampoon in which a Committee Against Pro-American
Activities investigates persons suspected of patriotism. One such suspect
is Merriwell Booh, high echelon policy chief of the State Department, who
is accused of being a "top drawer undercover agent of the pro-American
conspiracy." Defending himself, Booh insists that the phrase "this great
country of ours" was spoken "with broad sarcasm."[39]

There were also the usual loaded, lurid headlines and photos with tendentious captions. A random sampling of the former includes INSIDE STORY OF SPY FILMS TOLD BY EX-RED EDITOR, CHAMBERS SAYS HISS TOOK DATA FOR REDS, JURY GRILLS HISS BROTHER (Donald), and HISS HANDWRITING IDENTIFIED IN 12 SPY DOCUMENTS. Right after Hiss's indictment a picture of him was taken on the subway. The text below read "when some of the passengers recognized Hiss they moved away from him and hissed the man who is alleged to have turned State Department secret records over to the Communists."[40]

Of the nonpolitical writers, Igor Cassini let himself be distracted from the Hiss hunt on December 1, 1948, right after the 1949 *Social Register* came out. Under the headline NEW SOCIAL REGISTER PINK WITH PRO-REDS, Cassini charged that "Woolworth heir Frazier McCann and his wife... have been actively supporting Henry Wallace, leftist (New York Congressman) Vito Marcantonio, and have contributed heavily to Communist fronts." Cassini added that "other parlor pinks who have made the *Register* are Joe 'Submission to Moscow' Davies... and Mrs. Hester G. Huntington, who was the 'Angel' of Earl Browder, onetime chief of the American Communist Party."[41]

The only Hearst columnist who seemed somewhat out of sync during the anti-Hiss campaign was Walter Winchell. Because of attacks on him in *Time,* Winchell detested the Luce empire. This antipathy carried over to Chambers, a senior *Time* editor, and throughout the Hiss-Chambers controversy Winchell maintained a posture of malevolent neutrality.

To relieve his frustration, Winchell devoted most of October to one of those personal vendettas for which he was famous. We recall Pegler's homophobic animadversions on the dancer Paul Draper. Winchell's "Draper" was Serge Lifar, the Parisian ballet master who was planning a visit to the United States. In accusing Lifar of wartime pro-Nazi sympathy, Winchell was by no means off the mark. Lifar had a foul record as a collaborator, having "called on the Führer during a visit to Germany in 1942 (and) published articles praising the Nazis in the occupation press." Astoundingly, he got off with the wrist slap of being barred from his profession for a year.[42] Crowing over how accurately he had sized up Lifar, Winchell wrote that "some faces must be pretty cerise. They belittled my exposé of the Queereographer's pro-Nazi activities."[43]

On December 8 Winchell directed a sartorial sneer at Chambers ("his pants are too high over his knees") and, questioning Chambers's break with communism, commented that he wasn't "the only 'former' Communist working for Henry Luce."[44]

On December 16, the day Hiss was indicted, Winchell lamented that "a man with that sordid record was a senior *Time* editor since 1939. That fact alone deprived *Time* of the privilege of criticizing anybody!" Almost as an afterthought, Winchell added that this did not absolve Hiss.[45]

Even after Hiss's indictment, Winchell continued to snipe at Chambers and *Time*. On December 29 he wrote that "locals (read Winchell) are wondering why *Time* never got wise to Chambers. Don't they ever watch what their editors are doing?"[46]

Winchell's New Year's Eve column contained the interesting hypothesis that "if Hiss hadn't sued Chambers, it is doubtful if Chambers would have revealed (the Pumpkin Papers... Under a goading examination by Hiss's lawyer, Chambers blew."[47] William L. Marbury, one of Hiss's lawyers, had subjected Chambers to a probing interrogation in November.

There was a five-and-a-half month interval between Hiss's indictment and the first trial. As prosecution and defense made their preparations, there followed the inevitable lull in news coverage about – in Chambers's phrase – the two men "caught in a tragedy of history." But the *Journal-American* and *Mirror* writers would have little rest. On December 27, eleven days after Hiss's indictment, an event took place in Eastern Europe that unleashed an outpouring of anti-communist fervor which dwarfed even the emotions stirred up by the Hiss case.

The Ordeal of Cardinal Mindszenty

Several Catholic clerics had tainted records during the Second World War. In Slovakia, Monsignor Josef Tiso led a pro-Nazi puppet government and was executed in 1947. Also under a cloud was Archbishop (later Cardinal) Aloizije Stepinac. Accused of collaborating with the fascist Croatian regime of Ante Pavelic, Stepinac was sentenced to sixteen years at hard labor in 1946.

No such stigma ever touched Joszef Mindszenty. Though of German descent (the family name was Pehm), he was so repelled by Nazism that in 1941 he adopted the ultra-Hungarian and ultra-Catholic name of Mindszenty – "all saints."[48] A sympathetic biographer writes that when the Germans occupied Hungary, Bishop Mindszenty sheltered Jews and denounced anti-Semitism as "the basest tool of Nazi propaganda."[49]

This conflicts with the assertion of novelist Howard Fast, then a Communist, that Mindszenty was at times known to have made anti-Semitic remarks.[50] Arrested by the Nazis on September 27, 1944, Mindszenty was confined to Budapest's Vészprém Prison.

After the war, Mindszenty was elevated to cardinal and made Primate of Hungary. This set the stage for a collision with the Hungarian government. Though the Premier, István Dobi, belonged to the Smallholders Party, real power lay in the hands of Communist Deputy Premier Mátyás Rakosi. Rakosi was a ruthless Stalinist and Mindszenty, rigid and authoritarian, stood for the unbending anti-communism of the Church under Pius XII.

A portent of things to come was a November 27, 1948 speech by Rakosi. The Deputy Premier said Hungary would have to collectivize agriculture, claiming that farm prices in private holdings were 33-500 percent above the world market. Rakosi also denounced "spies, traitors, smugglers, and Fascists dressed in the robes of a cardinal." Mindszenty had been an outspoken opponent of collectivization.[51]

On December 27 Mindszenty and thirteen others were arrested on charges of plotting against the government, espionage, treason, and black market currency dealings. The *Journal-American's* headline read JAIL HUNGARY CARDINAL. The news account listed the charges and added that the "arrest had been freely predicted" since Rakosi's remark about "Fascists in the robes of a cardinal."[52]

The *Mirror,* by its own admission, followed a policy of 90 percent entertainment and 10 percent news.[53] So its December 28 Mindszenty headline – HUNGARY ARRESTS CARDINAL – was smaller than the one about the suicide attempt of actress Faye Emerson, then the wife of Elliott Roosevelt. The text noted that Hungary was 67 percent Catholic and recorded the lament of England's Cardinal Griffin that "the flag of freedom has been torn down in Hungary."[54]

On December 29 the *Journal-American* carried a page 2 story headed SPELLMAN CITES PLOT IN CARDINAL'S ARREST. The New York prelate said the arrest came after "months of plotting and threatening by the Red Fascists."[55] In "East Side, West Side" Frank Conniff recalled as prophetic his column of October 15, 1946, in which he described the conviction of Archbishop Stepinac as "the boldest tactical success yet accomplished in the Communist Party's... offensive against the Roman Catholic Church."[56]

The *Mirror's* contribution that day was a page 2 story headlined SAYS CARDINAL PLOTTED PRO-US KINGDOM. One of the charges against Mindszenty was that he had conspired with pretender Otto von Hapsburg to establish an Austro-Hungarian monarchy that would be a bulwark against communism in Eastern Europe.[57]

The next day the *Journal-American's* headline read POPE EX-COMMUNICATES CARDINAL'S PERSECUTORS. Pius pronounced "major excommunication" against all who participated in Mindszenty's detention, from Premier Dobi to the policemen who made the arrest. Major excommunication can be reversed only by the Pope.[58]

In the same issue, Frank Conniff angrily reacted to an Associated Press story that some "prominent Hungarian Catholics disapproved of Cardinal Mindszenty's militant anti-communism." These people, insisted Conniff, were not "prominent Catholics but prominent appeasers, collaborators, and quislings."[59]

The next day Conniff suggested that "American newspapers and wire services must devise some new approach to portray the rigged background against which Cardinal Mindszenty will be pinioned."[60] There was no doubt in anybody's mind that Mindszenty would be subjected to the confession-extracting techniques that had proved so successful during the Stalin Purge.

News and editorial coverage about the cardinal slackened in January. Through methods frightening and familiar, Mindszenty was being softened up for his show trial, which would begin in February.

The *Journal-American's* February 3 headline read CARDINAL DENIES REBEL PLOT. Underneath was a photo of Mindszenty and the caption "Admits Being 'Partly Guilty.'" While confessing to the other charges, Mindszenty denied plotting with the United States and Britain to overthrow Hungary's Communist government.[61] Concurrently, the Hungarian regime published a written "confession." This document was such a clumsy forgery that it contained over fifty misspellings, including such words as "Catholic," "monarchy," and "primate."[62]

MINDSZENTY DENIES DURESS was the *Journal-American's* February 4 headline. Directly above was a smaller caption, "Like Moscow Trials." The story noted Mindszenty's confession but reproduced the following International News Service bulletin: "At the Vatican, news that Cardinal Mindszenty repudiated a letter saying any confession of guilt would be the result of extortion, strengthened the conviction of Vatican officials that the Primate is testifying under extreme duress."[63]

The consensus remains that Mindszenty broke under drugs and not torture. On the stand the cardinal showed no signs of bodily mistreatment, sustaining views that his will to resist was destroyed chemically rather than physically.

The end of Mindszenty's trial, on February 6, was headlined CARDINAL'S DEATH TRIAL CLOSES in the *Journal-American* and CARDINAL'S TRIAL ENDS, ASKS DEATH in the *Mirror*.[64] The *Journal-American* noted Mindszenty's final plea that he was not an enemy of the Hungarian people, coupled with an admission that "some deeds ascribed to him conflicted with the Hungarian laws."[65]

The prosecution had asked for the death sentence. The prospect that Mindszenty might be executed drove New York's cardinal to one of his wildest flights of demagoguery. As a master of overripe prose, Francis Spellman was challenged only by Douglas MacArthur and the *Journal-American's* Harry H. Schlacht. February 6 was a Sunday and Spellman's sermon – "Rebellion to Tyrants Is Obedience to God" – was reproduced on the pictorial page of the *Journal-American,* flanked by pictures of Spellman in the pulpit and Mindszenty in the dock. The opening segment of this oration is so remarkable that it worth quoting almost in full:

> A new god has come to you, my people. His fiery eyes do not flash through clouds of incense or altar candles… The new god is not a stone statue worn smooth by the kisses of the faithful. He was not born in heaven… The new god is born from earth and blood – he strides ahead and under the thunder of his steps the globe trembles from East to West. This is the red god. The Seine shudders at his impact and tries to break its banks. Westminster trembles before him like Jericho, and across the green ocean his red shadow falls on the walls of the White House. Hosanna! New god.[66]

Spellman hastened to assure his audience that "these words are not mine." Instead, he attributed them to a "Hungarian Communist," a "Satan-bred man" who taught these "blasphemous lines" to "the youth of Red-enshackled lands."[67]

The words were in fact Spellman's – or those of an imaginative priest on his staff. Nobody with a minimal knowledge of history or an ear for Marxist prose could ever imagine a 1949 model Stalinist apparatchik uttering the piece of bombast that Spellman attributed to that conveniently unnamed "Hungarian Communist." But this was a more innocent age. Spellman shrewdly realized that thundering rhetoric about "fiery eyes" and a "red god" would play a lot better with the Knights of Columbus and sodality ladies in his audience than if he had factually reproduced some dry account of how "the progressive Hungarian masses are militantly resisting clerical reaction."

Spellman also sounded a thinly-veiled appeal for domestic repression: "When will the… American public, and the leaders in all phases of American life, religious, educational, political, labor, industrial, communications, yes, and in entertainment, when will free men raise their voices as one… and work against Satan-inspired Communist crimes?"[68] (In Spellman's lexicon, a "Satan-inspired Communist crime" could be placement of *The Nation* in a school library or a "dirty" movie like *Baby Doll*.)

That same day, at Spellman's behest, four thousand Catholic Boy Scouts marched down Fifth Avenue and three thousand Fordham students recited a rosary on behalf of Mindszenty.[69]

On February 8 a Hungarian court rejected the prosecution's death plea and sentenced Mindszenty to life imprisonment. In declining to execute the prelate, it took into consideration his confession and an apology he made to the government.[70]

LIFE FOR CARDINAL was the *Journal-American's* February 8 headline. An editorial commented that the trial was "part of a war being waged with savage severity against Catholics because their Church, under the inspired leadership of Pope Pius XII, has been the most effective opponent of World Communism."[71]

The *Mirror's* February 8 headline read REACH VERDICT ON CARDINAL. An editorial called attention to the trials of the twelve Communist leaders in New York, suggesting that Americans "contrast the brutal treatment accorded (Mindszenty) with the freedom of the prancing and heckling lawyers who... are being given ample time to mock justice."[72]

For all Spellman's fulminations about Mindszenty's "martyrdom," the Vatican could barely conceal its displeasure over his submissive behavior in court. Nobody, not even his severest critics, ever accused Eugenio Pacelli of being a bleeding heart. In a querulous address to the Sacred College, Pius remarked that Mindszenty's "vacillating mind" was inexplicable unless he had been injured physically or mentally.[73]

With his conviction, Joszef Mindszenty faded from the headlines, not to emerge till the 1956 Hungarian revolution. As for the Hearst writers, they had some unfinished business with Alger Hiss.

The Hiss Case: May 1949 to January 1950

The first Hiss trial opened at the Federal Courthouse in Manhattan's Foley Square on May 31. The judge, Samuel Kaufman, was a Truman appointee who would later draw criticism for alleged bias in favor of the defendant. The prosecutor was Assistant U.S. Attorney Thomas F. Murphy. Big, beefy, and walrus-mustached, Murphy looked like an old-time Tammany precinct boss. Murphy's populist image was reinforced by a family connection: he was the brother of "Fireman" Johnny Murphy, ace relief pitcher of the Yankees during the thirties.

The defense was captained by Lloyd Paul Stryker, a florid, silver-haired master of rolling cadences and dramatic courtroom techniques. The jury, ten of whom were male, represented "a cross-section of middle-class white America."[74]

On June 1 the *Journal-American's* headline read CHARGE HISS

GAVE RED SPY TOP SECRETS OF STATE DEPARTMENT. The story, written by ex-Communist Howard Rushmore, was completely slanted against Hiss. It contained references to how he "sat with pursed lips and glared at the prosecutor" and how Priscilla Hiss "moistened her lips nervously."[75] The "Red spy" in the article was Chambers. Rushmore identified him as a conduit to "a Communist 'apparatus' that existed among New Deal Reds."[76]

Stryker's opening day histrionics received minimal attention in Rushmore's story. Ecstatically praising his client, Stryker said that "I will take Alger Hiss by the hand, and... into the valley of the shadow of death I will fear no evil, for there is no blot or blemish on him."[77] Stryker was as theatrical in vilifying Chambers as in eulogizing Hiss. "In the warm southern countries... where they have leprosy, sometimes you will hear... a man crying down the street, 'unclean, unclean' at the approach of a leper. I say the same to you at the approach of this moral leper."[78]

Pegler, typically relating these events to his private agendas, wrote that the Hiss case "was proof that the Roosevelt administration was equally guilty or traitorously negligent."[79]

The *Journal-American's* June 6 headline read WADLEIGH ADMITS GIVING CHAMBERS STOLEN SECRETS. Henry Julian Wadleigh was a State Department employee who confessed espionage to the FBI in 1948.[80] An economist trained at British universities, he described himself as a Communist "sympathizer" but not a Party member.[81] At the Hiss trial, Wadleigh repeated his FBI testimony that he had handed over trade documents to Chambers and to another Communist agent named David Carpenter, alias David Zimmerman.[82]

On June 7 general topics writer Inez Robb commented that the dilemma of Alger Hiss "poses the personal problems of the... individual, either temporarily or permanently, in the American Communist Party."[83] Despite the column's "objective" tone, it reflects the *Journal-American's* certainty that Hiss was a Party member – a view not shared by many others who believed in his guilt.

Eleanor Roosevelt was one public figure who continued to believe in Hiss's innocence. Even after his conviction, when a majority of Democratic liberals reluctantly accepted the verdict, she refused to go along with their consensus.[84] The former First Lady's stand was a source of both outrage and delight to Westbrook Pegler. "Eleanor Roosevelt," he wrote on June 14, "has joined the Communists and other proximate defendants in the Hiss perjury case... trying to discredit Whittaker Chambers."[85]

The Hiss defense began on June 21. Following Murphy's skillful handling of the prosecution, and the testimony of such as Wadleigh, a mood seemed to prevail at Hearst headquarters that Hiss's conviction was a foregone conclusion. In a reflective what-might-have-been piece, Bob Considine opined that "Alger Hiss might have avoided... the present trial if he had taken different steps at several key moments in the case." Hiss, in Considine's view, should have immediately given HUAC a written statement about his activities at the time he knew "Crosley" and not delayed a month before suing Chambers.[86]

On June 27 Stryker conceded a discrepancy between Mrs. Hiss's statement that she had sold their typewriter to a junk dealer and a later defense admission that it had been given to the family of a maid who worked for the Hisses between 1935 and 1938. This machine was the famous Woodstock N230099, on which were typed the incriminating documents handed over to Chambers. Howard Rushmore wrote that this would help the prosecution "prove Alger Hiss a liar and purveyor of State secrets to a Communist spy ring."[87] In the same issue Pegler labeled the hated Eleanor Roosevelt "a figurative co-defendant of Alger Hiss."[88]

Both Stryker and Murphy made their final summations on July 6. The *Journal-American's* page 1 story reported that "Hiss shrunk in his chair as Murphy shouted his accusations branding (him) another Judas Iscariot, another Benedict Arnold."[89]

Due to a strike, the *Mirror* did not appear in June or July of 1949. So all the New York Hearst coverage on the first trial was in the *Journal-American*.

The trial ended in a hung jury, with an 8-4 vote in favor of conviction. Confident that Hiss would be found guilty, the Hearst writers reacted with rage and vindictiveness. PROBE OF HISS JUDGE DEMANDED IN CONGRESS, read the *Journal-American's* July 9 headline.

Howard Rushmore's story accused Judge Kaufman of "prejudice" and complained that he had not allowed Hede Massing, ex-Communist ex-wife of Gerhardt Eisler, to testify against Hiss. Among the congressmen calling for an investigation of Kaufman was Richard Nixon.[90] The same issue carried an interview with anti-Hiss juror James F. Hanrahan. Hanrahan characterized one pro-Hiss juror as "emotional," two as "blockheads," and one as a "dope."[91]

In an inexcusable ethical transgression, the *Journal-American* printed the names and addresses of two pro-acquittal jurors. One of them, Arthur L. Pawlinger, "claimed that he had received... threatening phone calls after the trial and asked the FBI to investigate."[93]

The second trial began on November 17, 1949. No sooner had the first ended than U.S. Attorney John F. X. McGohey, Murphy's superior, put the case back on the calendar. "When judges are available we'll try it again," said McGohey. "And Tom Murphy will try it. He has done a magnificent job."[94]

Murphy was the only holdover. The new judge, Henry W. Goddard, was a no-nonsense type who, unlike his predecessor, had no pronounced political leanings. Heading the defense was a Southern-born Boston attorney named Claude B. Cross. Dry and incisive, Cross was a Calvin Coolidge to the flamboyant Stryker's William Jennings Bryan. The second jury, like the first, was white and middle-class. The only difference was in gender proportion: eight of the jurors were women.

Robbed of victory in July, the Hearst papers were out for blood. A recurring theme in their reportage during the trial was Hiss's connection with alien subversives, the more alien and the more subversive the better. On November 21 the *Mirror's* headline was RED ORDERED HISS TO JOIN STATE DEPARTMENT. The "Red" in question was a sinister and mysterious figure known mainly as J. Peters but also by many other aliases. A Hungarian, Peters was identified by Chambers as chief Comintern representative in the United States and paymaster to Chambers and other America-based Comintern agents. According to the *Mirror's* story, "Whittaker Chambers asserted yesterday that Hiss entered the State Department on orders from 'J. Peters,' former leader of the Communist underground in the United States."[96]

The *Journal-American* also chronicled Hiss's links to unwholesome foreigners, its December 9 headline reading EISLER'S EX LINKS HISS TO RED RING. Hede Massing was an aging siren who had once been acclaimed the toast of Vienna.[97] As a Communist agent in Washington, she tried to persuade a young State Department employee named Noel Field to steal documents for her. Massing testified that in 1935 she had chided Hiss for "trying to get Noel Field from my organization and into yours." Hiss, taking the matter lightly, allegedly said: "So you are this famous girl who is trying to get Noel Field away from me." The article concluded with criticism of Judge Kaufman for refusing to "let Mrs. Massing testify in the first trial... and today her testimony proved dynamite."[98]

Three days later Hiss's cause was further damaged by the testimony of a former superior at State, Dr. Stanley Hornbeck. Hornbeck, originally a Hiss supporter, admitted that William C. Bullitt, former ambassador to the Soviet Union and France, had referred to Hiss as a "fellow traveler." The *Journal-American* headline read SAYS BULLITT CALLED HISS A PRO-RED.[99]

In both trials the Hiss defense used psychiatry as a weapon against Chambers. Thanks to Murphy, the weapon proved a boomerang. Over the prosecution's objections, the court had allowed Dr. Carl Binger to observe Chambers and take notes if he perceived signs of abnormal behavior. At the second trial, Dr. Henry A. Murray, a Harvard Medical School psychologist, was allowed to back up Binger.

Both Binger and Murray came off as men educated beyond their intelligence. Binger "had been certified as a psychiatrist only in 1946 and... his admission to the American Psychiatric Association had been twice deferred because of insufficient training."[100] Although Murray's credentials were more impressive, he appeared on the stand to be slow-thinking and easily confused.

On January 11, 1950 the *Journal-American* headline read QUIZ ENTANGLES HISS ALIENIST. Binger, who had characterized Chambers as a congenital liar, admitted to Murphy that he had once instructed his maid to tell a caller he wasn't in. Murphy asked him if this was any better than Chambers lying when he applied for a passport. With hauteur, Binger replied that "I don't compare a man of Chambers's education and background with our colored West Indian maid."[101] In the exchange, Binger looked like a bigot as well as a bumbler.

Binger also cited as a sign of mental instability Chambers's habit of frequently looking up at the ceiling. Murphy pointed out that Binger himself had looked at the ceiling fifty times in fifty-nine minutes.[102]

During the Second World War, Murray had prepared a psychological profile of Adolf Hitler for the Office of Strategic Services. When questioning Murray, Murphy speculated that "some of Hitler's speeches might have been written by Goebbels or (Ernst) Hanfstaengl." Murray replied that there was "evidence that Hiss helped Hitler in some of his writings." Murphy: "Doctor, I think you are a little confused. You mean Hess, as in Rudolf." Though Murray's only error was a slip of the tongue, Rushmore's account in the January 13 *Journal-American* was gleefully headed PROSECU-TOR RIPS SECOND HISS ALIENIST.[103]

On January 14, in the *Mirror*, Winchell called attention to "the news pictures showing how Alger Hiss has aged between trials. A horrible example of the effect that comes from worry."[104]

The fuddled psychologist was not the only Murray who contributed to Hiss's downfall. On January 18 a page 1 story appeared in the *Journal-American* under the heading MAID LINKS HISSES TO CHAMBERS. Written by Rushmore, it reported the testimony of Edith Murray that Alger and Priscilla Hiss visited the Chamberses in Baltimore in 1936. Hiss had denied that he and his wife ever visited Chambers in that city.[105]

Hiss was found guilty on January 21. On the 25th, following his sentencing, the *Journal-American* carried an enormous headline reading HISS GETS 5 YRS. The word "years" was abbreviated to make the headline bigger. Below the headline was a picture of Hiss exiting through the barred gates of a subway station. A gloating caption read: "The picture may be reversed shortly, with the sign reading 'Entrance' and the barred doors, those of prison gates."[106]

George Sokolsky's column, "These Days," had recently begun running in the *Journal-American.* The rightist pundit observed that "Alger Hiss is a symbol of a mad period in our government, a period during which administrative control had become so close that major policies were determined at low levels."[107]

On the day of Hiss's conviction, Secretary of State Dean Acheson made his generous but probably ill-advised remark that "I will not turn my back on Alger Hiss." The *Mirror's* headline – ACHESON WILL STAND BY HISS – was followed the next day by an editorial describing Acheson as a "dangerously incapable official (who is) unworthy of that office."[108]

Walter Winchell addressed the issue three days later. Under "Alger Hisstory," he noted that "Mrs. Dean Acheson contributed substantially to the Alger Hiss defense fund." The gossip also claimed that "Dr. Henry A. Murray (he testified for Hiss) has been a member of over 21 Communist fronts."[109]

On February 1 the *Journal-American* carried a burning editorial that could be described as a dress rehearsal for the McCarthy era – an era that would begin in eight days. The editorial shrieked that the verdict was not against "Alger Hiss alone" but against "FELLOW TRAVELERS of the Communists – in schools and colleges... in miseducated artistic and literary circles – who are MORE DANGEROUS than the Communists themselves." This foreshadows McCarthy's later denunciations of "anti-anti-communists," individuals who deny pro-communist sympathy but who continually obstruct the efforts of those truly fighting communism. The editorial also excoriated "every fool or knave who has supported... the Communist movement," and those who "mendaciously characterized Communist exposés as 'Witch Hunts' and 'Red Herrings.'"[110] The *pièce de résistance* that day was a Burris Jenkins cartoon depicting a pitchfork labeled "American Justice" being driven into the writhing body of a snake with hammer and sickle markings on its skin. As the prongs of the pitchfork find their mark, the dying serpent utters the outcry – HISS-SS![111] Few people knew the probable inspiration for that cartoon. In 1918 many

American newspapers were angrily denouncing William Randolph Hearst for his alleged pro-Germanism. That spring the *New York Tribune* began an acid-dipped weekly series with a cartoon captioned "Coiled in the Flag." Only this time the offending reptile was characterized as HEAR-S-S-T![112]

And Where was Joe?

Joe McCarthy had a great deal to say about Alger Hiss – but only after Hiss's status had changed from that of embattled accused to convicted felon. McCarthy's detachment from the great Hearst anti-communist crusades of the late forties is a phenomenon that has never been adequately explored. To correctly assess the totality of that detachment, it is necessary to examine four time frames: August 3 to December 16, 1948, the period between Chambers's initial accusations against Hiss and Hiss's indictment for perjury; December 27, 1948, to February 8, 1949, the time-segment between Cardinal Mindszenty's arrest and sentencing; May 31 to July 7, the first Hiss trial; November 17, 1949, to January 21, 1950, the second Hiss trial.

During the first period, those three-and-a-half months of confrontations, lawsuits, and pumpkin papers, McCarthy's main concern was with housing. On August 5, the day of Hiss's rebuttal to Chambers, McCarthy offered an amendment to a housing bill approved by the Senate Banking and Currency Committee that emasculated it of provisions calling for public housing, slum clearance, and assistance to paraplegic veterans.[113] McCarthy had long opposed public housing, believing that federally-funded projects were "breeding grounds for Communism."[114]

In mid-August, as the Hiss controversy was heating up, McCarthy was busy preparing a thirty-seven page article titled "Wanted: A Dollar's Worth of Housing for Every Dollar Spent." The article appeared in a ninety-four page booklet called *How to Own Your Own Home*. Publisher of the paean to private housing was the Lustron Corporation of Columbus, Ohio, a manufacturer of prefabricated dwelling units. Though McCarthy originally claimed sole authorship, he later admitted to receiving assistance.[115] But his fee – $10,000 – would have aroused the envy of the world's most successful authors.

The writer has been completely unsuccessful in his quest for any expression of support or sympathy for Cardinal Mindszenty on the part of McCarthy. I have consulted biographies, historical works, magazines, microfilmed newspaper collections, and the comprehensive FACTS ON FILE directory – all to no avail. I have also sought information from four leading academic authorities on the period and from a prominent conservative activist and former friend of McCarthy.

David M. Oshinsky is Professor of History at Rutgers University and author of *A Conspiracy So Immense: The World of Joe McCarthy.* Oshinsky says the possibility exists that McCarthy may have addressed the Mindszenty case in contacts with Hungarian-American groups in Wisconsin but of this he is not sure.[116]

The second McCarthy scholar with whom I communicated is Thomas C. Reeves, Professor of History at the University of Wisconsin-Parkside and author of *The Life and Times of Joe McCarthy.* His comment: "I have no recollection of McCarthy addressing himself to the issues in question. (The Mindszenty case and the controversy between Eleanor Roosevelt and Cardinal Spellman.) Indeed, he may only barely have known of them at the time."[117]

Michael O'Brien is Associate Professor of History at the University of Wisconsin Center - Fox Valley. His major work on the McCarthy era is *McCarthy and McCarthyism in Wisconsin,* published in 1980. He wrote: "It is possible that McCarthy commented on the trial of Cardinal Mindszenty. However, I never ran across it, and I looked carefully for any pre-1950 comments on communism. I doubt that he did comment."[118]

My fourth academic source is Richard M. Fried, Professor of History at the University of Illinois at Chicago and author of *Men Against McCarthy* and *Nightmare in Red.* Fried does not "recall McCarthy ever discussing Mindszenty" and adds that he is "hard-pressed to think of many references by Joe to specific events in Eastern Europe at all – aside, obviously, from Yalta."[119]

Outside the academy I communicated with Thomas A. Bolan, legal adviser to New York's Conservative party and former law partner of Roy Cohn. Bolan wrote that "I do not have any information on whether Senator McCarthy ever publicly expressed an opinion during the trial and sentencing of Cardinal Mindszenty." Later, during a personal interview, Bolan reaffirmed this position.[120]

In the absence of further information, the conclusion is inescapable that McCarthy's interest in the plight of Cardinal Mindszenty ranged from minimal to nil. This is particularly strange if we consider the image McCarthy would later project as a symbol of militant Catholic resistance to communism.

During the first Hiss trial McCarthy was sorely beset by troubles at home. Throughout late spring and early summer of 1949 the senator was being targeted by the Wisconsin Board of Bar Commissioners, a body concerned with the conduct of lawyers. The Board was "disturbed by political advertisements used by McCarthy and his backers in 1946 that solicited votes on the basis of decisions he had rendered as a judge."[121] The commissioners' complaint forced the hand of the state supreme court. On July 12 – five days after the Hiss trial ended in a hung jury – the court dismissed the case against McCarthy while at the same time ruling that he had violated his oaths as a circuit judge and as an attorney.[122]

McCarthy was further distracted from the Hiss case by Senate hearings on the World War II Malmedy massacre. Egged on by German-Americans in Wisconsin, McCarthy claimed that former Nazi SS troopers had been tortured into admitting complicity in the December 1944 atrocity that claimed the lives of eighty-three American prisoners. On June 6, shortly after the hearings ended, McCarthy angrily denounced them as a "whitewash" and followed up with a bitter personal attack on Connecticut Republican Senator Raymond Baldwin.[123] Baldwin was chairman of a subcommittee created to investigate the case.

The second trial saw McCarthy doing some serious redbaiting – but not against Alger Hiss or the persecutors of Cardinal Mindszenty. His foe was Cedric Parker, city editor of the *Madison Capital Times.*

Angered by Parker's disclosures about his financial manipulations and the lightning divorces he had handed down as a judge, McCarthy counterattacked on November 9. In a nine-page mimeographed document sent to newspapers and radio stations, McCarthy accused Parker of ties with Communist fronts and cited testimony from two ex-CP members that Parker was a Communist.[124]

Two days later, at a Shrine Club meeting, McCarthy claimed that Parker's boss, *Capital Times* managing editor William T. Evjue, had called Parker a Communist in 1941.[125]

Parker denied the charge and Evjue declared that Parker "has repeatedly assured the management of the *Capital Times* that he is not a member of the Communist Party." Evjue added that Parker had signed a non-communist affidavit and filed it with the National Labor Relations Board.[126]

McCarthy, in a preview of the style that would become his trademark, waved a letter from an NLRB official denying that the agency had ever received such an affidavit from Parker. "Throughout November and December," writes Michael O'Brien, "he kept the controversy alive and received more publicity as he constantly repeated his charges, challenged Evjue and Parker to start a libel action, and urged Evjue to debate him."[127] McCarthy loved headlines and was delighted that his attacks on Parker were not only being extensively reported in Wisconsin papers but that they had even rated a story in *Time.* With the recognition he was attaining from hounding Parker and Evjue, McCarthy had little time for Alger Hiss.

Also contributing to McCarthy's lack of focus on the Hiss case was his involvement in a dispute within the armed forces. In October Navy Captain John G. Crommelin released to the press three letters from high-ranking Navy officers protesting armed forces unification on grounds that it would weaken the naval air arm.[128] Reprimanded and transferred, Crommelin requested a court-martial in a November 18 letter to Chief of Naval Operations Forrest C. Sherman. The letter charged that the Army high command, filled with a "lust for power," was planning to usurp civilian control of the defense establishment.[129]

Leaping in on Crommelin's side, McCarthy accused the Army of planning to set up a "Prussian military dictatorship."[130] This little-known incident can be considered the opening skirmish of McCarthy's celebrated 1954 battle with the Army. Crommelin owed a debt of gratitude to McCarthy and would have a chance to pay it during the last great political battle of McCarthy's career, when he was threatened by a censure resolution in the Senate. In the fall of 1954, Crommelin (by now a rear admiral) served as chief of staff to a pro-McCarthy group called Ten Million Americans Mobilizing for Justice.[131]

"Macro" and "micro" are useful designations to describe the approaches of the Hearst press and Joe McCarthy to communism in 1948-49. The former sounded anguished outcries against high-placed traitors in government and saw Cardinal Mindszenty's fall as a metaphor for atheistic Marxism's assault on the Christian West. The latter, linking redbaiting to self-interest, ignored Hiss and Mindszenty as he keyed in on potential subversion in public housing projects, human rights abuses against Nazi SS troopers, and a pesky reporter in Wisconsin.

4. 1950: The Alliance Forms

To a dwindling legion of McCarthy loyalists, February 9, 1950 is a date with the same emotive significance as the 4th and 14th of July are to American and French patriots. In 1956, J. B. Matthews declared the date one of three great anniversaries in February – the others being Lincoln's birthday and Washington's birthday.[1] To critics, it is a "day of infamy" in the tradition of December 7, 1941. To all, it marked the beginning of what would become known as the McCarthy era.

That evening, in Wheeling, West Virginia, the Wisconsin senator addressed an audience of 275 at a dinner held in the Colonnade Room of the McClure Hotel. The function was sponsored by the Ohio County Women's Republican Club.

This was the first of five Lincoln Day appearances that the Republican National Committee had arranged for McCarthy. As a legislator held in scant esteem, the committee had given him the most mediocre of bookings. After Wheeling, his destinations were Salt Lake City, Reno, Las Vegas, and Huron, South Dakota. If McCarthy had such shattering news, wondered *New York Post* columnist William Shannon, why would he give it in a "Triple I League" town like Wheeling?[2]

It was in these unpretentious surroundings that McCarthy may or may not have uttered one of the most inflammatory statements in American political history:

> While I cannot take the time to name all the men in the State Department who have been named as active members of the Communist Party and as members of a spy ring, I have here in my hand a list of 205 – a list of names that were made known to the Secretary of State as being members of the Communist Party and who nevertheless are still working and

shaping policy in the State Department.

The element of doubt stems from the possibility that McCarthy never in fact spoke these words; he was notorious for departing from prepared texts. The sentence was attributed to him mainly because it appeared the following day in a story run by the *Wheeling Intelligencer.* But the author, reporter Frank Desmond, later told a Senate committee that he had obtained the quote from a manuscript McCarthy gave him before the speech.[3] Confusion was heightened by McCarthy's subsequent claims that he had the names of 57 State Department Communists (in Salt Lake City on February 10) and then 81 (before the Senate on February 20).

Whether or not McCarthy used the "205" figure in his first speech, that appearance in Wheeling ignited a political conflagration that would not subside till McCarthy's censure in 1954. In view of the national trauma induced on February 9, it is astounding how slight was the initial fallout and how slow the Hearst press was in making McCarthy's cause its own.

Norman L. Yost, managing editor of the *Intelligencer,* was also a part-time Associated Press correspondent. On the night of the 9th he phoned in the news of McCarthy's Wheeling speech to Charles R. Lewis, night editor of the AP bureau in Charlestown, West Virginia. The next day eighteen newspapers carried the AP story. Twelve were in Wisconsin and the other six were the *Chicago Tribune, Buffalo News, Baltimore News-Post, Newark News, Lowell Sun,* and the *Nashville Banner.*[4]

Of these, only the *News-Post* was a Hearst paper. But coverage was brief and there was no editorial comment. The first mention of McCarthy in the *Journal-American* came on February 16. The slant was hardly designed to encourage McCarthy partisans. Headlined SAYS SEN. MCCARTHY LIES, the story began: "President Truman asserted that Senator McCarthy (R.-Wis.) had not spoken the truth when he stated there were 57 card-carrying Communists in the State Department."[5] The nine-line article appeared on page 2.

On February 21 the *Journal-American* carried two more stories, both on page 2, that presented McCarthy in a negative light. The first, headlined DENIES LEFTIST IS TRUMAN AIDE, stated that "(Press) Secretary Charles G. Ross denied McCarthy's assertion that a 'speech writer' is a member of a Communist-front organization."[6]

Equally unsympathetic was an article under the smaller heading ACHESON HITS BACK AT MCCARTHY. It reported that "Acheson declared that there is not one word of truth in the GOP senator's charge that there are 81 card-carrying Communists in the State Department."[7] These stories appeared the day after McCarthy had changed his numbers for the second time, declaring in the Senate that the total of Communists in the State Department was 81 rather than 57 or 205.

The accused "leftist" was presidential assistant David Demarest Lloyd. Lloyd was Case #9 of McCarthy's 81 "Communists." He had belonged to the Washington Book Shop and the National Lawyers Guild but resigned when he learned they were Communist fronts. Lloyd was also a founder of the anti-communist Americans for Democratic Action.[8]

In an irony that has been widely overlooked, the first favorable reference to McCarthy in a Hearst paper appeared in the column of a man who would become one of his most implacable enemies. On February 25, Drew Pearson wrote that McCarthy had received a call about four hundred alleged subversives in government. Though McCarthy disclosed this information only to Richard Nixon on his private line, a reference to the four hundred was made on the Senate floor by Scott Lucas of Illinois, a strongly anti-McCarthy Democrat. Pearson's implication was that the Democrats were tapping McCarthy's phone.[9]

Pearson's support for McCarthy was short-lived. His assistant, Jack Anderson, had been on friendly terms with the senator. In response to McCarthy's urgent request, Anderson gave him a "raw" file on David Demarest Lloyd, one that contained unfounded allegations of subversive activity along with such concrete evidence of anti-communism as Lloyd's role as a founder of ADA. Typically, McCarthy emphasized the former but ignored the latter. He claimed, for example, that Lloyd had "a relative who has a financial interest in the *Daily Worker.*"[10]

The relative in question was Lloyd's great-aunt, Caroline Lloyd Strobell, who died in 1941. A wealthy eccentric, her "financial interest" in the *Worker* came to exactly one dollar. By contrast, she had a $14 million dollar interest in the far-right *Chicago Tribune.*[11] Disgusted by such irresponsibility, Pearson "swiftly severed relations with McCarthy and became the first syndicated columnist to attack him."[12] Their mutual hostility became notorious and escalated into a violent physical confrontation later that year.

As February gave way to March, there was a perceptible shift in Hearst coverage from negative to neutral. The February 25 *Journal-American* carried a page 2 story headlined SEN. TYDINGS NAMED HEAD OF RED PROBE. The eleven-line article noted that Tydings would "head the investigation of charges by Senator Joseph McCarthy... that Communists have infiltrated the State Department."[13] The impartiality of the story contrasts sharply with the pejorative headlines SAYS SEN. MCCARTHY LIES and ACHESON HITS BACK AT MCCARTHY.

On the same day, George Sokolsky attacked Dr. Philip C. Jessup, the State Department's ambassador-at-large, but did not mention McCarthy. (Jessup would later become a prime McCarthy target.)[14]

Tydings had been appointed by Tom Connally, Texas Democrat and chairman of the Senate Foreign Relations Committee. Other members of what would become known as the Tydings Committee (it was actually a subcommittee) were Democrats Brien McMahon of Connecticut and Theodore F. Green of Rhode Island and Republicans Henry Cabot Lodge of Massachusetts and Bourke B. Hickenlooper of Iowa.

A page 2 *Mirror* story on the 26th was friendly to Tydings without being hostile to McCarthy. Headlined 5 TO HUNT REDS IN STATE DEPARTMENT, it noted that the subcommittee would be "looking into McCarthy's charges that 81 persons he said were Communists or fellow travelers have been or are employed in the State Department." Approvingly, the article also stated that "Tydings told reporters there would be 'no witch hunt and no whitewash' in the probe of charges made by Senator Mc-Carthy."[15]

Equally neutral was a February 27 story in the *Mirror* headlined PROBE STATE DEPT., FBI URGED. "The Senate," it began, "has ordered a Foreign Relations Subcommittee (the Tydings) group to... subpoena the loyalty files of 57 State Department employees accused by Senator McCarthy of being Communists."[16]

The first sign of a swing toward McCarthy can be detected in a page 6 *Journal-American* article on February 28. The headline was HITS WHITE HOUSE AIDE AS PRO-HISS. The aide in question was David Demarest Lloyd and his attacker was Joe McCarthy. The senator charged that "Alger Hiss would probably be back in the State Department if the decision were up to a White House aide, David Demarest Lloyd."[17]

In composing partisan headlines, it is common practice to make a sympathetic figure of the aggressor while placing the "villain" under attack. In the "anti" headlines of February 16 and 21, McCarthy was called a liar by Truman and rebutted by Acheson. Now he was on the offensive against Lloyd, accusing him of what in the early 1950s was a cardinal sin: softness on Alger Hiss.

McCarthy's role as headline aggressor was clearly apparent in two March 9 entries. A page 4 story in the *Mirror* was headed SENATOR TIES DOROTHY KENYON TO 28 PRO-COMMUNIST GROUPS.[18] Kenyon, a former New York municipal court judge, had served a three-year term on a United Nations commission but had no connection with the State Department. Though she had joined groups that were later identified as subversive, she got out of them as soon as she learned of their procommunist inclination.[19] Kenyon had also "resisted efforts by the Communists to take over the American Labor Party" and, at the UN, "had sparred repeatedly with Soviet representatives and been severely criticized by Moscow."[20]

In the *Journal-American,* on page 10, the headline read MCCARTHY FLAYS SENATE PROBERS. Specifically, he accused the Senate investigating group of being "a tool of the State Department."[21] The March 12 *Journal-American* carried a page 8 story in which McCarthy said he had received a "sizeable (sic) number of new leads" about Communist infiltrators in government.[22] But an article on the next page showed that the Hearst directorate had still not committed itself entirely to McCarthy. The headline read MISS KENYON HITS USE OF HER NAME ON LEFTIES' LIST. Kenyon claimed on several occasions her name was placed on letterheads of suspect groups without her permission. Under Kenyon's picture appeared the caption: "Perhaps I was a sucker."[23] This indicates a belief that Kenyon was a dupe rather than a subversive – an opinion contrary to the one held by McCarthy.

Two days later both the *Journal-American* and *Mirror* were back on the McCarthy track. A page 1 headline in the *Mirror* read M'CARTHY LISTS 4 MORE PRO-REDS. The four were Esther Brunauer, a member of the State Department's UN staff, Haldore Hanson, a State Department scientific and cultural official, Noel Field, the alleged object of contention between Hede Massing and Alger Hiss, and Johns Hopkins professor Owen Lattimore. McCarthy described Lattimore as one whose background "makes him an extremely poor security risk." That background, according to McCarthy, "included affiliation with numerous Communist organizations."[24] Though inflammatory, this accusation was mild compared to what McCarthy would be saying about Lattimore in a few days.

Up to March 14, the only column reference to McCarthy had been that allusion to wiretapping by Drew Pearson on February 25. He was mentioned in no other column and in no editorial. All that changed between the 14th and 16th. The first glowing endorsement by a New York Hearst columnist came on the 14th in Frank Conniff's "East Side, West Side." Conniff wrote that "the grass roots reaction to the badgering and baiting tactics aimed at Senator McCarthy, a Marine combat flyer who still carries Jap splinters in his legs, changed the administration's merry tune the moment this sentiment began to waft its way back to the Capital."[25] (Like many others, Conniff did not then know that McCarthy's claims to having been wounded in action were spurious.)

While embracing McCarthy, the *Journal-American* had not yet given up on Tydings. On the same day as Conniff's endorsement, Igor Cassini defended Tydings while getting in a lick at his favorite punching bag. Explaining that Tydings was "the son-in-law of ex-ambassador Joe 'Submission to Moscow' Davies," he added that "I had always remained on excellent terms with Tydings, who never seemed to hold a grudge when I took pot shots at his Stalin-loving father-in-law."[26]

On the 15th the *Mirror* made McCarthy beneficiary of that journalistic technique known as "blanketing," where a back page adverse story about a subject is eclipsed by a favorable one on the front pages. Blanketing Dorothy Kenyon's spirited denial of McCarthy's charges against her was a page 2 story headlined MCCARTHY NAMES CONSUL, 29 OTHERS AS PRO-REDS. The consul was John Stewart Service, a veteran career diplomat then serving in Calcutta.[27] The same story had appeared a day earlier in the *Journal-American*, in a front page headline reading M'CARTHY SAYS CONSUL FAILED ON LOYALTY CHECKUP.[28]

The praise in Conniff's March 14 column was followed by a plug from Fulton Lewis the following day. On the *Journal-American's* editorial page, Lewis wrote that "Senator Joseph R. McCarthy has dusted off for public inspection the Communist-front affiliations of individuals attached to the State Department in one way or another."[29]

If there was a formal Hearst blessing for McCarthy and his cause, it was an editorial in the March 16 *Mirror*. Headed GO TO IT, JOE MCCARTHY, it declared that "the Senate investigation of the State Department, forced by Senator Joseph R. McCarthy, fighting young senator from Wisconsin, is one of the most important events of our time...." Elsewhere McCarthy was described as one who fought "the Japs as a Marine flyer in the Pacific, where he was subsequently wounded." Ending on a hortatory note, the editorial warned that "the people are tired of being bamboozled. They want the mess cleaned up. Go to it, Joe McCarthy."[30] With that, the alliance between the Hearst empire and the wild-swinging senator became official.

Though the focus in this work is on the two New York papers, the out-of-town Hearst journals faithfully followed the *Journal-American* and *Mirror* in backing McCarthy after the GO TO IT editorial. In 1951 William Randolph Hearst Jr. would issue a policy statement about "dispersal of power." But this autonomy was largely limited to local coverage.[31] In the fevered spring of 1950, with the Red hunt a national obsession, it would have been as likely for a Hearst paper to oppose the McCarthy endorsement as for the *Daily Worker* to support it.

The Hearst organization's delay in extending that endorsement had nothing to do with any lapse in anti-Red fervor. Coverage on communism in the Hearst papers was as lurid as ever. On February 12, three days after the Wheeling speech, the *Journal-American's* front page banner headline was PLAN WARTIME ROUNDUP OF 4,000 REDS. The same story carried an account of a Catholic priest's warning to an American Legion audience that "Communists and their dupes" had taken over American foreign policy and that radio networks had been infiltrated by Communists. Later that week the *Journal-American* accused a hundred American scientists of being Soviet agents and charged that they were being protected by "some mysterious political power."[32] On February 19 the *Journal-American* printed a doctored photograph depicting what New York would look like after being hit by a Russian atomic bomb.[33]

On the same day, in the *Mirror,* Walter Winchell adhered to his usual pattern of frenetic redbaiting while remaining friendly toward members of the Roosevelt family. "The Daily Scummunist," he shrilled, "hasn't printed one word yet on the arrest of atomic spy (Klaus) Fuchs. Free press, huh?" On a more respectful note, he saluted a recent TV appearance by the former First Lady as an indication "that Mrs. FDR is giving television something you rarely find in that medium: intelligence."[34]

There are two explanations for the Hearst press's tardiness in endorsing McCarthy. One is advanced by Edwin R. Bayley, dean of the Graduate School of Journalism at Berkeley and author of a book about McCarthy and the press. Bayley, a former reporter who was once called a Communist to his face by McCarthy, thinks that the Hearst press was living in another era during the period immediately following the Wheeling speech. "Oddly," he writes, "some newspapers that later became McCarthy's most vigorous tub-thumpers – notably the Hearst papers – carried no McCarthy editorials during the first month. (After Wheeling.) The Hearst papers, in fact, carried very little news of the McCarthy controversy. Even though they came out every day, they looked as if they had been printed in an earlier time; their editorials and some of their columnists railed at the long-dead Roosevelt, while other columnists harried their own well-worn packs of Communists and fellow travelers."[35]

If Bayley perceived the Hearst press as living in the past, Adela Rogers St. Johns saw it as looking elsewhere before settling on McCarthy. St. Johns served two generations of the Hearst family as a Kissinger-like operative and, by this account, played a key role in attempting to recruit a leader for the Red hunt: "We made one fatal mistake," she wrote. "We were looking for a senator to carry the ball. I went down to get Millard

Tydings... he said, 'Nooo, nooo, they'd beat you to death before you were through'.... Other senators wouldn't come anywhere near it. The only guy who would go was McCarthy. We didn't know he was a drunk. If McCarthy hadn't been an alcoholic the whole story would have been different, because we had the material but he kept blowing it. He'd get drunk and say things he shouldn't."[36]

If this account is true, it explains the Hearst papers' respectful attitude toward Tydings in the five weeks between the Wheeling speech and the GO TO IT, JOE MCCARTHY editorial. Perhaps the Hearst organization was still hoping that Tydings would be its Richard Lionheart in the crusade against subversion.

But why Tydings? The choice was not illogical. Though a Democrat, Tydings was conservative, anti-New Deal, and had withstood a 1938 effort by Roosevelt to purge him from the Senate. Nor can the circumstances of Tydings's kinship with Joseph E. Davies be ignored.

For all the flowery prose they had to write, most of the Hearst writers were worldly men with a sardonic sense of the absurd. What better joke on their *bête rouge,* Joe "Submission to Moscow" Davies, than to have the Red hunt led by his own son-in-law? Moreover, if Igor Cassini is correct, Tydings wasn't particularly troubled by attacks on his wife's father.

This leaves one unanswered question: did the Hearst press come to McCarthy or did McCarthy come to the Hearst press? St. Johns's account suggests the former. Yet there is evidence that it was McCarthy who made the initial overture.

When McCarthy spoke at Wheeling, William Randolph Hearst had eighteen months to live. But he was in his dotage and power was in the hands of the ambitious Richard E. Berlin, who served as president of the Hearst Corporation, and a seven-man committee of top news executives that included two of Hearst's sons. Serving as vice-chairman, and heir apparent, was William Randolph Hearst Jr. (Though young Hearst eventually became chairman, he had to thwart a power play by Berlin that would have given the chairmanship to *Baltimore News-Post* editor William Baskervill.)[37]

Bill Hearst and McCarthy had been friends since 1947. According to Hearst's recollection, they were introduced by the beautiful Austine ("Bootsie") McDonnell, then the estranged wife of Igor Cassini.

Hearst and Bootsie were married in July 1948, with McCarthy as a wedding guest. The newlyweds introduced him to Berlin and the two formed a friendship based on a shared "Irish heritage, political leanings, and fondness for booze."[38] Berlin frequently invited McCarthy to his Fifth

Avenue apartment and there the senator met such figures as George Sokolsky.[39]

So McCarthy already had a Hearst connection when he launched his "era" at Wheeling. It was completely natural for him to go to his friend Bill Hearst for help when he saw things spinning out of control.

As Hearst recalls it, "Joe gave us a call not too long after the (Wheeling) speech. And you know what? – he didn't have a damn thing on that list. Nothing. He said, 'My God, I'm in a jam.... I shot my mouth off. So what am I going to do now?' So I guess we fixed him up with a few good reporters...."[40]

Unfortunately, Hearst's account does not disclose the exact date of McCarthy's call. What did he mean by "not too long?" A few days? A week? Two weeks? Precise information would help clear up the mystery of that thirty-five day lapse between the Wheeling speech and the GO TO IT, JOE MCCARTHY editorial.

A clue is furnished in a book about the Hearst empire by Lindsay Chaney and Michael Cieply. The authors state that "it was hardly surprising that McCarthy thought of Hearst when, in the wake of his Wheeling address, Democratic senators Herbert Lehman and Scott Lucas began pressing him to produce the names of his 205 subversives."[41]

The inquisition of McCarthy took place on February 20. Badgered mercilessly by Lucas, Lehman, and Brien McMahon of Connecticut, McCarthy floundered badly and at one point accused Lucas of "making a farce" of the proceedings by playing a "silly numbers game."[42]

The preceding does not jibe with Adela Rogers St. Johns's claim that it was Hearst who made the initial overtures. Of all the versions about the launching of McCarthy's career, St. Johns's is perhaps the weakest. She states, for example, that McCarthy kept "blowing it" because "he was a drunk." Yet there is an overwhelming consensus among students of that period that alcohol never de-railed McCarthy till the last sad phase of his career, after he had been censured and his name was no longer in the headlines. "His drinking prowess," writes Richard Rovere, "was in fact notable. He could 'belt a fifth'... between midnight and five a.m., catch a couple of hours of sleep, and be in his office at eight or nine, ready for a hard day's work leading the populace to mischief with empty words."[43]

The most logical explanation for the five-week lapse is that the Hearst high command was sharply divided about McCarthy. Bill Hearst, his champion, would not become chairman for another year and a half and the presence of an opposition faction can be deduced from the three anti-McCarthy news stories and the continued favorable treatment of Millard

Tydings.

Who led the opposition? It may have been J. B. Matthews. To a Hearst colleague, Matthews had expressed contempt for "the Johnnie-come-lately anti-Communist who plunges into battle with no knowledge of what he is up against."[44] Could there be a more accurate description of McCarthy? McCarthy was an embarrassment to many sophisticated right-wing ideologues, especially those who had leftist antecedents and a grounding in Marxism. Eugene Lyons, an ex-Soviet sympathizer who could be described as an ideological twin to Matthews, originally considered McCarthy a disaster. Though Lyons later reversed course, his initial response was to write that the "luck of the Communists... held good" when a man as ignorant and irresponsible as McCarthy entered the lists against them.[45] What particularly shocked Lyons, Matthews *et al.* was that McCarthy had never heard of Earl Browder till the former Communist leader was called to testify before the Tydings Committee.[46]

Whatever happened behind the scenes, the issue was resolved by mid-March. J. B. Matthews opened his files to McCarthy, leading to the senator's expression of gratitude for "J. B.'s encyclopedic memory." The "few good reporters" included Howard Rushmore, an ex-Communist, Larry Kerley, a former FBI agent, and Ray Richards and Kent Hunter, who had "worked on the investigation of *Amerasia* magazine, a (pro-communist) publication which had come into possession of State Department documents."[47]

For his part, J. Edgar Hoover furnished McCarthy with a chief investigator named Donald A. Surine. The outwardly prudish Hoover had recently fired Surine for sexual involvement with a prostitute during a white slavery investigation in Baltimore. This was a decision made more in sorrow than anger. Still respecting Surine's investigative skills and anti-communist zeal, Hoover enthusiastically recommended him to McCarthy. From that time on, Surine functioned as liaison between the senator and the FBI chief.[48]

"About March 23rd or 24th, 1950," McCarthy first conferred with a man who would become another powerful supporter.[49] Though he lived in Bronxville, Alfred Kohlberg was an important associate member of the "New York crowd" that included Sokolsky and Matthews. Kohlberg, a wealthy importer, was the unofficial head of the so-called China Lobby, a group dedicated to advancing the interests of Chiang Kai-shek's Nationalist government and discrediting all foes of that regime. Natural enemies of the China Lobby were McCarthy targets Owen Lattimore and John Stewart Service, men who had a connection with China and strong reservations about Chiang.

After March 16, it would be a long time before any anti-McCarthy material surfaced in the *Journal-American* and *Mirror*. On that day the *Journal-American* carried a page 14 news story about Fulton Lewis's radio broadcast of the day before. John S. Service, American consul in Calcutta had just been summoned to the United States to answer McCarthy's charges against him. Lewis observed that Service's recall "has given a big boost to Senator Joseph R. McCarthy's charges that the State Department is harboring bad security risks."[50]

On March 18 George Sokolsky cautiously attempted to shield McCarthy from some of the flak he was taking over Dorothy Kenyon. Her spirited defense – and the prominence of some of her defenders – had created considerable public sympathy for the feisty attorney. Sokolsky began by listing some of the leftist organizations that Kenyon had belonged to. His purpose, he explained, was to establish a "pattern of activity." The pattern, he added, "does not necessarily make Miss Kenyon a Communist, but it does open to question her judgment and her associations."[51]

McCarthy had been attempting to revive the *Amerasia* case, doubtless savoring the flavor of a controversy involving purloined government documents and an admittedly pro-communist magazine. "If the State Department succeeds in smearing Senator McCarthy," editorialized the *Mirror*, "in whitewashing their own boys, in keeping secret the names of admitted homosexuals and Communists, the *Amerasia* case will remain a dead letter."[52]

The *Journal-American's* March 21 headline read M'CARTHY LINKS TOP RED SPY TO 'RING' IN STATE DEPARTMENT. Though no name was mentioned, the "spy" was tantalizingly described as the "boss" of an espionage ring of which Alger Hiss was merely "one of the links."[53] Tydings immediately summoned a closed-door session of the committee, at which McCarthy told his stunned colleagues that the man he was about to finger was Owen Lattimore. The next day, without naming Lattimore, McCarthy announced that he "willing to stand or fall on this one."[54]

In the same issue, Sokolsky indulged himself in a bit of highbrow homophobia. Avoiding the barnyard invective of Winchell and Pegler, he voiced a view widely held in 1950 by inquiring as to "what part did these homosexuals, subject to blackmail, play in the formulation and conduct of these erroneous policies?"[55] In the *Mirror*, Victor Riesel also seized on this theme. "Analysis of 3,000 letters to Senator McCarthy," he wrote, "reveals as much concern over infiltration of homosexuals as worry over Stalinists."[56]

Since Drew Pearson had already broken the story, McCarthy now named Lattimore as the "top Russian agent" in America. On March 27 the *Mirror* headline read CALLS LATTIMORE TOP RED AGENT. Because the accusation was so sensational, the page 1 story was not slanted toward McCarthy and even mentioned that Mrs. Lattimore had "hotly denied McCarthy's public charges."[57] (Lattimore himself was on a government mission in Afghanistan.)

The day before, in the *Journal-American,* an item in Igor Cassini's column demonstrated that the Hearst organization had still not completely given up on Millard Tydings. Assuring readers that McCarthy **ws** "honest and fearless," he warned that the Wisconsinite would have a difficult time going up against "the impeccable Millard Tydings, son-in-law of ex-ambassador Joe 'Submission to Moscow' Davies."[58]

Victor Riesel's March 29 column showed McCarthy's influence seeping into the labor relations area. Riesel wrote that the State Department, prodded by McCarthy, had "directed its security agents to get out into the big cities (especially New York) and discover everything possible about Communist-led white-collar workers' outfits."[59]

The next day McCarthy made his charges against Lattimore on the Senate floor. But there was no mention of the Johns Hopkins professor being a "top Russian spy." Lattimore had been downgraded to a "policy risk," the "architect of our Far Eastern policy," and one of a "small but dominant percentage of disloyal... thinkers who are rendering futile the Herculean efforts of the vast majority of loyal Americans."[60] In this speech McCarthy also made the most unintentionally funny remark of his career. As the press galleries rocked with laughter, he assured listeners that they could "ask almost any school child who the architect of our Far Eastern policy is, and he will say 'Owen Lattimore.'"[61]

If McCarthy was funny without intending to be, the exact opposite can be said of Pegler. Seeking to bolster McCarthy's assaults on the State Department, his March 31 column took the form of a crudely gay-bashing poem titled THREE WHOOPS AND A YOO HOO FOR THE STATE DEPARTMENT. An excerpt reads:

> How could he help it if parties both unusual and queer
> Got into the State Department, which all patriots hold dear?
> To hear the dastards tell it, they are true to Uncle Joey
> And call each other female names, like Bessie, Maude, and Chloe.[62]

Lattimore appeared before the Tydings Committee on March 31. He stoutly defended his views on China and attacked McCarthy for "instituting a reign of terror among officials and employees of the United States government." Lattimore had previously sent a telegram from Afghanistan in which he characterized "McCarthy's off-record rantings" as "pure moonshine."[63]

The next day the *Journal-American* sought to defuse Lattimore's attacks with a blanketing maneuver. On page 1, next to an article headed LATTIMORE HERE, FLAYS M'C, there appeared the larger headline LEFT-WING PROF IN SUICIDE LEAP. The suicide was Harvard American Literature professor F. O. Matthiessen. The story, far longer than Lattimore's rebuttal, contained three subheadings: "His Final Note" (he was a "Christian and Socialist" depressed over world conditions); "Backed Wallace" (he was a delegate to the Progressive Party convention in 1948); "Supported Many Red Front Groups" (followed by a listing).[64]

On April 4 Frank Conniff commented that "Senator Joe McCarthy's determined fight to expose the nest of Communists and queers seems likely to establish the junior senator from Wisconsin as the Republic's most valuable asset in the following Congressional elections."[65]

Two days later a *Journal-American* editorial bitterly assailed Republican moderate Henry Cabot Lodge, a member of the Tydings Committee, who had stated that "none of (McCarthy's) charges have been proven." The editorial railed that this "was a mean and dirty maneuver to pull on a colleague who has stubbornly carried the ball for the Republican Party in breaking the State Department mess into the open."[66] This was the first attack on a Republican centrist; up to now, the victims had been Democrats and "subversives."

On April 20 an important anti-Lattimore witness took the stand. Louis F. Budenz was an ex-Communist and former editor of the *Daily Worker*. Budenz charged that Lattimore belonged to a "Communist cell" that had infiltrated the Institute of Pacific Relations and that "Party disciplinarian Jack Stachel had advised him to consider Owen Lattimore... a Communist."[67] The *Mirror's* April 21 headline read LATTIMORE IN RED SPY CELL: BUDENZ.[68]

On the same day Pegler returned to a theme that never ceased to fascinate him. His April 21 column was an open letter to Dean Acheson. "Have you checked with Harvard recently," he asked, "on the courses that are offered for young men of distinction who have heard the call of the (Oscar) Wilde and are planning careers in the State Department?"[69]

Budenz, considered a disreputable sort, came under attack from all sides. The ex-Communist had returned to the Catholicism of his youth and nobody denounced him more fiercely than Dennis Chavez, the Roman

Catholic senator from New Mexico. On May 12, in a virulent personal attack, Chavez revealed that Budenz had had three children out of wedlock. "I believe in clemency toward sinners," he concluded, "but with repentance should go humility... My ancestors brought the Cross to this hemisphere. Louis Budenz has been using the Cross as a club."[70]

The Hearst papers defended Budenz against all comers. On April 22 a *Mirror* editorial ridiculed the elderly Senator Green for asking Budenz why he wasn't used in the trial of the eleven Communist leaders. "He was," gloated the editorial, "testifying for ten days. Was Senator Green's face red? It was purple."[71]

On May 17 Frank Conniff addressed Chavez's attack on Budenz. Deploring efforts "to inject the religious issue in the campaign to discredit Senator Joseph McCarthy," he charged that Chavez's speech "had obviously been prepared for him" because the senator stumbled over words. Conniff concluded that "(Fordham President) Father Laurence McGinley's forthright endorsement of Louis Budenz comes at an apt moment."[72] McGinley had characterized Chavez's remarks as "lower than a *Daily Worker* editorial" and branded the senator a "modern Pharisee" who is "always ready to point a self-righteous finger at their (sic) fellow man."[73]

While McCarthy was undoubtedly gratified by this Catholic support, he soon made it clear that he was aiming at a broader constituency. On May 25, in an address to a group of Catholic editors in Rochester, New York, he denied being a Catholic spokesman and repeatedly emphasized the "Protestant-Catholic-Jew" theme. Father Donald Crosby S. J., the author of a book about McCarthy and the Catholic Church, comments that "he was trying to rise above the 'Catholic issue' and his Catholic audience by attempting to appeal to all of American society."[74]

Walter Winchell Comes Aboard

Walter Winchell was the last Hearst columnist to commit himself to McCarthy. Where the rest of the organization got in line with the GO TO IT, JOE MCCARTHY editorial of March 16, Winchell held out till April on the air and May in his column. When Drew Pearson, then his friend, heard Winchell laud McCarthy on his April 23 broadcast, "he could only say in bewilderment that 'Walter really must think he's slipping.'"[75]

In the column, between February and May, Winchell continued his usual two-track approach: redbaiting but being equally rough on extreme rightists; bashing Truman but revering Roosevelt. In his February 27 column, under the heading INVESTIGATING THE INVESTIGATORS, Winchell scored Congress for not being vigorous enough in preventing the escape of accused Comintern agent Gerhardt Eisler and for "nice-nellying

Franco."[76]

As late as May 1, Winchell still appeared to have reservations about McCarthy. Eleven days after Budenz's testimony, he wrote that "a New York newspaperman will be a surprise witness against Budenz for Lattimore."[77]

By May 12, all Winchell's doubts had ended. That day he described a party in New York attended by one of McCarthy's targets in the *Amerasia* case. "'What's going to happen next?' the accused Red was asked...' 'Probably,' cracked a reporter, 'the Pumpkin.'"[78] This was a reference to the hollowed-out pumpkin on Whittaker Chambers's farm, in which he kept the microfilms that he used against Alger Hiss.

Six days later, the bulk of Winchell's column was devoted to an attack on the "fat cats" who bankrolled neo-Nazi Joseph Kamp and fascist sympathizer Merwin K. Hart. Winchell ended with this quote: "'I think a tremendous amount of harm has been done by calling... liberals Communists.' Who said that? Senator McCarthy, on April 3, 1947."[79] This seems like an effort at self-justification. To rationalize his support for McCarthy, Winchell sought to invest the Wisconsin brawler with liberal credentials.

What made Winchell go over to McCarthy? A Winchell biographer, Bob Thomas, believes the columnist was blackmailed. Writes Thomas: "Whatever doubts Winchell may have had about getting behind McCarthy were resolved by a simple threat. The McCarthy forces informed Winchell that unless he fell into line he would be a forthcoming target for the junior senator from Wisconsin." Thomas goes on to say that "Winchell was excessively vulnerable" because of his "premature anti-fascism, always suspicious to Red hunters."[80]

This version is disputed by another Winchell biographer, Herman Klurfeld. "On the personal level," writes Klurfeld, "Winchell... found McCarthy likable. More important in Winchell's judgment, J. Edgar Hoover was an ardent admirer of McCarthy. Further, Walter believed Communist infiltration of government to be a fact, and he thought McCarthy was right in contending that Communists should be ferreted out of high places as vigorously as pro-Nazis. Finally, McCarthy was anti-Truman, which won brownie points with Winchell. Thus he failed to see – or deliberately ignored – the menace of McCarthyism."[81]

Though Winchell may have been a draftee, once he committed himself he acted like the most enthusiastic of volunteers. As the Red hunt intensified, Winchell served McCarthy as combined bloodhound and pit bull, sniffing out "subversives" with single-minded dedication and going after them with no-quarter ferocity.

Korea and the Tydings Committee Report

"The picture of treason which I carried in my briefcase to that Caucus Room was to shock the nation and occupy the headlines until Truman declared war in Korea...."[82] As McCarthy saw it, Truman, the coddler of Communists in government, was trying to detract attention from McCarthy's anti-communist crusade by ordering troops into a shooting war against Communist armies in Korea.

That conflict broke out on June 25, when well-armed North Korean forces crossed the 38th parallel and began to roll up the poorly-equipped South Koreans opposing them. The invasion was condemned by the U. N. Security Council on June 27 and on the 30th President Truman ordered American ground units into Korea.

At first, McCarthy seemed resigned to being pushed out of the headlines. "My only forum is page one," he told a reporter. "I don't have that now, so I'll keep quiet."[83]

McCarthy's silence was brief. In early July he told Wisconsin political boss Tom Coleman that "the war situation makes it difficult to continue the anti-Communist fight effectively – at least temporarily. I am inclined to think," he added, "that as casualty lists mount... (the people) can't help but realize that there was something rotten in the State Department."[84]

McCarthy gauged the situation accurately. Though American forces would continue to be hard-pressed till MacArthur's Inchon landing in September, public interest in the war was beginning to wane. All that was needed to re-focus attention on McCarthy was a series of dramatic political developments.

These took place in mid-July, when the Tydings Committee was drafting its final report. Prelude to the explosive events of the next few days was an unusually silly entry in the Cholly Knickerbocker column. John E. Peurifoy, Deputy Undersecretary of State and outspoken foe of McCarthy, had just been named ambassador to Greece. Cassini described the appointment as "a reward for being the Department's leading hatchet man of (sic) Senator McCarthy's charges." Then, in a haughty *non sequitur,* he sniffed that during the Depression Peurifoy had been "a cashier at a Childs restaurant in New York."[85]

The Tydings Committee report came out the following day. It was signed by three Democratic senators – Tydings, Green, and McMahon – but not by the Republicans Hickenlooper and Lodge. The report contained some of the bluntest language ever used in an official document. McCarthy had perpetrated "a fraud and hoax on the Senate" and his accusations represented "perhaps the most nefarious campaign of half-truths and untruths in the history of this republic." Of McCarthy's principal targets, Lattimore and Jessup were completely exonerated and Kenyon was adjudged guilty of nothing more than "naiveté and perhaps gullibility."[86]

Release of the report was followed by one of the most acrimonious sessions in the history of the Senate. This recrimination-filled meeting included a particularly nasty encounter between Senator Kenneth Wherry of Nebraska and committee counsel Edward Morgan, who helped prepare the report. After failing to get Morgan ejected from the Senate, Wherry called the attorney a "dirty son of a bitch" and threw a punch at him.[87]

This tempestuous session took place on the 20th. On the 18th the *Mirror* had run a page 2 story headlined 'FRAUD, HOAX' SAY DEM SENATORS TO MCCARTHY. The article quoted McCarthy as saying that "the Tydings-McMahon report is a green light to the Red Fifth Column in the United States."[88] The *Journal-American,* in a page 4 story headed END MCCARTHY STATE DEPARTMENT PROBE, printed another McCarthy statement, that the report "gave a favorable signal to the traitors, Communists, and fellow travelers in our government."

The following day, even before the dramatic Senate session, the *Journal-American* took the unusual step of denouncing the report in a front page editorial headed A SHAMEFUL PERFORMANCE. The editorial characterized it as "probably the most disgracefully partisan document ever to emanate from the Congress of the United States" and added that "it verges on disloyalty."[90]

The report, the Senate brawl, and the accompanying headlines combined to diminish the newsworthiness of the Korean fighting. From now on, the war's primacy in the news would be pretty much related to such historic reversals of fortune as the Inchon landing and the Chinese intervention. But it would never again, on a sustained basis, eclipse the political wars of Joe McCarthy.

Getting Millard Tydings

November was less than four months away and Millard Tydings was up for reelection. That front page editorial marked the end of any kindly feelings the *Journal-American* and *Mirror* had for Tydings. Henceforth the conservative Marylander would occupy the same place in the Hearst doghouse as his father-in-law.

On July 20 *Journal-American* Washington bureau chief Kent Hunter quoted adverse Republican reaction to the report and denounced the document itself as a "vindictive and bitter attack on Senator Joseph McCarthy." In the same issue, George Rothwell Brown described the report as a "brazen... job of partisan whitewashing."[91]

On the 21st a *Journal-American* news story by Glenn M. Green noted that the liberal Republican Senator Irving Ives of New York had charged the Tydings Committee with "dereliction of duty" for issuing such a report. In "The Political Parade," George Rothwell Brown wrote an obituary for the "'Truman Honeymoon' that followed commitment of troops to Korea." What killed the honeymoon was that "attempted whitewash by the hand-picked Tydings Committee."[92]

The next day Pegler denounced "the disgraceful report of the Tydings Committee" which "proves that the party which administers our government... still suffers from this apathy toward Communists."[93] On the 24th a *Mirror* editorial charged that the report was "so obviously untruthful as to border on the obscene."[94]

This press barrage was the curtain raiser to the election campaign against Tydings, a campaign rarely paralleled in viciousness and dirty tricks. His little-known opponent, a Baltimore attorney named John Marshall Butler, compensated for his obscurity by bringing Joe McCarthy to Maryland to campaign for him. In top form, McCarthy labeled the Democrats "Commiecrats" and charged Tydings with "protecting Communists for political reasons."[95]

Tydings's foes reached the ethical nadir when a composite photo was circulated showing what appeared to be Tydings and Earl Browder in friendly conversation. The caption read:

> Communist Earl Browder, shown at left in the composite picture... was cajoled into saying Owen Lattimore and others accused of disloyalty were not Communists. Tydings (right) answered, "Oh, thank you, Sir." Browder testified in the best interests of the accused, naturally.[96]

While the picture was identified as a composite to avoid the possibility of legal action, it was assumed that the word would get by many voters, which it obviously did. But there was one fraudulent emendation. Where Tydings dismissed Browder with a curt, "Thank you, sir," in the caption a fawning "Oh, thank you, Sir" is attributed to him.[97]

Tydings lost by 43,100 votes. Ironically, a contributing factor to the defeat of this "Communist coddler" was his unpopularity with organized labor and blacks. Like most Southern and border legislators of his day, Tydings had a dismal record on civil rights.[98]

On November 8, after Tydings's defeat, the *Journal-American* commented that "Senator Joseph McCarthy was credited indirectly with the feat the late President Roosevelt couldn't accomplish – 'purging'... Millard Tydings from the U.S. Senate."[99] Three days later the same paper editorialized that "Mr. Tydings suffered (a) humiliating but well-deserved chastisement."[100]

In that tense fall, fear and repression were spreading. Few people incarnated the *zeitgeist* better than one of the *Journal-American's* "non-politicals," the entertainment editor Gene Knight.

Knight, a little bully who would have functioned efficiently as a block committee leader under Stalin, wrote on October 19 that "it might interest a downtown nightclub owner that his singer is listed in *Red Channels* as being associated with five organizations labeled as Communist fronts by the U.S. Attorney General."[101] Two days later Knight crowed that "on October 1 I stated that a singer in a downtown nightclub is listed in 'Red Channels'... The singer is no longer there."[102]

Winchell, Pearson, and McCarthy

Walter Winchell and Drew Pearson had been friends and allies during the days of the New Deal and the Second World War. Both hated Nazis, Fascists, and the isolationist enemies of FDR. The McCarthy era brought that friendship to an end. Pearson turned against McCarthy in early March; Winchell embraced him in April (on the air) and May (in his column). Apart from differences of opinion over McCarthy, there were other reasons for the break. Winchell had been giving hints about the title of a "mystery tune" on the popular radio show "Stop the Music" and became angry when Pearson followed suit.[103] Moreover, Pearson had offended Winchell by contradicting his statement that Truman had been a member of the Ku Klux Klan.[104]

Between May and December Winchell continued to mingle redbaiting with anti-fascism while at the same time becoming increasingly laudatory about McCarthy. On June 6 he identified "Washington's hottest romance" as one between "Martha Rountree, producer of 'Meet the Press'... and Senator Joe McCarthy, the Red Menace."[105]

In early July, in a show of independence, he challenged the official Hearst policy on Franco Spain. On July 1 a *Mirror* appeared under the heading LET'S MAKE UP WITH SPAIN. "What a travesty," it read, "that we deny Spain the usual international courtesies while extending them to... ruthless Red Fascist countries."[106] The very next day Winchell declared that "in a speech Franco said Spain is a democracy. Yes, sir, and he can show you the graves of those who said it isn't."[107]

Through most of July and August Winchell was on vacation. On his return, he attacked an unnamed "undesirable" in the media. "A femme radio writer at a major network," he wrote, "has been fired for giving her scripts a Moscow flavor."[108]

Column plugs from Winchell were a treasured commodity. With regal impartiality he conferred them on restaurants, singers, and nightclub comics as well as on political favorites. On October 29 the gossip noted that "Boris Shuh's *The Choice* is rough on comrats. It had the Daily Scummunist reviewer shrieking like a wounded pansy."[109]

On December 22 Winchell reproduced part of a letter McCarthy had sent him on the 18th. The senator wrote that "the cabal of smear artists who have objected to my fight against Communism have been carefully looking into every nook and cranny, hoping they could find something they could label anti-Semitic."[110]

McCarthy's letter was manna to Winchell. By being able to present McCarthy as an anti-anti-Semite and foe of right-wing extremism, Winchell could more easily fend off criticism of his support for him.

That column came nine days after an incident that showed McCarthy at his most brutish. On December 13, at Washington's tony Sulgrave Club, McCarthy and Drew Pearson were seated at the same dinner table.

A well-oiled McCarthy told Mrs. Pearson that his forthcoming attack on her husband would cause her to divorce him. Pearson responded by taunting McCarthy about his income tax chiseling. McCarthy invited Pearson to come outside, an invitation the columnist declined. Later, in the cloakroom, McCarthy trapped Pearson, and, according to varying accounts, either slapped, punched, or kneed him. The fight was broken up by Richard Nixon.[111]

The Hearst press, which normally thrived on sensationalism, was strangely reticent in reporting the Pearson-McCarthy encounter. Perhaps the organization, now so committed to McCarthy, was embarrassed by his behavior. On December 14 the brawl was dismissed on page 4 of the *Journal-American* as an incident of "physical violence (that) erupted between Senator Joe McCarthy and Drew Pearson...."[112]

On the 15th McCarthy went after Pearson on the Senate floor. In a verbal attack as savage as his physical one, he described the columnist as "a Moscow-directed character assassin," an "unprincipled liar and fake," and a man of "twisted, perverted mentality." McCarthy also called for a boycott of the Adam Hat Company, Pearson's sponsor.[113]

The boycott was taken up by Fulton Lewis on his radio program and ten days later Pearson's sponsorship was dropped. Though the company president claimed that the decision had been made prior to the Sulgrave Club incident, his statement aroused vast skepticism.[114]

Pegler, in his December 26 column, wrote that "Senator McCarthy has started (sic) an important public service by going after Drew Pearson."[115]

A different view was taken by Arnold Forster, chairman of the Anti-Defamation League. Forster, a friend of Winchell, wrote the columnist urging that he oppose McCarthy's efforts to drive Pearson off the air. "When Joe McCarthy demands that people boycott the stores which sponsor his broadcasts, the Senator is denying Pearson's right to earn a living...." Forster also stated that Pearson's "right to freedom of speech is vital to all of us."[116]

Forster's appeal fell on deaf ears – as did a personal one from Pearson. "When Pearson sought help in saving his sponsorship from McCarthy's threats, Winchell told Pearson to 'go to hell.'"[117] Both Winchell's biographers agree that his attitude stemmed more from pique over Pearson dispensing quiz show tips than from political differences.[118]

The Anna Rosenberg Affair

Fulton Lewis and J. B. Matthews, two of McCarthy's good heralds in the Hearst organization, almost succeeded in getting him in a pile of trouble in the waning months of 1950. On November 10 Lewis told his radio audience that Anna Rosenberg, a respected New York businesswoman recently nominated to be an Assistant Secretary of Defense, had once been a member of the Communist John Reed Club. Matthews followed up by disseminating a nine-page sheet linking Rosenberg to four Communist-front organizations.[119] McCarthy, seeing no reason to doubt his mentors, called on Republican Senate floor leader Kenneth Wherry to block Rosenberg's nomination.

At this point some strange specimens began to crawl out of the political fever swamps. One was the career bigot Gerald L. K. Smith, perennial godfather to right-wing hate groups. Another was an unemployed microfilm technician named Ralph De Sola, who claimed to have seen Rosenberg at John Reed Club meetings. From a clinical standpoint, probably the most interesting of these newcomers was Benjamin H. Freedman. A self-described "excommunicated Jew," Freedman was an ally of Smith in distributing anti-Semitic literature. Wealthy from the sale of the Woodbury Soap Company, Freedman bankrolled a Jew-baiting tabloid called *Common Sense*.[120]

With enemies like Smith, De Sola, and Freedman, Rosenberg didn't need friends – though she had them to spare. In appearances before the Senate Armed Forces Committee, Freedman and De Sola rivaled each other in looniness. The former disclosed that he had sued Bernard Baruch, Senator Herbert Lehman, and Thomas J. Watson, president of IBM, for conspiring with Cardinal Spellman to keep him out of the Catholic Church. The latter heard himself described by his ex-wife as "completely unstable, and haunted by a mother complex which caused him to blame... successful women for his own shortcomings."[121]

Sensibly cutting their losses, Lewis and Matthews abandoned the anti-Rosenberg camp. Lewis repudiated Smith while Matthews denounced Freedman as "rabidly anti-Semitic." Taking his cue, McCarthy reversed himself and voted for Rosenberg's confirmation. A bitter valedictory to the distasteful episode was furnished by Smith. Sensing betrayal most foul, he contended that Lewis "has demonstrated one thing: that he fears the Jews more than he hates Communism."[122]

Thanks to the agility of Lewis and Matthews – and the support of Walter Winchell – McCarthy did not suffer excessively from the Rosenberg controversy. He had opposed the nominee when it seemed she was liable to serious charges of Communist affiliation – then abruptly changed course when he learned that she was the victim of a smear by the anti-Semitic lunatic fringe.

McCarthy's rejection of Freedman and Smith won him an accolade from the liberal scholars Moshe Decter and James Rorty. In their book on the McCarthy movement, they write that "Senator McCarthy publicly eschewed anti-Semitism... during the period when anti-Semitism... might have been exploited in organizing a movement. This fact testifies... to the absence of this particular virus in the senator's political makeup."[123]

Nineteen fifty witnessed the sealing of the Hearst-McCarthy compact. Though the Hearst organization was a reluctant warrior in the beginning, once aboard it became the most staunch and devoted of allies. In measuring this evolution, landmark events were the GO TO IT, JOE MCCARTHY editorial of March 16 and, over April and May, the winning of Walter Winchell.

5. 1951-52: The Alliance at High Noon

Moshe Decter and James Rorty, in their study of McCarthy and the Communists, point out that in the late forties McCarthy's voting record was moderately internationalist and in favor of the bipartisan foreign policy. He supported Harold Stassen's presidential campaign in 1948, spoke against the candidacy of Douglas MacArthur, and was in no way aligned with that group of Republican reactionaries which included John Bricker of Ohio, Kenneth Wherry of Nebraska, Styles Bridges of New Hampshire, Homer Capehart of Indiana, and Bourke Hickenlooper of Iowa.

In 1947 McCarthy was paired against an amendment to reduce interim foreign aid, in 1948 he supported the European Recovery Program, and in 1949 he opposed a 10 percent cut in Marshall Plan funds.[1]

All that changed after Wheeling and the Hearst endorsement. In 1951 McCarthy favored an amendment to cut foreign aid by $300 million, in 1952 he backed a measure to reduce the Mutual Security Fund by $300 million, and in 1953 he opposed the Eisenhower nominee, Charles E. Bohlen, for the post of ambassador to the Soviet Union.[2] After Wheeling, McCarthy not only shared the anti-communist fervor of the Republican rightists but also their neo-isolationism and pinchpenny economic views.

The Hearst-McCarthy honeymoon lasted a little over three years, beginning with the GO TO IT, JOE MCCARTHY *Mirror* editorial on March 16 1950, and showing no signs of strain till late March of 1953. High plateau of the alliance was 1951-52, when – to paraphrase John Kennedy's witticism – anti-McCarthy material was as scarce in the Hearst papers as criticism of the Pope in *Osservatore Romano*.

As 1951 opened, McCarthy was heavily under fire for his participation in the backstreet campaign that unseated Millard Tydings. Disgust over tactics used against Tydings culminated in public Senate hearings that ran between February and April. What particularly angered foes of the anti-Tydings coalition was the composite picture showing Tydings in what appeared to be friendly discourse with Earl Browder. The strength of this sentiment put the Hearst-McCarthy forces on the defensive. On February 2 Fulton Lewis lamely protested that "it was labeled in the (campaign) publication as a composite, or split picture. The newspaper staff (of the tabloid in which the picture appeared) has been harassed ever since."[3] McCarthy was also covering his rear, explaining to Wisconsin Republican boss Tom Coleman that he had nothing to do with the picture. Coleman had labeled the composite "inexcusable and needless."[4] Later, McCarthy denied the picture did Tydings an injustice, citing the Marylander's allegedly "cooperative" relationship with Browder.[5] The incident is significant because it shows the Hearst press willing to defend McCarthy against a powerful Republican conservative like Coleman.

On February 12 Walter Winchell approvingly noted that "Senator McCarthy has repudiated Upton Close, the coattail rider."[6] McCarthy had bowed to the wishes of Wisconsin Jewish leaders and expunged from the Congressional Record an article Close had sent him. The story criticized two prominent Jews, Felix Frankfurter and Harold Laski, for their influence on State Department personnel.[7]

Truman v. MacArthur

On April 11 President Truman relieved General Douglas MacArthur of his command in the Far East. The general had been persistently sniping at the administration's policies, feeling that there was too much focus on Europe and not enough on Asia. On October 15, 1950, Truman met MacArthur on Wake Island to try and reach an understanding. When the general continued his criticisms, Truman issued a gag order on December 6, 1950, directing that MacArthur make no more speeches or issue any further press releases till they had been cleared by the State or Defense Department. MacArthur ignored the directive. The final straw came when he sent a letter to the House minority leader, Congressman Joe Martin of Massachusetts, in which he endorsed an inflammatory speech Martin had made on February 12. Martin declared that the "Truman administration should be indicted for the murder of thousands of American boys" if the president failed to allow Chinese Nationalist troops to "open a second front in Asia."[8] Martin sent a copy of his speech to MacArthur, inviting him to comment "on a confidential basis or otherwise."[9]

That MacArthur had no interest in confidentiality is evinced from the fact that Martin read his reply on the House floor. Congratulating the congressman on having "lost none of your old-time punch," the general assured that there was nothing in his speech in conflict with logic. In a pointed reference to Truman and his advisers, he commented on how "strangely difficult (it is) for some to realize that here in Asia is where the Communist conspirators have elected to make their play for world conquest...." MacArthur concluded his letter with the now famous phrase, "there is no substitute for victory."[10]

In the face of such open insubordination, it is difficult today to understand the outrage that was provoked by MacArthur's dismissal. To many Americans in 1951, MacArthur seemed to incarnate that indispensable leadership quality that another general, Charles de Gaulle, articulated in *The Edge of the Sword:* "Prestige cannot be without mystery." Though flamboyant, MacArthur was never familiar.

Deigning to come home after accepting the Japanese surrender, he mystified all by deferring his hero's welcome and staying on as America's proconsul in the Far East. Exaggerated reverence for MacArthur was not confined to the unsophisticated. Herbert Hoover compared him to "a reincarnation of St. Paul" and Congressman Dewey Short of Missouri described him as "a great hunk of God in the flesh."[11]

And now the Man of Glorious Mystery was coming home – not in triumph, as was his due, but in official disgrace after being fired by a little wardheeler who had accidentally risen to the presidency.

While the more sober opponents of the administration saw Truman's move as a blunder, the Hearst press regarded it as a sacrilege. Awe of MacArthur and contempt for Truman – that had always been the Hearst posture and now these emotions were exponentially intensified.

But it had not always been McCarthy's. In 1948, when Harold Stassen was making his bid for the Republican nomination, the Hearst organization strongly supported MacArthur. McCarthy, on the other hand, was chairman of a Wisconsin Stassen-for-President club. In a snide and condescending campaign letter, he conceded that "General MacArthur has been a great general" but added that "he has been out of touch with civilian problems of government" and should not "undergo the strain of years as President of our country in this difficult time." McCarthy also played on the feelings of Wisconsin's large Catholic and Lutheran populations by emphasizing that the general's first marriage had ended in divorce.[12] McCarthy's about-face on MacArthur demonstrates how he now endorsed the agendas of the Hearst press and the Republican right.

On April 11 the *Journal-American's* headline read MACARTHUR FIRED. The news story made no pretense to objectivity. The general's firing, it declared, was a "crushing blow to America long prepared by a clique of administration officials who seem determined on a course of appeasement toward Communist Russia and Communist China." On page 7, McCarthy denounced the dismissal as "a black day for America and a great day of rejoicing and victory for Communism."[14]

On April 12 Winchell wrote that "the greatest scandal in American history is now out in the open. The scandal is not the dismissal of General MacArthur; it is the foreign policy that made it inevitable."[15] The *Mirror's* editorial on the 12th lamented that "the greatest general of our day, Douglas MacArthur, has been dismissed to please the cupidity of Great Britain, the ignorance of Dean Acheson, the jealousy of General George Marshall...." It added that "we not include Harry Truman in this listing... because he is too small...."[16]

On the same day, the *Journal-American* gave free rein to McCarthy's talent for vulgar innuendo. In a page 2 story headed M'C HINTS TRU-MAN TIPSY, the senator charged that "Truman is surrounded by the Jessups, the Achesons, and the old Hiss crowd" and his firing of Mac-Arthur "shows the midnight power of bourbon and benedictine."[17]

The April 13 *Mirror* contained a follow-up story on page 9. Under M'C SAYS WHITE HOUSE 'TRAITORS' DO IT WITH BOURBON, it quoted McCarthy's claim that "most of the tragic things are done between 11:30 and two in the morning, when they've had time to get the President cheerful." McCarthy concluded that "the pals of Alger Hiss are still running the State Department."[18]

Extremism was running rampant that spring, with respected legislators using words they would have flinched at before MacArthur's dismissal. On April 27 Dean Acheson found himself pounced on by a fellow Yale man and longtime symbol of conservative integrity. In a page 1 *Journal-American* story, under TAFT DEMANDS ACHESON OUSTER AS APPEASER, Mr. Republican charged that "the State Department, from the beginning, wanted the Communists to win in China."[19]

McCarthy v. Marshall

On June 14, thanks largely to McCarthy, a second general burst into the news. George C. Marshall, then serving as Secretary of Defense, was described by Harry Truman as "the greatest living American." Richard Rovere characterized him as "the least assailable American," a status earned by his "vast and palpable dignity" and a reputation never touched by scandal.[20] In a less flamboyant manner, Marshall was as Olympian a figure as MacArthur.

This did not deter McCarthy. Though McCarthyism has become a synonym for repressive conformity, McCarthy himself had a mischievous and anti-establishment side to his nature. The bigger an enemy, the more he enjoyed cutting him down. And now he was tweaking the nose of "the greatest living American."

McCarthy's attack on Marshall took the form of a 60,000-word speech which was later expanded into a book titled *America's Retreat from Victory: The Story of George Catlett Marshall.* McCarthy read only a third of the speech on the Senate floor, the other 40,000 words being published in the Congressional Record. In leaving such a large section of the speech unread, McCarthy was motivated partly by boredom and partly by a desire to accommodate his fellow senators – "I do not wish them to miss the ball game this evening."[21]

The speech was a radical departure from the norm of McCarthy's political attacks. It contained none of the "Red Dean of fashion" rhetoric with which he belabored Acheson or recommendations that "the son of a bitch ought to be impeached" – one of his comments when Truman fired MacArthur. Instead, the largely unread address was a scholarly analysis of Marshall's errors in policy, strategy, and judgment. Though pointedly critical, the speech at all times remained on a lofty academic plane.

Where the barnyard abuse of Acheson and Truman was authentic Joe McCarthy, the Marshall speech saw the senator in the role of Charlie McCarthy. The "ventriloquist" was first thought to be one of the "Georgetown School," conservative historians under the leadership of Charles Callan Tansill and Stefan Possony.[22] While McCarthy steadfastly claimed that he and his "staff" wrote the speech, his friend and associate Robert Morris identified the author as a fiercely polemical anti-communist journalist named Forrest Davis.[23]

Despite its lack of personal invective, the speech was condemned almost as strongly by moderate Republicans as by Democrats. Senator Leverett Saltonstall of Massachusetts called it "sickening, simply disgusting." "An offense against good taste and good sense," was the judgment of the Republican *New York Herald-Tribune,* while a smaller GOP journal, the *Youngstown Vindicator,* labeled the Davis-McCarthy effort a "Stink Bomb."[24]

But the Hearst press held fast. On June 14, the *Journal-American's* headline read MCCARTHY LAYS U.S. CRISIS TO MARSHALL. A page 1 story noted that McCarthy "accused the Defense Secretary of 'participating in an administration conspiracy so (the United States) will fall victim to Soviet intrigue...." As a partner in the conspiracy, McCarthy identified Dean Acheson, "Russian as to heart, British as to manner."[25]

Since the *Mirror* was an evening paper, its coverage on any important story usually came a day later than the *Journal-American's*. In even stronger language, a page 2 story was headlined M'C BLASTS GEN. MARSHALL AND ACHESON AS LIARS. Along with carrying a truncated version of McCarthy's truncated speech, it quoted McCarthy as saying that Acheson's testimony on MacArthur was "a piece of organized fabrication."[26]

While his Senate speech was widely denounced, some of the mud thrown by McCarthy at Marshall managed to stick. If a figure as seemingly unassailable as Marshall could be attacked with impunity, then who was safe? The boldness of McCarthy's assault emboldened others. No man is perfect and now little chinks were discovered in Marshall's armor. Immediately before Pearl Harbor, he had been horseback riding when he should have been in constant touch with the commanders in Hawaii. Like other grand planners, he was not a talented troop commander. His World War I record had not been as distinguished as MacArthur's, leading to the *Mirror's* editorial comment about Marshall's alleged "jealousy" of his former superior. When Marshall retired as Defense Secretary in the winter of 1951, he was still venerated by a great number of Americans. In 1953 he would win the Nobel Prize. But his reputation would never again be the seamless garment it had been before the daring attack of McCarthy, Forrest Davis, and the Hearst-Patterson-McCormick press.

McCarthy v. Benton

In 1951-52 McCarthy's most energetic and steadfast enemy in the Senate was a Connecticut Democrat named William Burnett Benton. A co-founder of the advertising agency of Benton and Bowles, he became a millionaire on Madison Avenue and then decided to devote himself to public service - as did his partner, Chester Bowles. Between 1945-47 Benton served as Assistant Secretary of State for Public Affairs. In 1949 the governor of Connecticut - his old friend Bowles - appointed Benton to serve out the unexpired term of retiring Senator Raymond Baldwin.

Benton was bright, liberal, Yale-educated, and a former Rhodes scholar. Despite this sophisticated background, his loathing for McCarthy was primitive and uncomplicated. He was particularly angry over McCarthy's role in the Maryland campaign. On August 7, 1951, Benton introduced a resolution "requesting an investigation by the Rules Committee to determine whether or not (McCarthy) should be expelled from the Senate."[27] On August 8 the *Journal-American* took notice of Benton's resolution in a page 2 story headlined M'CARTHY OUSTER MOVE ADVANCED. The article complained that the move by Sen. Benton... to expel Sen. McCarthy was put in the hands of the same subcommittee which denounced last fall's senatorial campaign and noted McCarthy's part in it."[28] This was a subcommittee headed by Senator A. S. ("Mike") Monroney, Democrat of Oklahoma, which so strongly denounced the "backstreet" campaign in Maryland.

After flashing back at Benton ("Connecticut's mental midget," "the hero of every Communist and crook in and out of government"), McCarthy created one of those headline-grabbing diversions for which he was famous. In the August 9 *Journal-American,* under M'CARTHY CALLS VINCENT RED SPY, the opening sentence read: "Sen. McCarthy... charged in the Senate today that John Carter Vincent had engaged in 'espionage activity' while serving as U.S. Minister to Switzerland."[29]

Even by McCarthy standards, this was wild and way out. Vincent was one of the "old China hands" who had served there in wartime and were now being pilloried for having been insufficiently ecstatic about Chiang Kai-shek. Far from engaging in espionage while in Switzerland, Vincent was himself the victim of a sleazy scam perpetrated by one of McCarthy's spies in Europe. This operative was an unstable young black man named Charles Davis, who had been discharged from the Navy for homosexuality. A former Communist, Davis had switched sides in 1949 and been hired by a McCarthy representative in Paris named John E. Farrand. Seeking to discredit Vincent, Davis sent him a telegram under the signature of Swiss Communist leader Emil Stampfi. The imposture was discovered and Davis was arrested and jailed by the Swiss authorities.[30]

Benton was beside himself with glee. "Here," he declared, "we have an admitted homosexual ex-Communist convicted as a personal spy on Senator McCarthy's payroll, trying to frame an American diplomat – with a false telegram linking him to Communists."[31]

The Connecticut senator would enjoy few other satisfactions in his fight with McCarthy. However much McCarthy was disliked by many legislators, there was a strong tradition in the Senate against expulsion of one of its own. A two-thirds vote was required and no senator had ever been expelled.

Benton's resolution was considered in late September by a subcommittee on Elections and Privileges headed by Iowa Democrat Guy Gillette. Declining to respond to Benton's attack, McCarthy told Gillette that "the Benton type of smear material can be found in the *Daily Worker* almost any day of the week."[32] Gillette was a timid man and he later resigned the subcommittee chairmanship after McCarthy threatened to go into Iowa and campaign against him.[33]

By April 1952 McCarthy had taken the offensive against Benton. When Benton accepted McCarthy's challenge that he waive immunity on his charges, McCarthy sued him for $2 million. Though he had no chance of winning, he wanted to "reverse the roles, to make himself the accuser and Benton the accused."[34]

On April 10 the *Journal-American's* headline read MCCARTHY URGES PROBE OF BENTON. Among McCarthy's accusations were that Benton, while in the State Department, defended persons accused of Communist affiliation before a loyalty board and that he purchased "lewd and licentious material that followed the (Communist) party line." This was a reference to Edmund Wilson's *Memoirs of Hecate County,* then considered a controversial work.[35]

On July 3 McCarthy made his only personal appearance before the subcommittee. It was still headed by the irresolute Gillette, who did not resign till McCarthy's September 9 victory in the Wisconsin primary. Another member was the Missouri Democrat Thomas Hennings, a man with a serious drinking problem.[36] So the cards were stacked against Benton, who had made the unhappy transition from hunter to hunted.

The *Journal-American's* July 3 edition carried a page 12 story headed BENTON SHIELDED REDS, SAYS MCCARTHY. McCarthy claimed that "the chameleon from Connecticut," while serving in the State Department, had "sheltered a number of Communists, fellow travelers, and complete dupes." Though McCarthy didn't claim that "Mr. Benton is a member of the Communist Party," he accused him of following all its directives and added that "his soap selling abilities are worth ten million dollars a year" to the Communists.[37]

The vicious Benton-McCarthy controversy in the Senate ended with Benton's defeat in November 1952. Though the ex-senator continued to attack McCarthy from the outside, sitting in his seat was a pro-McCarthy Catholic Republican named William Purtell. The scalps of Millard Tydings and William Benton were the ones McCarthy most cherished. At the Appleton Hotel, while McCarthy and his friends celebrated, "the election board in the reception room bore the terse announcement, 'Benton went to hell at 8:30.'"[38]

In the November 6 issue of the *Journal-American,* Connecticut native Frank Conniff wrote that "Benton knew so little about the Nutmeg mores... that he campaigned throughout the state baying about 'McCarthyism,' not realizing that thousands of Connecticut residents... think

McCarthy is a fine old Irish name that shouldn't be bandied about too loosely."[39]

Entertainers Under Fire

In 1951-52, glory years of the Hearst-McCarthy alliance, the ideologically committed "nonpolitical" writers bore approximately the same relationship to their political counterparts as guerrillas do to regular forces. Guerrilla wars are always crueler and there was more blood shed and more careers destroyed among entertainment figures than among legislators, government officials, and academics who were normal targets of the political columnists.

Some of the bloodletting was literal. Barry Gray, a radio talk show host who had offended Winchell, was twice beaten up, once suffering a fractured skull.[40] He also had to endure the sort of career damage and personal ostracism that would have been impossible in the case of a politician or a professor. "Winchell had the power to kill someone professionally," said Gray in an interview. "I lost two television shows... actors stopped coming on my program. I was a pariah. A week before, I had gone into Lindy's and it was 'Hi, how are you?' I walked into Lindy's then, and there was a silence. I felt like I was in *High Noon*. I was ostracized."[41] So intense was Winchell's antagonism against Gray that at times it even assumed the form of anti-Semitism. In the manner of Rankin's references to "Lipshitz," he informed readers in one column that Gray's original name was Bernard Yaroslaw.[42]

Winchell was the leader of the guerrilla forces. His chief lieutenants were Lait, Mortimer, and Jack O'Brian, with Dorothy Kilgallen filling the role of reluctant camp follower. Cassini was a special case, his main quarry being politically incorrect socialites.

The impact of McCarthyism outside the political arena should never be underestimated. Brooks Atkinson, theater critic of the *New York Times*, said McCarthy "had driven all good playwrights to silence of triviality."[43] A rabbi, interviewed by the *New York Herald-Tribune* in 1952, even blamed college "panty raids" on McCarthyism. This cleric declared that McCarthyism made dissent on major issues dangerous, causing students "to find expression for their bottled-up energies in foolish and unseemly 'raids' upon dormitories."[44]

In the February 2, 1951 "Voice of Broadway," Dorothy Kilgallen gave a good example of her token redbaiting – enough to pay her dues but avoiding any comment that might damage the careers of show business friends. Picking on a safe target – the fugitive Comintern agent Gerhardt Eisler – she wrote that he wanted to go back to the United States for a "highly specialized stomach operation."[45]

Three days later Cassini chronicled some transatlantic high jinks. He wrote that "London aristocracy is cheering John Fox-Strangways who kicked Labor Minister Aneurin Bevan at the exclusive White's Club."[46] Bevan was an extreme leftist in the Labour party. The fact that Fox-Strangways's action got him expelled from his posh club would indicate that the cheers came more from Cassini than from a broad spectrum of London's *beau monde.*

That spring the theatrical adaptation of *Darkness at Noon,* Arthur Koestler's celebrated indictment of Stalinism, was having a rather rocky run on Broadway. The cast was riddled with dissension, a condition noted by Kilgallen in another dutifully anti-communist but non-controversial sally: "If Stalin and his pals were having as much trouble as the 'Communists' at the Royale (Theater), how lovely."[47]

Of Winchell's journalistic flatterers, there were few as obsequious as the *Mirror's* Nick Kenny. Ironically, an item in Kenny's June 23 column may have done Winchell more harm than good. Kenny wrote that "Tee Vee is buzzing over Walter Winchell's wonderful video MC job for Sherman Billingsley on the Stork Club show the other night. WW is as impressive before a TV camera as he is in front of a radio mike."[48]

He wasn't. It was in fact television that destroyed Winchell. The staccato voice and the clicking telegraph key, so effective on the air, failed to work their magic on the tube. Additional minus factors were the columnist's vulturine profile and ever-present hat. One of Winchell's biographers, Bob Thomas, records these comments when he first appeared to his public. "So that's what he looks like...." "Look, he operates that key himself...." "Why is he wearing a hat?...."[49] Had Winchell's hubris not been inflamed by such as Kenny, he might have avoided a disastrous error.

Though the preceding is peripheral to McCarthyism's impact on the entertainment world, it is significant that Winchell's decline began in 1952 – that peak year of the McCarthy era when the gossip's listeners also became his viewers.

As a labor columnist, Victor Riesel belonged to the "regular forces" rather than the "guerrillas." But the political writers had ample latitude to pontificate on what was wrong in the entertainment world – and they often did.

In April 1952 Riesel was closely monitoring a Hollywood investigation by Senator Pat McCarran's Internal Security Subcommittee. On the stand was actress Judy Holliday, who had won an Oscar for her portrayal of a dumb blonde in the hit comedy *Born Yesterday.* The hearing was going well for Holliday. Not only were the senators convinced of her repentance (she had supported some suspect organizations) but particularly impressed when she told them that she had actually hired people to investigate her. "You watch it now, don't you?" said Senator Arthur Watkins approvingly. "Ho, do I watch it now," replied Holliday. The flinty McCarran, normally a merciless inquisitor, remarked mildly that "Communism fastens itself like a leech on the careers of prominent entertainers," adding the comforting observation that "we do not want to accuse anyone of guilt by association."[50]

This was too much for Riesel. Detecting bleedingheartism among McCarran and his colleagues, he addressed an angry message to the actress in his column: "This is to let Hollywood's Oscar-winning blonde, Judy Holliday, know that we weren't born yesterday... she says, in effect, that she was played for a sucker... Now she's to resume her career. But what will Judy Holliday (and others) do for the world which was besmirched by those to whom they lent their names like casual endorsements of toothpaste?"[51]

One in the guerrilla ranks whose ferocity matched Riesel's was Jack O'Brian. On August 7, 1952 the *Journal-American's* radio-TV columnist cast a cold eye at Clifton Fadiman, a donnish author, critic, and moderator of the highbrow "Information Please" program. Branding Fadiman a snob as well as a subversive, O'Brian charged that he "insisted everyone around 'Information Please' call him MISTER Fadiman while sports writer Red Barber preferred to be called 'Red.' Perhaps Fadiman feared that someone might get him mixed up with Barber's nickname."[52]

Five days later O'Brian posed an indignant question. "Watcha mean, there's a 'blacklist' for Red Channelites? If true, far left Adelaide Klein wouldn't have been hired by Channel 9's Harvey Marlowe for 'Trapped'...."[53] Klein had belonged to six suspect groups and had also endorsed the Stalin Purge Trials.[54]

The September 5 *Journal-American* contained a hand-rubbing prediction by O'Brian that "there'll be pink-tinted tea from the September 29 hearings of the HUAC in Hollywood, with 20 studio writers, directors, and actors to be called in first."[55]

Even at this high tide of McCarthyism, O'Brian believed that Communists and fellow travelers still had the power to damage an anti-Red film at the box office. On October 19 he wrote that "when *My Son John* was released as a movie the lefties slung their worst epithets and... it did not win the success it might have."[56]

On the 23rd O'Brian's efforts earned him that most coveted of prizes, an accolade from Winchell. In a bouquets-and-brickbats entry, the columnist lauded O'Brian as the "radioracle" while castigating John Crosby, the *Herald-Tribune's* liberal radio-TV commentator, as "the radiogre."[57]

The 1952 Election

As early as 1950 Harry Truman had made up his mind not to run for reelection. On April 16 he wrote in his diary that "I am not a candidate for nomination by the Democratic convention." In addition, Mrs. Truman was known to be strongly opposed to her husband seeking another term.[58]

The official announcement was not made till almost two years later. On March 29, 1952, at a Jefferson-Jackson dinner in the Washington Armory, Truman began a fighting speech by attacking the "dinosaur school of Republican strategy" that would "pull out of Korea... abandon Europe, and let the United Nations go to smash...." The president warned that the Republican campaign would not address the issues but be full of "phony propaganda" with McCarthy as the GOP's real spokesman. Then it came:

> Whoever the Democrats nominate for President this year, he will have this record to run on. I shall not be a candidate for reelection. I have served my country long, and I think honestly and efficiently. I shall not accept a renomination. I do not feel it is my duty to spend another four years in the White House.[59]

I WON'T RUN, SAYS TRUMAN was the *Mirror's* March 30 headline. The story was factual and unslanted. The next day the *Mirror* spoke from the heart. Its editorial concluded that "Harry S. Truman, toward the end of a tawdry and labored political speech, took his party off the hook with the long awaited announcement of his intentions... But Truman the man, was not the issue, he was the symbol... in the nature of a political obituary, it is charity to say, 'History, take him away!'"[60]

On March 31 the *Journal-American* addressed Truman's announcement in a front page editorial. It ended with the pronouncement that "his decision not to run is no tragic or irreplaceable loss to the country."[61]

Margaret Truman writes that Adlai Stevenson was the Democratic front runner as far back as the Jefferson-Jackson dinner.[62] If so, he was front runner by elimination. Truman's first choice had been his good friend Chief Justice Fred A. Vinson. But Vinson, happy on the Court, declined Truman's overtures.[63] The president then considered other potential candidates. Senator Richard Russell of Georgia had "all the qualifications as to ability and brains" but his segregationist views made him "poison to Northern Democrats and honest liberals."[64] Truman also ruled out a more liberal Southerner, Estes Kefauver of Tennessee. "What a president this demagogic dumb bell (sic) would make," he said scornfully. Truman disliked "Cow Fever" because his crime investigations had hurt Democratic machines in large cities.[65] Senator Robert Kerr of Oklahoma, a staunch defender of Truman during the MacArthur controversy, was "a grand man, a good administrator... but he has a gas record." Kerr was a spokesman for the big natural gas interests in his home state.[66] Truman also had a sentimental attachment to Alben Barkley, his vice-president. But Barkley's age was a fatal obstacle. "I wish he could be sixty-four instead of seventy-four... My good friend Alben would be dead in three months if he should inherit my job."[67] A final possibility was Averell Harriman. Truman considered him "the ablest of them all" but doubted if the voters would "elect a Wall Street banker and railroad tycoon president of the United States on the Democratic ticket."[68]

So it narrowed down to Stevenson. Truman was not enthusiastic about the Illinois governor. A hard-charging, pragmatic politician, he was driven to near frenzy by Stevenson's indecision. On July 24, three days after the Democratic convention opened, Stevenson called Truman and asked if the president would be embarrassed if Stevenson allowed his name to be placed in nomination. "I've been trying since January to get you to say that," exploded Truman. "Why would it embarrass me?"[69]

Another problem was Stevenson's status as a divorced man. This difficulty was compounded by a whispering campaign launched by the candidate's vindictive and unbalanced ex-wife. The former Mrs. Stevenson said "she wouldn't have minded if he had left her for a woman, but could not tolerate his leaving her for a man."[70] Even Walter Trohan, Bertie McCormick's bureau chief in Washington, dismissed this canard as the manifestation of "a woman's vicious wrath."[71]

The 1952 campaign was the dirtiest in American history. McCarthy was riding high, the Democrats were being openly assailed as the party of treason, and the sensitive, introspective Stevenson must have listened to the Hearst-Patterson-McCormick tom-toms with the feelings of an isolated planter in the jungle.

As in 1948, the Hearst press's first choice was MacArthur. The Republican convention opened on July 7, with the general as keynote speaker. William Manchester describes the address as "the worst of his career – banal and strident in content, wretchedly delivered... whenever he mentioned God, which was often, his voice had a disconcerting way of rising an octave and breaking, and he had developed a peculiar habit of jumping up and down and pointing his right finger toward the ceiling for emphasis. Halfway through it the delegates began babbling so loudly among themselves that he could hardly be heard."[72]

That keynote address was MacArthur's political swan song. But the Hearst organization continued to support its hero – as did McCarthy. Where in 1948 the sixty-eight-year-old MacArthur was too old to be president, in 1952 the seventy-two-year-old MacArthur was not. On July 9 a page 2 *Journal-American* story carried the headline MCCARTHY URGES M'ARTHUR AS NOMINEE. While expressing admiration for Eisenhower and Taft, the Wisconsinite described MacArthur as "a man who combined the qualities of both."[73]

From the Hearst coverage, one would get the impression that McCarthy's endorsement was the main point of his speech. In reality, it was an adventitious supplement to a rancorous attack on the "Acheson-Truman-Lattimore party" that limits the Korean War "to the area to which the Communists want it limited."[74] Entering the convention hall to the strains of "On Wisconsin" and the "Marine Hymn," he enlivened his speech with such publicity gimmicks as having cronies march around the hall with placards bearing red herrings and the names "Acheson," "Lattimore," and "Hiss."[75] These antics were described in a page 8 story under M'CARTHY BLASTS TRUMAN GROUP, along with McCarthy's conclusion that the Truman administration was guilty of either "abysmal stupidity or treason."[76]

In the same issue E. F. Tompkins noted, and quite correctly, that the "GOP liberals" didn't want McCarthy addressing the convention. His column that day also contained a rave for *McCarthyism: The Fight for America,* a cut-and-paste job that appeared under the senator's name in that election year.[77] Elon Farnsworth Tompkins, born in 1887, was the *Journal-American's* senior political writer both by age and longevity. A Hearst employee since 1927, he became the *Journal-American's* chief editorial writer in 1937.

On July 10 the *Mirror* focused on another part of McCarthy's convention speech. Under MOSCOW-DC AXIS ALLEGED BY MC-CARTHY, the text carried his comment that "the same men who delivered nearly half the world to Communist Russia are still in control in Washington and Moscow."[78]

The same day Winchell launched an attack on James Wechsler, editor of the *New York Post,* every bit as sulphurous as McCarthy's on the "Acheson-Truman-Lattimore party." Winchell and Wechsler were old enemies. On January 7, 1951 the *Post* began a 24-part series on Winchell. The series was a broadax job, an exercise in overkill in which the columnist "was pictured as perverse, coarse, an unmitigated liar… a plagiarist, a demagogue whose cynicism put him on the right side for the wrong reasons, an unethical newspaperman who violated the principles as well as the amenities of his craft – in brief, an all-around monster."[79] Individual segments of the series were devoted to such topics as Winchell's ghost-writers, his extramarital affairs, and his friendship with mobsters.[80]

Winchell, accustomed to adulation, was so taken aback by the *Post's* broadside that at first he didn't respond. Then, "after eighteen of the articles had appeared, it was announced that Winchell was suspending his column because of ill health."[81]

The *Post*, wishing to avoid the appearance of picking on a sick man, temporarily suspended the series. Winchell recuperated and the attacks were resumed. By now the columnist had recovered his nerve as well as his health. The defining feature of his counterattack was to paint the *Post* red. Wechsler, in his youth, had been a member of the Young Communist League. Much was made of this, and little of Wechsler's subsequent career as a dedicated anti-communist. In fact, Winchell's strategy was to depict Wechsler's conversion as phony. In his July 10 column, Winchell referred to Wechsler as "this Ivan character who claims he is a 'former' Communist." The article also referred to Wechsler's paper as the *Postitute*.[82] (On other occasions, he called it the *Compost*.)

Confirming E. F. Tompkins's view that Republican liberals were displeased by McCarthy's presence at the convention, New York governor Thomas E. Dewey instructed his delegation to remain seated during the standing ovation that followed McCarthy's speech. In the July 10 *Journal-American*, Fulton Lewis raged that Dewey's action was "a new low in convention politics." [83]

Though Eisenhower was McCarthy's third choice (after MacArthur and Taft), he reacted to Ike's nomination like a good party loyalist. "I think Eisenhower will make a great president," he said, adding that "one of the finest things I've ever seen is Eisenhower going to Taft's headquarters and accepting Taft's offer of cooperation."[84]

As for the Democratic candidate, the tone of McCarthy's campaign was set by a crude remark he made when told that Stevenson had called on Eisenhower to repudiate him: "Horsemeat Adlai should brush the odor of Alger Hiss off his toga before he advises Eisenhower."[85]

Both candidates had defended General Marshall in August appearances before the American Legion. Pegler took notice of this on September 2, referring his readers to McCarthy's ghosted book about Marshall and defending it as "objective, precise, and truthful." Pegler also charged that Stevenson found (a) pro-Communist atmosphere salubrious during his service with the Red Bureaucracy of the Roosevelt-Truman regime."[86]

The next day Frank Conniff spoke for his own constituency, the mostly blue-collar Catholic-ethnic Democrats who remained loyal to the party for economic reasons but were singularly unresponsive to appeals against McCarthyism. Conniff's mother had been an active Democratic worker and the columnist covered a Connecticut function in her honor. With satisfaction he noted that "there was nary a mention of Joe McCarthy or the phony issue of McCarthyism." Conniff concluded that "Democratic sentiment at the grass-roots level is liable to be heavily with Joe, for these Democrats are fiercely anti-Communist."[87]

In a slightly different form, this sentiment was echoed on September 4 by E. F. Tompkins. Apparently ascribing extremism only to McCarthy's enemies, Tompkins opined that "by violently campaigning against Senator McCarthy… Governor Stevenson and his left-wing advisers are making the courageous Wisconsin crusader a foremost citizen."[88]

History has slighted E. F. Tompkins. Elderly and relatively obscure, overshadowed by the Peglers and Sokolskys, his motivating role in one of McCarthy's most famous speeches has been widely overlooked. Just as Forrest Davis was behind McCarthy's book on Marshall, so did the little-known Tompkins provide the original inspiration for McCarthy's celebrated "Alger – I mean Adlai" speech. On September 5, fifty-seven days before McCarthy's attack on Stevenson, Tompkins's column was headed "Adlai and Alger: A New Deal Mystery." Tompkins first dismissed Stevenson's denunciations of McCarthyism, declaring that it was "a very good synonym for anti-Communism." Then locking into his main theme, Tompkins pointed out that "Adlai and Alger" had served together in the Agricultural Adjustment Administration in 1933-34 and that Hiss had nominated Stevenson as a delegate to a 1942 conference sponsored by the Institute of Pacific Relations. IPR, whose membership included Owen Lattimore and Frederick Vanderbilt Field, was a favorite target of the Red hunters.[89]

Characteristically, McCarthy added embellishments of his own when he made the famous speech. The "Alger – I mean Adlai" quip was delivered at least four times by a giggling McCarthy.[90] Other flights of fancy included McCarthy's claim that the *Daily Worker* had endorsed Stevenson and that Stevenson had lied about membership in Americans for Democratic Action. But the original inspiration clearly came from Tompkins, senior Red hunter at the *Journal-American* and a man whose contributions were always underrated.

On September 8 McCarthy found himself lauded by another member of the Hearst old guard. George Rothwell Brown, the contemporary of De

Casseres, devoted his column that day to the Wisconsin primary. Brown was certain that "the people of Wisconsin are too intelligent to fall for the distortion that has been employed by Left Wing dupes and stooges who are trying to destroy Joe McCarthy."[91]

Brown's optimism was well-founded as McCarthy scored one of his most impressive victories. His opponent, Len Schmitt, was an attorney of German descent with a good war record. A former Progressive, Schmitt had hoped to attract a large number of crossover votes from liberal Democrats. This was not to be. The Democratic primary winner, Thomas Fairchild, was a favorite of party liberals and some GOP leaders estimated that he soaked up 50,000 votes that might otherwise have gone to Schmitt.[92]

SEN. M'CARTHY WINS BY LANDSLIDE was the page 1 headline of the September 10 *Journal-American.* This was no exaggeration. McCarthy swamped Schmitt by a 515,281-313,701 margin and carried 69 out of 71 counties. The editorial noted that "the vote in Wisconsin... is a rebuke to those myopic Americans who would rather belittle and degrade Joe McCarthy than face the rude facts of Communist intrigue...." It concluded that "Joe McCarthy is a fighting guy with roots deep in the emotions of contemporary Americans. This newspaper is proud that it has supported him."[93] The same issue carried a picture on page 4 of a grinning McCarthy; the caption was WINNING SMILE.[94]

As passions mounted and partisanship escalated during this meanest of campaigns, Hearst writers were no longer satisfied with merely attacking open enemies of McCarthy. Also under fire were Republicans considered guilty of insufficient enthusiasm about the senator. On October 1 Frank Conniff took a fellow Connecticut native, Representative Clare Boothe Luce, to task for not welcoming McCarthy when he came to their state. This lapse, scolded Conniff, "may square Mrs. Luce with her social and · intellectual friends, but people who understand the long, rugged road Joe McCarthy has braced will not be impressed."[95]

Today it is well known that Joseph P. Kennedy, a friend and supporter of McCarthy, persuaded him to stay out of the race in Massachusetts where John Kennedy was running against the moderate Republican Henry Cabot Lodge. If Pegler is to be credited, there was in fact pressure on McCarthy to give Lodge a helping hand. "The Republican National Committee," he wrote, "has been quietly whining for Joe McCarthy to go up to Massachusetts and save Henry Cabot Lodge." Pegler, who disliked centrist Republicans almost as much as he did Democrats and Communists, predicted that if McCarthy did go, Lodge would say that treason is a bad thing but McCarthy's methods were not just right.[96]

Sokolsky, on his pundit's perch, could afford to remain somewhat above the kneeing and gouging of this unusually vicious campaign. Taking a retrospective look at Harry Truman, he described him as a man of "vindictive tenacity" whose hatred for McCarthy, McCarran, and Jenner "was not as much due to a vast difference of opinion over policies as refusal to recognize that any can be right that originates among those who oppose him."[97]

On October 27, day of the "Alger – I mean Adlai" speech, the *Mirror* heralded the event in a page 2 story headed M'CARTHY DRAFTS EXPOSE OF ADLAI. The article predicted that McCarthy would not call Stevenson a Communist or pro-Communist but just give the candidate's history and let the people decide.[98]

The speech was reported on page 1 of the October 28 *Journal-American,* under the headline ADLAI AIDED RED CAUSE – M'CARTHY. There was no mention of "Alger – I mean Adlai" but considerable coverage on McCarthy's denunciation of Stevenson's "left-wing advisers." These included Arthur Schlesinger, Wilson Wyatt, Archibald MacLeish, and Bernard de Voto, whom McCarthy called "Richard" de Voto. The page 1 text carried McCarthy's accusation that Stevenson, while serving in the government, had rejected an admiral's advice that he fire Communist radio operators on merchant ships.[99]

As the campaign entered its last days, the Hearst papers did everything they could to maximize McCarthy's role. "The Republican most feared by the Democrats and their rapscallion followers," wrote Pegler, "is not Eisenhower but Joe McCarthy."[100] Many of McCarthy's foes would have agreed with this evaluation.

In October, as invective on both sides mounted in stridency, a strongly anti-McCarthy book hit the stands. Though it was brought out by a little-known house in Boston (other publishers were afraid to touch it), it quickly became a best-seller. Titled *McCarthy: The Man, the Senator, the "Ism",* it was written by Jack Anderson, Drew Pearson's chief assistant, and a Wisconsin reporter named Ronald May. To his credit, Anderson made no pretense that this was anything but a special hatchet job in connection with the campaign. "The scheme of the book," he wrote, "was to bring together all the verifiable offenses in the McCarthy record... the early promise, the ruthless ambition, the switched allegiances, the trampled friends, the quickie divorces, the tax scams, the faked war record, the conflicts of interest, the shady backers, the false charges, the corrupt pattern."[101] Later historians have uncovered errors of fact in the Anderson-May book. For example, the authors claimed that McCarthy, in 1946, said that "Communists have the same right to vote as anyone else...."[102] McCarthy denied ever making such a statement. David Oshinsky, after failing to uncover the source of the quote following an extensive search, wrote that "my feeling is that McCarthy was correct, that he never uttered such a comment."[103]

Yet "the fear and loathing of McCarthy within liberal-intellectual circles was such... that the volume was greeted with great seriousness in important newspapers and journals."[104] The book's ascension into the best-seller lists was fueled by laudatory reviews in the *New York Times, New York Herald-Tribune, Saturday Review,* and *Washington Post.* The book was also praised by respected academics. A favorable review by Professor Robert K. Carr of Dartmouth drew an angry cannonade from Pegler. Denouncing Anderson as a "private detective and stooge for Drew Pearson's strange activities," Pegler characterized the review as "dishonest" because "there is not the slightest reasonable doubt that Carr... knew the anti-McCarthy book was written by an agent of an enemy of McCarthy."[105]

Pegler's attack on Carr was not the only reaction to the Anderson-May book by a Hearst organ. Shortly after the book came out Ronald May was attending a banquet in Milwaukee at which McCarthy was a speaker. When McCarthy denounced him as a Communist spy, May was roughed up by the senator's supporters and ejected from the premises. The scene was photographed by the Hearst-owned *Milwaukee Sentinel,* with the caption: MCCARTHY POINTS FINGER AT SNOOPER: CHARGES HE IS SEEKING SMEAR MATERIAL.[106]

Eisenhower's victory was greeted by a gloating editorial in the *Journal-American.* Stevenson's attacks on McCarthy had turned out to be a "boomerang," since "McCarthyism was chiefly responsible for Democratic defeats in Connecticut. Illinois, and New York."[107]

In his own race, McCarthy won 54 percent of the vote and defeated Fairchild by a 870,444 to 731,402 margin. While the victory was duly recorded by the *Journal-American* and *Mirror,* there was no mention that McCarthy placed last of eleven candidates on the Republican ticket.

Though Eisenhower won in 39 of 48 states, the Republicans had the slimmest of margins in Congress, 48-47 in the Senate and 221-213 in the House. But this was enough to qualify McCarthy for chairmanship of a committee. In a holiday mood, he accepted a plaque from a band of well-wishers at New York's Astor Hotel on December 11. The group included such McCarthy stalwarts as Pegler, Matthews, and Rabbi Benjamin Schultz of the American Jewish League Against Communism, as well as Major General Charles Willoughby, MacArthur's former chief of intel-

ligence. The *Mirror* covered the event in a page 2 story headed NO LETUP
IN HIS BATTLE V. REDS: M'C. McCarthy, amid cheers, said that "the
anti-communist battle cannot abate until we have won the war or civilization has died."[108]

Year's end brought another satisfaction to the Hearst-McCarthy
forces. John Carter Vincent, the quarry that had eluded McCarthy in
Switzerland, was recalled as Minister to Tangier after the Civil Service
Loyalty Review Board recommended his dismissal by a 3-2 vote. On
December 17 a *Journal-American* editorial jubilantly observed that Vin-
cent would be summoned to appear before "several committees of the
Congress." The editorial exulted that "the news from Washington is hot
and good, and Senator McCarthy's stature is increasing daily."[109]

Nineteen fifty-two was the zenith of the Hearst-McCarthy alliance.
The ease with which pro-McCarthy material could be inserted into Hearst
papers is demonstrated by an incident that took place in late summer, as the
campaign was getting underway. A young Communist defector named
Harvey Matusow walked into McCarthy's office and volunteered his
services. He offered to write a story about attending a Communist meeting
at which the term "McCarthyism" was allegedly coined. Jean Kerr, Mc-
Carthy's secretary and future wife, liked the idea. "In a moment she was
on the phone to Jack Clements (Hearst public relations director) in New
York. She told Clements about my suggestion and asked him whether he
could make a story of it. Hanging up the phone, she turned to me and said:
'Will you write the story and send it to me this week. I'll see to it that it gets
published.'"[110]

Nineteen fifty-three promised to be another bright year for the
Hearst-McCarthy alliance. The Democrats were out and the Republicans
were returning to the White House after "twenty years of treason." True,
Eisenhower had no love for McCarthy. Also true that the popular general
had not been the Hearst organization's first or even second choice. But
these tensions seemed to have evaporated. Eisenhower, after his nomination,
delighted the Hearst ideologues by adopting a "no-enemies-on-the-right"
strategy. During the campaign, Eisenhower, McCarthy, and the Hearst
papers were united in an effective coalition against the hated "Acheson-
Truman-Lattimore party." In the euphoria of victory, there was little
reason to suspect that this coalition might break down. Yet to come were
the days when differences between the new president and the Wisconsin
senator would create an agonizing dilemma for the Hearst directorate.

6. 1953: The Alliance Cracks

The new year began with a conspicuous demonstration of the Hearst press's solidarity with McCarthy. One of the most damaging allegations against him was that he had faked his war record. A desk-bound intelligence officer, McCarthy later stated that he had gone on bombing raids as a volunteer tail gunner and aerial photographer. In 1944 he claimed fourteen missions; in 1947, seventeen; in 1951, thirty-two.[1] He also claimed to have been wounded. On one occasion he told a Wisconsin audience that he carried "ten pounds of shrapnel in this leg."[2] Later, realizing that this defied medical logic, he announced that he had been injured "in a plane crash at Guadalcanal."[3] In reality, his injury came during a "shellback" ceremony when his ship, the seaplane tender *Chandeleur,* was crossing the equator. With a bucket attached to his foot, McCarthy fell down a stairwell and sustained a fracture.[4]

While in the Senate, McCarthy was troubled by the discrepancy between his tales of heroism and the lack of accompanying medals. If he had flown thirty-two missions, why didn't he have the Distinguished Flying Cross, awarded for twenty-five? If he had been wounded, why didn't he have the Purple Heart? McCarthy had in fact been pestering the Navy Department for these decorations. After several rejections, the medals finally came through in November 1952. Instrumental in this unprecedented arrangement – where nonexistent achievements were made part of the historical record – was an assistant secretary of the Navy who had formerly worked for the Chicago Tribune's law firm.[5]

On New Year's Day, the *Mirror's* headline read SEN. M'CARTHY DENIES HE ASKED NAVY FOR MEDALS. The story noted McCarthy's declaration that the Navy Department had informed him he was eligible for the decorations but that he "did not seek the initiative in obtaining them." Also mentioned was the reaction of Harry S. Truman. The World War I artillery captain was "displeased" by the awards to McCarthy – as well he might be.[6]

In those early days of the Eisenhower administration, the Hearst press found itself in the unaccustomed role of peacemaker and mediator. It liked McCarthy but had no intention of going against the popular new president. With the soft-on-subversion Democrats out of power, the Hearst leaders' fondest hope was that McCarthy would become a team player and Eisenhower would remain the born-again, hard-line redbaiter he had been during the campaign.

The *Journal-American* and *Mirror* continued to cheer McCarthy when he went after Democrats and promised new exposures of "subversives" in government. But the cheers rapidly faded when he trained his guns on Republicans – even liberal Republicans like Senator Robert Hendrickson of New Jersey.

Hendrickson was a member of the Gillette-Hennings Committee looking into the Benton charges against McCarthy. McCarthy had been constantly pressuring its members, either to resign or to delay their deliberations indefinitely. In September 1952 he succeeded in getting Gillette to relinquish the chairmanship by threatening to go into Iowa and campaign against him.[7]

Next he went after Hendrickson. The New Jersey senator, who didn't relish the prospect of a back-alley fight with McCarthy, had been thinking of leaving Privileges and Elections and taking a seat on the noncontroversial Library of Congress Committee. Hearing of Hendrickson's intentions, a smiling McCarthy accosted him in the Senate cloakroom. "You're doing the right thing, Bob," he said. "It's the only thing to do with your prejudice."[8] Angered at being patronized as well as bullied, Hendrickson abruptly changed his mind.

The Committee's final report came out on January 2, 1953. It criticized McCarthy's efforts to obstruct its workings but concentrated more on his financial manipulations than on his political misdeeds. There was no mention of the Wheeling speech, the assault on Marshall, or his accusations of subversion against people in government. By the time the report was issued, the committee was down to three members – Hendrickson, the Arizona Democrat Carl Hayden, and Hennings, whose lapses into insobriety were strongly resisted by Drew Pearson and other McCarthy foes.[9]

McCarthy continued to badger Hendrickson, to the extent of once berating his twenty-one-year-old daughter over the telephone.[10] In the end, persuaded by a now sober Hennings, Hendrickson signed the report. A raging McCarthy denounced Hayden and Hennings as "lackeys" of Truman and described Hendrickson as "a living miracle... with neither brains nor guts."[11]

When the report came out, the recently defeated William Benton cheerfully predicted that "the Senate will be compelled to unseat Senator McCarthy."[12] Benton's optimism was misplaced. The Republicans now controlled Congress; moreover, McCarthy warned that any attempt to block his seating would lead to an investigation of the narrow and disputed election won by Senator Dennis Chavez in New Mexico.

The Hearst press was far from pleased by McCarthy's savaging of Hendrickson. There was no direct criticism of McCarthy, and his investiture was reported in a page 2 *Journal-American* story under MCCARTHY TAKES SEAT WITHOUT ANY CHALLENGE. But the same story was slanted favorably toward Hendrickson, carrying his response to McCarthy's insulting word-portrait: "Maybe something could be said about my brains, but I'd hate to have it said that I have no guts after this report."[13]

When the Republicans took over the Senate, McCarthy's seniority qualified him for the Senate Appropriations Subcommittee. Instead, he announced in late November 1952 that he would lead the seemingly less influential Committee on Government Operations. What attracted McCarthy was not so much the committee as one of its component parts.

This was a Permanent Subcommittee on Investigations with the widest range of discretionary powers. Up to now, the subcommittee had concentrated on export policy and homosexuals in government.[14] But its mandate was a great deal broader and McCarthy had every intention of exploiting that mandate to the limit.

His first move was to make some additions to the subcommittee's staff. On January 5 this item appeared in Cassini's column: "Young Bob Kennedy, son of former ambassador Joseph P. Kennedy, and a lawyer by profession, is one of the ace investigators in (sic) Senator Joe McCarthy's anti-Red team."[15]

The selection had been forced on McCarthy by Kennedy's powerful father. Calling in markers for past personal and political favors, the elder Kennedy phoned McCarthy in December 1952 and asked that his son be named chief counsel to the committee.

Two people were unenthusiastic about the idea. One was Senator John F. Kennedy. He told his assistant, Theodore C. Sorenson, that he hoped his brother would not take the job. An Irish Brahmin, Kennedy considered McCarthy the epitome of shanty vulgarity.[16]

The other was McCarthy himself. His first choice for chief counsel had been Robert Morris, an able, diligent Red hunter then serving with Pat McCarran's Senate Internal Security Subcommittee. When Morris declined, McCarthy hired a twenty-five-year-old *wunderkind* named Roy Cohn. A graduate of Columbia University Law School at nineteen, Cohn was already a veteran of legal battles against accused subversives, having aided in the prosecution of William Remington, the Rosenbergs, and the twelve Communist leaders.

Then there was the question of rank within the subcommittee. Despite Joe Kennedy's importunings, McCarthy wanted the experienced Cohn as chief counsel and not a young man just out of law school. Robert Kennedy was hired – but as Cohn's assistant.

The unequal relationship was noted in the January 14 *Journal-American,* in a page 4 story headed ROY COHN TO AID SENATE PROBERS. Next to a picture of Cohn was an item that "Senator McCarthy named Robert Kennedy, brother of Senator Kennedy (D.-Mass,) as Cohn's assistant."[17] Not mentioned was the explosive situation created by McCarthy's chain of command. Between these two ambitious, strong-willed young men, it was hatred at first sight. Tension was exacerbated as Cohn, never known for tact, treated Kennedy more like a gofer than a legal associate. "By asking the Kennedy kid to fill the coffee cups," writes Nicholas von Hoffman, "Roy had invited Nemesis into his life. From then on… Roy was tracked, stalked, and hunted by a man who was as much of a hater as he…."[18] Robert Kennedy's vendetta against Cohn would not end till Kennedy's death.

Other additions to the committee were Don Surine, Daniel F. Buckley, a former Tydings Committee staffer who defected to McCarthy, and Howard Rushmore. Rushmore, who continued to contribute regularly to the *Journal-American,* served as liaison between the Hearst organization and McCarthy. Since Cohn was now McCarthy's fair-haired boy, Rushmore saw fit to eulogize him in a sycophantic article that appeared in the February issue of the *American Mercury.* The *Mercury,* in decline since the glory days of H. L. Mencken, was now a political organ of the extreme right.

Rushmore's article, titled "Young Mr. Cohn," presented a picture that would not have been recognizable to many who had had dealings with Cohn. "His name is Roy M. Cohn… He has the kind of vivacious charm that has won him friends from all walks of life. A list of Roy Cohn's boosters reads like a *Who's Who* and includes Senator Homer Ferguson, Walter Winchell, Leonard Lyons, and George Sokolsky." Did Cohn have enemies? Yes, but they were all the right enemies or, in this case, left enemies. "John T. McTernan, chief counsel for the comrades (Communist leaders on trial)... was heard to remark: 'Where did the government pick up that brat?'" Rushmore, who would later regret his oleaginous words, concluded that "he is a ripe twenty-five years old and he's hated by every comrade from the State Department to Minsk."[19]

In the same month, at Cohn's insistence, the subcommittee took on one of his close friends as an unpaid "chief consultant." G. (for Gerard) David Schine was a handsome, air-headed millionaire's son of twenty-six. An *habitué* of nightclubs and escort to starlets, Schine had somewhere acquired the fantastic notion that he was an expert on communism. His father owned a chain of hotels and, as a dutiful filial gesture, David wrote a slim pamphlet which he titled *Definition of Communism.* This work was placed in every Schine hotel room. Though the pamphlet was only six pages long, Schine "managed to put the Russian Revolution, the founding of the Communist Party, and the start of the first Five Year Plan in years when these events did not occur; he gave Lenin the wrong first name, hopelessly confused Stalin with Trotsky, Marx with Lenin, Alexander Kerensky with Prince Lvov, and fifteenth-century utopianism with twentieth-century communism."[20]

McCarthy was a wretched administrator and a lenient boss. Though unimpressed by Schine ("he is a good boy but there is nothing indispensable about him"), he was mightily impressed by Cohn.[21] And if Schine was what Cohn wanted... well, why should he begrudge his brilliant chief counsel a collaborator who was drawing no salary?

It is not exaggeration to say that McCarthy's haphazard hiring practices not only damaged his alliance with the Hearst press but ultimately planted the seeds of his destruction. The hatred between Kennedy and Cohn, the antics of Cohn and Schine, a rancorous split between Rushmore and Cohn – all these hastened McCarthy's downfall.

One wonders how much longer McCarthyism would have survived if McCarthy had succeeded in winning Robert Morris away from the Senate Internal Security Subcommittee. Cohn may have matched Morris in ability but Morris had none of Cohn's dedication to the private concerns which in the end proved so harmful to McCarthy.

The Hearst press was 100 percent behind McCarthy's investigation of the Voice of America. This agency, filled with Democratic appointees, was a natural prey for those determined to expunge every trace of the

"Acheson-Truman-Lattimore" influence from government. On March 2, as the VOA probe got underway, the *Mirror* ran an editorial headed THE VOICE OF WHAT? It rejoiced that McCarthy's subcommittee was planning to investigate the agency, deducing that "out of these... hearings it seems reasonable that we will get a Voice of America that is an American voice. Another victory for McCarthyism."[22]

That same day, in the *Journal-American,* E. F. Tompkins ignored the VOA furor to take aim in an unexpected direction. The object of his displeasure was Mr. Republican, Robert Taft, who had voiced the heretical view that Communists should be allowed to teach astronomy, though barred from such fields as history and political science. Then, without identifying him, Tompkins alluded to a prominent astronomer at Harvard. "Does the use of his name by Communist fronts seem to put the accolade and approval of Harvard upon them?" The man in question was Dr. Harlow Shapley, a scholar who was challenged only by Frederick L. Schuman of Williams College for the title of America's leading academic fellow traveler. William F. Buckley was correct when he wrote that the records of Shapley and Schuman suggest a "personal contest" to see who could join more Communist-front groups.[23] If Taft had his way, Schuman (whose field was history) would have been out of a job but not Shapley. Tompkins, a fiercer ideologue, would have fired both.

In the same issue, Frank Conniff expressed satisfaction with McCarthy's behavior on the first day of the VOA hearings. "Senator Joe," he wrote, "was hardly the ogre he's been depicted in the 'liberal' press."[24]

This view was not shared by Reed Harris, acting chief of VOA's International Information Administration. Subjected to a brutal grilling by McCarthy, Harris's protests were noted on March 3 in a page 2 *Journal-American* article. Under TOP VOICE AIDE CHARGES SMEAR ACT BY M'CARTHY, Harris claimed he had been pilloried for VOA's decision to close down its Hebrew desk.[25] McCarthy also chivvied Harris over some youthful indiscretions when he was a student at Columbia. These minor sins could have been committed by any bright, inquisitive young man with a concept of anti-establishment behavior on a level more sophisticated than that expressed through panty raiding and animal house fraternity antics. Though Harris insisted that he had recanted his heretical views (mainly lampoons on the American Legion and overemphasis on football), McCarthy acted as though his campus career dated back to yesterday. Of McCarthy's major investigations, his third degree of Reed Harris was the most unfair and the one most characterized by *ad hominem* hostility.

The *Journal-American* editorial that day also addressed the VOA investigation. Under SHOCKING, it denounced VOA's 1952 decision to close down the agency's Hebrew desk. "At the time the Acheson regime gagged the Voice (by discontinuing the Hebrew broadcasts)... the powerful stations in Prague and Moscow were pouring their anti-Semitic venom into Israel and the Arab nations of the Middle East."[26]

At this point the Voice investigation was pushed off the front pages by a fateful event in the Soviet Union. On March 3, in what was arguably the worst-timed comment in journalistic history, Louis Sobol wrote that "Hitler is still alive. Only now he known as Joe Stalin."[27] Even as this was being written, Stalin was on his death bed. The next day, as the news crossed the Atlantic, the *Journal-American's* headline read STALIN IS SINKING, AIDES TAKE OVER. "I hope it's nothing trivial," was the comment of William Randolph Hearst Jr. in a front page editorial.[28]

Back at the VOA investigation, Reed Harris responded to attacks on him for closing down the Voice's Hebrew desk. The beleaguered administrator defended the action on grounds that "comments about the anti-Semitic activity of the Soviets and their satellites... was getting into Israel very, very effectively through the American news services, through broadcasts in a number of other languages in the Voice."[29] The Hebrew broadcasts were therefore discontinued as an economy measure.

A VOA official who opposed suppression of the broadcasts was Dr. Sidney Glazer, chief of the Hebrew desk until it was discontinued. Glazer, understandably, was less than enthusiastic about the abolition of a bureau over which he presided. When interrogating Glazer, McCarthy referred to the Slansky trial in Czechoslovakia, in which a group of mostly Jewish Communist officials were executed during a Stalin-style purge. McCarthy suggested that since the Communists had become "openly anti-Semitic," the Hebrew broadcasts would have been a "tremendous counterpropaganda weapon." Not surprisingly, Glazer agreed.[30]

In the March 8 *Journal-American,* Sokolsky complained that he had been unable to view Glazer's televised testimony. Though the hearing was shown in other parts of the country, in New York it was pre-empted by a "dull, vapid meaningless mass of time-consuming emptiness called 'The Wife of Monte Cristo.'"[31]

McCarthy got what he wanted from the VOA investigation: the scalp of Reed Harris. A few weeks after the hearings, Harris "resigned" from government service. His boss at IIA, Dr. Robert Johnson, "sent him a note of regret – but only after conferring with State Department officials who privately praised Harris to the skies."[32]

Throughout the Eisenhower years, the Hearst organization had a perpetual finger in the air to see which way the wind was blowing from the White House. Since the VOA investigation attracted no opposition from the president or his advisers, the Hearst papers cheered on McCarthy as he went after Reed Harris and the Voice's other Democratic appointees. Then came a controversy in which the Hearst-McCarthy alliance was put to its initial test.

First Break: The Bohlen Appointment

On February 5 the White House announced that Charles E. ("Chip") Bohlen was the president's choice for the post of ambassador to the Soviet Union. Bohlen, a forty-eight-year-old career diplomat, had been a foreign service officer since 1929. He spoke Russian and French, had done two prewar tours of duty in Moscow, and was one of Roosevelt's advisers at the Yalta Conference. Bohlen had met Eisenhower in Paris while the latter was commanding NATO forces. Ike liked and respected the poised diplomat and believed that his skills and fluency in Russian ideally qualified him for the Moscow post.

The president's friendly feeling toward Bohlen was not shared by McCarthy. With his Eastern prep school and Harvard background, Bohlen was instant anathema to the man who had washed dishes to put himself through Marquette. Then there was the matter of Yalta – where one of Bohlen's colleagues had been Alger Hiss.

The initial Hearst reaction to Bohlen nomination must have dismayed McCarthy. On March 16, in "East Side, West Side," Frank Conniff cautiously approved the president's choice. As for Bohlen's role at Yalta, he doubted "if anyone would contend that an interpreter of his relatively junior rank was in a spot to influence big diplomatic decisions."[33]

The prospect of having to oppose Bohlen without unanimous Hearst support did not deter McCarthy. M'CARTHY URGES BOHLEN LIE TEST was the *Journal-American's* March 23 headline.[34] On that day the Senate began debating Bohlen's nomination. McCarthy, citing the efficacy of polygraph tests, recalled the success with which he used the device in Wisconsin.[35] Senator Ralph Flanders, Vermont Republican and future McCarthy foe, called on his colleague to give the Eisenhower administration a chance.[36]

On the same day, Secretary of State John Foster Dulles testified on Bohlen's behalf. His testimony was reported the next day in a page 4 *Mirror* story under BOHLEN LOYAL WITHOUT ANY DOUBT: DULLES.[37] Though this sounds like a ringing endorsement, such an impression is misleading. Dulles and Bohlen disliked each other and

Dulles's statement before the Senate was more dutiful than enthusiastic. On the way to the confirmation hearings, Dulles insisted that they ride in separate cars so they wouldn't have to be photographed together.[38]

The *Mirror* also quoted McCarthy's remark that Dulles had "ordered" R. W. Scott McLeod, the State Department's security chief, not to testify at the confirmation hearings.[39] McLeod, an ex-FBI agent and fervent McCarthy supporter, had reportedly opposed Bohlen as a security risk after reviewing his FBI file.[40]

The *Mirror's* headline on the 24th read BOHLEN SHOULD TAKE LIE TEST: MCCARTHY. McCarthy wanted Bohlen questioned on charges about his private life. The story also noted that Senator Walter George, Democrat of Georgia, claimed that the file contained allegations that Bohlen had associated with "dissolute persons."[41] This was a code expression for sexual misconduct and may have been a reference to Bohlen's brother-in-law, Charles W. Thayer. Thayer, formerly consul general in Munich, had resigned from the Foreign Service rather than face a public hearing on charges of both heterosexual and homosexual improprieties.[42]

McCarthy continued his attack, now charging Bohlen with excessive friendliness toward the Soviets. On March 25, the *Journal-American's* headline read M'C SAYS REDS CALLED BOHLEN FRIEND. McCarthy "quoted a former (unnamed) Soviet official as saying that secret documents obtained by the Kremlin indicated that Bohlen was 'friendly' when he served in Russia before World War II."[43] Even by McCarthy norms, this was a reckless and unfounded charge. The "former Soviet official" was a chameleon-like opportunist named Igor Bogopelov who had gone over to the Nazis during the Second World War. After the war, he looked to the West. Moving to the United States, he was earning a living as a professional anti-communist informer when Bohlen was nominated to the Moscow post.

It may have been McCarthy's reliance on such a dubious figure that brought about an open attack on him in the Hearst press. Ironically, his first critic was Frank Conniff – who in March 1950 had been his first supporter. Regarding the charge that Bohlen was "friendly" to the Soviets, Conniff pointed out that in 1943 *"Time* (magazine) voiced reservations on Bohlen's appointment to accompany (Secretary of State) Hull's mission to Moscow on the grounds that he was 'prejudiced' against the Communists." Conniff asked why McCarthy had distanced himself on the nomination from such Republican conservatives as Taft, William Knowland of California, and Homer Ferguson of Michigan. The columnist concluded that McCarthy's "blitzkrieg against Bohlen has brought him a stunning setback from the standpoint of prestige."[44]

On March 26 an editorial appeared over the signature of William Randolph Hearst Jr. It began: "The Hearst papers invariably have supported Senator Joseph McCarthy, the hard-swinging Wisconsin Republican, in his campaign to force Communists and fellow travelers from positions of authority in the State Department." Hearst added that such pro-confirmation rightists as Taft, Knowland, and Ferguson had "trained their sights on the Communist menace long before the Wisconsin senator" and concluded that "Joe McCarthy has pulled a strategic boner in his opposition to the Bohlen appointment."[45]

The reference to Taft, Knowland, and Ferguson confronting the communist menace long before McCarthy can be interpreted as criticism of McCarthy's indifference to the Hearst anti-communist crusades of the late forties. The rift with McCarthy also demonstrated something else: that the Hearst organization was no longer a monolith. True, the parameters were limited and no Hearst writer could have got away with, say, defending the Truman-Acheson foreign policy or pleading the innocence of Alger Hiss. But dissent was permitted from the right. Not all Hearst columnists supported the Conniff-Hearst Jr. position and they voiced their opinions with complete freedom.

Bohlen was approved in the Senate on March 27, by a 74-13 vote. On that day, George Rothwell Brown lamented that Bohlen's "confirmation by the Senate will not mark the ending of a completely unnecessary break with the new State Department." This rupture, according to Brown, was caused by "an entirely new theory laid down by Taft that (Bohlen), who had been confirmed by the Senate, could not be interrogated by the Senate (and) that all the information must come from... Mr. Dulles himself."[46] Taft had offered a compromise whereby the FBI summary on Bohlen would be handed over by Dulles to a panel of two senators – himself and a Democrat, John Sparkman of Alabama. Brown obviously believed that Bohlen would have had rougher sledding if he had been interrogated by the Senate instead of having the FBI summary reviewed by two sympathetic senators.

George Sokolsky also refused to endorse the Conniff-Hearst position on Bohlen. In his March 30 column he complained that Bohlen had never been approved by a blue ribbon panel of emeritus foreign service officers. On a more philosophical note, he added that "Bohlen is no better or worse than many others in the State Department and has wide experience as an interpreter for Roosevelt and Truman." Sokolsky ended with the caveat that the Republicans "dare not evade the issue of getting rid of the remnants of the Acheson gang."[47]

Even more than William Randolph Hearst Jr., Frank Conniff showed courage in defying McCarthy and, by extension, his own fervently anti-communist Irish-Catholic constituency. On April 1, Conniff admitted that mail was running 5-1 against him for his criticism of McCarthy. Conniff conceded that McCarthy "has the largest personal following in recent American history." But he warned that the senator "will be ill-advised if he takes this following for granted...." He should "realize that many Americans who supported him also cherish high regard for President Eisenhower, Senator Taft, and other national leaders."[48]

Yet pro-McCarthy mail continued to come in, some of the entries printed in the *Journal-American's* "In the Mailbox" section. One such letter grieved that "the usually conservative press, including the New York *Journal-American*, has smeared Joe McCarthy for his fight against Bohlen's appointment."[49]

Throughout that spring Winchell followed a policy of supporting McCarthy while giving maximum free rein to his private vendettas. On April 2 he attacked the hated *New York Post* for praising American-born Viscountess Astor when she insulted McCarthy at a cocktail party. "I hope there is poison in your drink," she said, causing the *Post* to "rejoice that she has learned to scent a demagogue." Winchell described Astor as a "Nazi appeaser and High Priestess of London's Cliveden set," a charge that was essentially true.[50]

In that same month the *Post's* managing editor, James Wechsler, appeared before McCarthy's subcommittee. Though Wechsler was generally defiant of McCarthy, in early May he did turn over to the subcommittee a list of persons he had known to be members of the Young Communist League.[51] On April 29 Winchell wrote that Wechsler, "using standard smear techniques... argued that Senator McCarthy questioned because his rag had criticized McCarthy" rather than because "it followed the Party line."[52] McCarthy told Wechsler he believed his conversion from communism was phony and "that you are serving (communist ideals) very, very actively."[53] In any event, Wechsler giving up the names made little difference to Winchell. The gossip's hatred for the *Post* was more personal than political and no amount of anti-communist activity on Wechsler's part would have caused Winchell to let up on him.

While Winchell continued to flail away at the *Post*, other Hearst columnists were closing ranks around McCarthy in defiance of Conniff and Hearst Jr. On April 6 Fulton Lewis, under SHE HATES MCCARTHY, presented a highly unflattering word-portrait of Mrs. Agnes Meyer, widow of *Washington Post* publisher Eugene Meyer. Mrs. Meyer, as Lewis saw it, was "superficial, uninformed," and a "bush league version of Eleanor Roosevelt."[54]

The next day E. F. Tompkins unmasked another batch of McCartho-phobes. These were exponents of communism, socialism, and New Deal collectivism who "hate McCarthy because he peers through their intrigues and ruthlessly exposes their well-salaried hypocrisies."[55]

Sokolsky's April 22 column took the form of an "Answer to Mc-Carthy Haters." He concluded that "I have yet to come up with the name of an innocent man who has been smeared."[56]

After the first crack in the alliance caused by the Bohlen nomination, the Hearst directorate was anxious to avoid further criticisms of McCarthy, while remaining friendly with the administration. In attaining this in-creasingly difficult goal, it was aided by Eisenhower's above-the-battle attitude. The president detested McCarthy and privately told advisers that "I will not get into the gutter with that guy."[57] Publicly, he followed a policy of smoothing over disputes between his aides and McCarthy. This let the Hearst organization off the hook, postponing for a long time the unpleasant reality of having to choose between Eisenhower and McCarthy.

On March 28 McCarthy announced that the subcommittee had negotiated a deal with a group of Greek shipowners. Under its terms, 242 merchant ships would stop trading with China, North Korea, and other Communist countries. Two days later an enraged Harold Stassen, Ike's Mutual Security Administrator, denounced McCarthy's action as one that undermined his agency's activities.

At last it seemed as if the break had come. A high administration official had strongly and publicly attacked McCarthy. Though there were no editorials that could be interpreted as partisan, the *Mirror* on March 31 ran a page 2 story headed STASSEN RIPS INTO M'C SHIP PACT. The article quoted Stassen's accusation that McCarthy's move undermined efforts to halt East-West trade.[58] With this, it appeared as if the Hearst press was moving toward a pro-administration position.

It was Eisenhower who defused the tense situation. He did so by undercutting Stassen in a humiliating manner. At an April 1 press con-ference, he told reporters that Stassen had probably meant "infringed" rather than "undermined" and that the entire controversy was "a little incident" that "is not going to disturb me."[59]

The day before, McCarthy had lunched with Secretary of State Dulles. Afterwards, a joint statement was issued. It declared that while foreign policy was the responsibility of the chief executive, McCarthy's action was nevertheless "in the national interest."[60] In the end, the only person undermined was Stassen. Taking his cue from the president, he admitted that his choice of words had been poor.[61] The Hearst leadership was delighted. Thanks to the president's peacemaking skills, the façade of unity between the Eisenhower and McCarthy factions had again been preserved.

The next crack in the Hearst-McCarthy alliance was caused by an internal dispute. On April 4 Cohn and Schine had been sent on a quickie seventeen-day tour of Europe. Their purpose was to "purify" American overseas libraries of subversive books. The mission was both a disaster and a joke. Intense hostility and derision from the European press were compounded by the clownish antics of the two young investigators. On one occasion Schine was reported to have pursued Cohn through a hotel lobby, swatting him over the head with a rolled-up magazine.[62] The British press was particularly cruel. Turning Cohn and Schine into a Gallagher and Shean comedy team, an English paper composed a lampoon with every verse ending in, "Positively, Mr. Cohn! Absolutely, Mr. Schine!" At an interview, a London journalist asked them what credentials they had to investigate communism. The dull-witted Schine, misunderstanding the question, pulled out his wallet and flashed a card accrediting him as a committee investigator. The next day this mocking headline appeared: LOOK MA, WE GOT CREDENTIALS – SCHINE.[63]

Though other Hearst writers rallied round the luckless duo, Howard Rushmore did not. Obviously burning with shame over his February puff piece on Cohn, Hearst's man on the McCarthy subcommittee now denounced Cohn and Schine as "bumbling publicity seekers."[64] From a series of run-ins that predated the European trip, Rushmore had developed an intense dislike for Cohn. The altercation was followed up by Rushmore's "resignation" from the subcommittee. Though he continued to praise McCarthy in his *Journal-American* articles, Rushmore rarely passed up an opportunity to slam Cohn and Schine. Given McCarthy's admiration for, and reliance on, Cohn, Rushmore's persistent sniping at his trusted assistant did not make for harmony between the Hearst and McCarthy forces.

The departure of Rushmore from the subcommittee was followed by a true resignation: that of Robert Kennedy. He disliked Cohn as much as Rushmore did and also disliked Cohn's influence on the subcommittee. "Most of the investigations," he wrote, "were instigated by some preconceived notion of the chief counsel (Cohn)...."[65] Kennedy eventually ended up as counsel for the minority Democrats on the subcommittee.

Exit Doc Matthews

The alliance was soon to suffer another setback. This time controversy revolved around the shadowy figure of Joseph Brown Matthews. As godfather of the "New York crowd" and Hearst's master of the files, Matthews had long operated as an *éminence grise*. Now it was felt that he should play a more open role. With Rushmore's semi-defection, it is possible that McCarthy wanted to reinforce the Hearst alliance by working more closely with Matthews. On June 22 McCarthy appointed him staff director of the subcommittee.

Matthews had barely taken over before he became embroiled in an explosive controversy with overtones of religious bigotry. In the July issue of the ex-Menckenite, now McCarthyite *American Mercury,* Matthews had published an article titled "Reds in Our Churches." The tone of the piece was set by its opening sentence: "The largest single group supporting the Communist apparatus in the United States today is composed of Protestant clergymen."[66]

In his adulatory book about McCarthy, Roy Cohn claimed that Matthews had not written that inflammatory first sentence. The real culprit was an editor on the *Mercury,* who put it in to give the story more punch.[67] Whether this is true or not, there can be no denying the article's impact. What ensued was a conservative, Bible Belt revolt against McCarthy. Among the powerful Southern legislators who denounced Matthews were Burnet Maybank of South Carolina, John Stennis of Mississippi, William Fulbright and John McClellan of Arkansas, and Harry Flood Byrd of Virginia, who called Matthews a "cheap demagogue."[68] Among these men, Matthews was considered not only a demagogue but a traitor. An ordained Protestant from the South, Matthews was one of their own.

McCarthy's first impulse was to stick by Matthews; fair-weather friendship was not one of his faults. But a July 7 meeting of the subcommittee – in which four members demanded Matthews's immediate ouster and another wavered – convinced him that Matthews would have to go. To simplify matters, Matthews himself offered to resign.[69]

Then events took an unexpected turn. On July 9 Eisenhower received a telegram from an inter-faith trio of prestigious religious leaders: Monsignor John A. O'Brien, president of Notre Dame University; Rabbi Maurice Eisendrath, president of the Union of American Hebrew Congregations; and Dr. John Sutherland Bonnell, pastor of New York's Fifth Avenue Presbyterian Church. It read:

THE SWEEPING ATTACK ON THE LOYALTY OF PROTESTANT CLERGYMEN AND THE CHARGE THAT THEY ARE THE

LARGEST SINGLE GROUP SUPPORTING THE COMMUNIST APPARATUS IS UNJUSTIFIABLE AND DEPLORABLE.[70]

The telegram had in fact been inspired by White House political strategists. Their plan was to have Eisenhower respond favorably to the clergymen's message before McCarthy announced Matthews's resignation. This would make it look as if McCarthy had dumped Matthews as the result of White House pressure. The plan worked mainly due to the efforts of Richard Nixon and Deputy Attorney General William Rogers. Lured into Nixon's office, McCarthy was plied by him and Rogers with solicitous questions. Finally McCarthy made for the door. "Gotta rush now," he said, "I want to be sure I get the news of dumping Matthews to Fulton Lewis in time for him to break it on his broadcast."[71]

He was too late. While Nixon and Rogers were distracting McCarthy, this telegram had gone off from the president to the three clerics:

I WANT YOU TO KNOW AT ONCE THAT I FULLY SHARE THE CONVICTIONS YOU STATE... GENERALIZED AND IR-RESPONSIBLE ATTACKS THAT SWEEPINGLY CONDEMN THE WHOLE OF ANY GROUP OF CITIZENS ARE ALIEN TO AMERICA. SUCH ATTACKS BETRAY CONTEMPT FOR THE PRINCIPLES OF FREEDOM AND DECENCY.[72]

The Matthews controversy put the Hearst press in a difficult position. Within the organization, Matthews was something of an icon. With his massive files, he had rendered services of incalculable value during the crusades of the late forties and to McCarthy when he was endangered by his indiscretions at Wheeling. Moreover, Matthews commanded equal respect as ideologist and theoretician as for his bureaucratic talents. On the philosophical level, he was the Bukharin of the hard-line anti-communist American right.

To abandon Doc Matthews was unthinkable – however much this loyalty might jeopardize the Hearst-Eisenhower relationship. On July 5, as hot winds of resentment against Matthews were blowing out of the Bible Belt, the *Mirror* carried a story about a telegram received by McCarthy from a fundamentalist group in Oklahoma. Under the headline CHURCH COUNCIL OKS MATTHEWS, it read: WE NEED MORE NOT FEW-ER MEN LIKE DR. MATTHEWS.[73]

The July 7 meeting of the subcommittee had ended without a decision on the status of Matthews. McCarthy, trying to make the best of a hopeless situation, "defended his right to hire and fire staffers, then adjourned the meeting before a vote could be taken."[74] This action was noted on July 8 in a page 1 *Mirror* story headlined M'C BLOCKS MATTHEWS FIRING. More significant was another article on the same page, under the smaller headline PROBE NAMES 'RED' CLERGY. Testifying before HUAC was Archibald B. Roosevelt, fiercely conservative son of Theodore. Doing some rough riding of his own, Roosevelt declared that "the Communist Party has effectively infiltrated the clergy."[75]

The next day, in an almost identical statement, the *Mirror* quoted Ohio Republican Congressman Gordon Sherer's observation that "communism has succeeded in infiltrating the American clergy."[76]

It was on the same day, July 9, that Eisenhower received the telegram his aides had elicited from Msgr. O'Brien, Rabbi Eisendrath, and Dr. Bonnell. The telegram coincided with a strong defense of Matthews by George Sokolsky. Sokolsky, an intensely vain man, began with some self-congratulatory remarks about his insights into communism. Then, deferring to another for one of the few times in his life, he added that "I should not say that my knowledge in this field is comparable with that of J. B. Matthews... his files are so complete that many check their data against (them). Matthews is respected by every person who works in this field."[77]

On July 10 Winchell made an oblique defense of Matthews that contained a particularly scurrilous innuendo. "The attack on J. B. Matthews... followed his order to subpoena Leo Huberman. Leo appears to have a peculiar friend (in the Senate) who objected to the subpoena."[78] Huberman, an editor of the Marxist magazine *Monthly Review,* "was known for his rare willingness to criticize the Communist Party."[79] In Winchell's vocabulary, "peculiar" meant homosexual.

The final word on the J. B. Matthews controversy came from Howard Rushmore on July 11, two days before Matthews's ouster. Though Matthews replaced Rushmore as the Hearst-McCarthy liaison, Rushmore apparently bore no animosity. He charged that "the Democrats on Joe McCarthy's committee forced Dr. J. B. Matthews's resignation and thereby performed a service worthy of the Order of Lenin."[80]

The Matthews affair was a bad experience for both McCarthy and the Hearst press. McCarthy, tricked by Nixon, had been made to look as if he dumped Matthews under pressure from the White House. The Hearst organization, defending Matthews, had had to fight what it knew was a losing battle.

This was not a happy summer for McCarthy. He had wanted to investigate William P. Bundy, an assistant deputy director of the CIA, on grounds that Bundy contributed $400 to the Alger Hiss defense fund. CIA Director Allen Dulles, fearing that secret operations might be compromised by a McCarthy investigation, called his brother at State and asked him to do something. Foster Dulles turned the matter over to the reliable Nixon, who worked out a face-saving solution. McCarthy would "forgo" the investigation and turn over his information on Bundy to Allen Dulles for evaluation. Since it was already known that Dulles considered the information worthless, the episode was considered by the columnists Joseph and Stewart Alsop as "a total, unmitigated, unqualified defeat for McCarthy."[81] In Wisconsin, William Evjue of the *Madison Capital Times* rejoiced that "for the first time, McCarthyism is on the defensive."[82]

During an August probe of the Government Printing Office, McCarthy was made to look ridiculous. He was fond of talking about "Fifth Amendment Communists"; now he came up against a Fifth Amendment bookmaker. An elderly printer named Carl Lundmark was accused of operating a betting parlor on GPO property. Lundmark invoked his constitutional privilege. As a red-faced, spluttering McCarthy warned of how a "major gambling ring" could "subject a government worker to blackmail," spectators in the galleries laughed and hooted.[83]

McCarthy's travails were interrupted by marriage, on September 23, to his longtime assistant Jean Fraser Kerr. The newlyweds departed on a three-week honeymoon on a remote key in the British West Indies, where the only communication was by radio. Roy Cohn had the call number, with instructions to use it only in case of emergency. One week into the honeymoon, Cohn radioed McCarthy. A critical security situation had developed at the Army Signal Corps base at Fort Monmouth, New Jersey. McCarthy broke off his honeymoon and returned to the United States on the next plane.[84]

Fort Monmouth

The Fort Monmouth investigation gave the Hearst-McCarthy alliance a much needed shot in the arm. The Hearst press had sundered over Bohlen, experienced nervous moments during the Greek ship deal, been embarrassed by the Cohn-Schine fiasco in Europe, and forced to back a losing horse in the Matthews controversy.

Now it was like old times again, a return to the golden days of 1952 when McCarthy was hounding Reds and Eisenhower's men were giving him encouragement and support. As early as Labor Day, even before McCarthy's wedding, Secretary of the Army Robert T. Stevens wired the senator that he would "offer my services in trying to correct anything that may be wrong."[85] On October 13, shortly after McCarthy interrupted his honeymoon, Stevens attended closed hearings on Fort Monmouth at McCarthy's invitation and then issued a statement that "the Army is cooperating in every way."[86] With this spirit prevailing, the Hearst press could back McCarthy's new Red hunt to the hilt without fear that its friendly relations with the White House might be damaged.

Reports about a dangerous situation at Fort Monmouth had been trickling into McCarthy's office throughout the long, hot summer of 1953. Some came from the FBI, some from the right-wing press, and some from that band of anonymous informers in government that McCarthy called the Loyal American Underground.[87] More information came from Major General Kirke B. Lawton, the security-conscious, pro-McCarthy commander at Monmouth.[88] The first hearing, in September, was pretty small potatoes. Though McCarthy made appropriately indignant noises (he was "shocked beyond words" at the situation), the most dangerous subversive he uncovered was a civilian employee who "had access to invoices and requisitions which would indicate where food was being shipped at various Army bases."[89]

Cohn's radio message, sent on October 10, followed a story by Willard Edwards in the *Chicago Tribune* that top scientists engaged in developing radar secrets had been suspended as security risks. On the 12th McCarthy flew to New York to begin hearings at the Federal Courthouse on Foley Square. Thus began the "new" Fort Monmouth hearings, accompanied by reams of journalistic ballyhoo. McCarthy's main theme was that a spy ring organized by Julius Rosenberg still existed at the base. This motif was quickly taken up by the Hearst papers. On October 16 the *Mirror's* headline read ROSENBERG LED SPY RING AT FORT MONMOUTH: M'C. Despite the Rosenbergs' execution, insisted McCarthy, "there is a strong possibility that the ring is still in operation." McCarthy added that he would go to the federal prison at Lewisburg, Pennsylvania, to interview David Greenglass.[90] Greenglass, Rosenberg's brother-in-law, had been sentenced to fifteen years for his part in the conspiracy.

The trip to Lewisburg was actually made by Cohn and Schine. Greenglass, anxious to reduce his sentence, gave McCarthy's young men a deposition that added fuel to the investigative flames. "As far as I know," it read, "these (espionage) operations never stopped and could very possibly be continuing to this very day."[91]

The *Journal-American's* October 17 editorial was headed DIG, JOE. In ominous tones, it warned readers that "as the pieces are fitted together, it is clear that Senator McCarthy has begun to dig up something big and ugly and dangerous in his investigation of a radar spy ring at Fort Monmouth, New Jersey."[92]

The same theme was taken up by Sokolsky six days later: "...when the whole story of the Monmouth spy ring is disclosed, a case not dissimilar to the Rosenberg spy apparatus... will be discovered... This apparently is what the McCarthy committee is checking with some success."[93]

Then came a highly unexpected expression of support. "Joe McCarthy will almost drop dead when he reads this, but in my opinion he is absolutely right in probing the leaks of Signal Corps radar secrets at Fort Monmouth."[94] The author of this encouraging message was Drew Pearson.

If Pearson was an unforeseen McCarthy supporter, Lee Mortimer and Victor Riesel were not. Mortimer praised Fort Monmouth's commandant, "Major General Kirke Lawton (who) cooperates to clean up the mess with Senator McCarthy."[95] Riesel, ruminating on "the Rosenberg spy ring," wrote that "we could have saved millions of dollars... simply by mailing all our ultra-secret weapons blueprints directly to the Kremlin."[96]

While the Fort Monmouth investigation undoubtedly succeeded in tightening up previously lax security procedures, it was a textbook case of the witch hunt. There was no "Rosenberg spy ring," people were fired for their beliefs rather than for their actions, and the charge against one luckless employee was of having attended a lecture by the anti-communist liberal *New York Post* columnist Max Lerner.[97]

On October 24 both the *Journal-American* and the *Mirror* printed an endorsement for McCarthy from America's most powerful Catholic prelate. The page 1 *Journal-American* story was headed SPELLMAN BACKS PROBES ON REDS. The cardinal considered "published reports that Yugoslavia is exercised over McCarthyism" to be "particularly ironic to Americans... This from a country of tyrants and slaves."[98] Spellman, himself exercised, was still smarting over the imprisonment of collaborationist Archbishop Stepinac.

SPELLMAN IN EUROPE, DEFENDS RED PROBES was the headline of a page 4 *Mirror* story. To an audience of four thousand Catholics at the Brussels Palace of Fine Arts, the cardinal declared that the "anguished cries and protests against 'McCarthism' (sic) are not going to dissuade Americans from their desire to see Communists exposed and removed from positions where they can carry out their nefarious plans."[99]

In an editorial, the *Journal-American* lauded Spellman's "forthright words," adding that "one of our outstanding churchmen has done this country a great service by speaking out as he did."[100] In praising Spellman's praise of McCarthy, the Hearst press knew it had the administration over a barrel. If Ike and his advisers were circumspect about crossing McCarthy, they were downright panicky about doing anything that might offend Spellman. Nixon was particularly deferential to the cardinal – and this policy paid off. Though Spellman was considered by many to be the embodiment of aggressive Catholic power-seeking, in 1960 he supported the Quaker vice-president against the only successful Catholic aspirant to the presidency.[101]

Whatever Eisenhower may have thought privately of Spellman's comment, he was in no position either to publicly denounce the cardinal's support for McCarthy or the Hearst press's endorsement of that support. To effectively cut the ground out from under McCarthy, the president's men wanted to show that they could be just as tough as he was in ferreting out subversives and repudiating the policies of Truman and Acheson. On November 6 Attorney General Herbert Brownell told a group of business executives in Chicago that in 1946 Truman had appointed Harry Dexter White executive director of the International Monetary Fund despite FBI warnings that he was a Communist. Truman's angry response, delivered on national television, rated a caustic headline in the November 17 *Mirror*. Under BROWNELL LIED, HST TELLS US, the story noted Truman's claim that "he retained White in his job to aid an FBI investigation." A skeptical editorial in the same issue doubted Truman's story and charged that Truman used the FBI as little as possible from resentment "over FBI investigation of election frauds in Kansas City."[102]

That same day, J. Edgar Hoover appeared before the Senate and gave Truman the lie. This was long-awaited revenge: Hoover had hated Truman since the ex-president had tried to turn some of the FBI's functions over to the Civil Service Commission back in 1947. "I did not enter into agreement to shift White from his position in the Treasury Department to the International Monetary Fund," he told the senators. "At no time was the FBI a party to any agreement to promote Harry Dexter White... The decision to retain White was made by higher government authority."[103] With these words, Hoover branded his ex-boss a liar and coddler of subversives.

Hoover's message was duly noted by his *muezzin*. On November 18, Winchell chortled that "G-man Hoover's knockout rebuttal is the talk of the town."[104] Truman's speech also contained a furious denunciation of McCarthyism, which he claimed the administration had embraced. In some of the strongest language ever heard in a political speech, he described the "ism" personified by the Wisconsin senator as "the corruption of truth... the use of the big lie... the rise to power of the demagogue who lives on untruth," and concluded that "this horrible cancer is eating at the vitals of America...."[105]

McCarthy gave back as good as he got. His November 24 rebuttal, also televised nationally, was covered in a page 1 *Mirror* story headlined HST PUT PARTY OVER COUNTRY. Above the headline, in smaller print, were the words: "McCarthy Charges." McCarthy called Truman a "defeated and discredited politician" and said his administration had been "crawling with Communists." As for the term "McCarthyism," it had originated with the *Daily Worker.* In a tit for tat, McCarthy defined "Trumanism" as "the placing of your political party above the interests of your country, regardless of how much the country is injured thereby."[106]

Then McCarthy went further. "The raw, harsh, unpleasant fact," he said, "is that communism is an issue and will be an issue in 1954." This was open defiance of the administration, a direct refutation of Eisenhower's recent statement that the internal security problem would be solved by the time of the 1954 elections. McCarthy's speech also contained an insulting rhetorical question. Addressing the problem of American prisoners in Korea, he asked: "Are we going to continue to send perfumed notes, following the style of the Truman-Acheson regime?"[107]

Two days later the *Mirror* editorialized that "Senator Joe McCarthy's speech on Tuesday night needed to be spoken... as a contribution to national morality." The editorial also reminded readers that "to ferret out conspirators is not an easy task (that) can be done in the refined atmosphere of intellectual teas or cocktail parties."[108]

It would be hasty to interpret these statements as a sign that any Hearst organ was now tilting toward McCarthy and away from the administration. On November 25, the day after his nationally televised speech, McCarthy tempered his rhetoric of the 24th with a statement that he was not challenging the president's leadership. Referring to Eisenhower as "an honorable man," McCarthy called on Americans to send telegrams to the White House protesting the "blood trade" with Communist countries.[109]

Nineteen fifty-three was a year of strain for the Hearst-McCarthy alliance. During the Bohlen confirmation hearings, Frank Conniff and William Randolph Hearst Jr. split off from Sokolsky and George Rothwell Brown. A fissure also threatened over the Greek ship deal, when Stassen's defiance of McCarthy resulted in an anti-McCarthy headline in the *Mirror.* (The lesion was healed, ironically, by Eisenhower's undercutting of Stassen.) Another divisive factor was the squalid internecine feud between Howard Rushmore and Cohn and Schine. Back at the *Journal-American,* Rushmore continued to laud McCarthy. But he never made the slightest effort to conceal his hatred of Cohn or contempt for Schine.

The darkest episode that year was the controversy over J. B. Matthews, when the Hearst organization was forced to the wall in a no-win battle. By contrast, the brightest hour was the Fort Monmouth investigation. Armed by widespread popular support, McCarthy went after the "Rosenberg spy ring" with the cooperation of Army Secretary Stevens and the blessing of such an unlikely supporter as Drew Pearson.

As 1953 drew to a close, the Hearst-McCarthy alliance was still intact. But it would never again be the strong, unbroken phalanx that it had been in the three years between the GO TO IT, JOE MCCARTHY editorial and the nomination of Charles E. Bohlen.

133

Journal-American cartoon commemorating the 30th anniversary of J. Edgar Hoover as head of the FBI. Though Hoover had by now turned against McCarthy, the Hearst press never slackened in the fawning adulation it heaped on the Director.

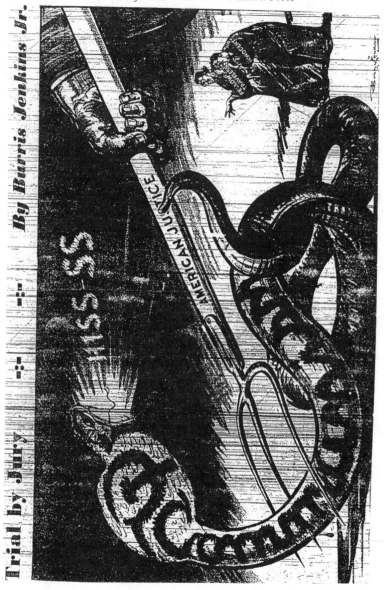

This appeared immediately following the verdict in the Hiss trial. Few were aware of the similarity between this cartoon and one that appeared in 1918 in the New York *Tribune*. Caption was COILED IN THE FLAG and the offending reptile was characterized as "Hears-s-s-t."

7. 1954: Fragmentation

Public opinion has a way of lagging behind political reality. As 1954 began, Joe McCarthy's career was on a clearly irreversible downgrade course. Seemingly unbeatable in 1950-52, in 1953 he had been roundly trounced on the Bohlen nomination, outmaneuvered in the J. B. Matthews controversy, and rebuffed in his efforts to investigate the CIA. In addition, he had aroused feelings of fear and loathing among a powerful group of White House insiders. Presidential assistant C. D. Jackson, a former editor of *Time,* called for a declaration of war against McCarthy in November 1953.[1]

Jackson's hostility was fully shared by influential publishers and business leaders who had the president's ear. These included William Robinson of the *New York Herald-Tribune,* Palmer Hoyt of the *Denver Post,* and CEOs Philip Reed of General Electric and Paul Hoffman of Studebaker. Hoffman wrote that McCarthyism had escalated from a "nuisance" to a "deadly menace."[2]

This antagonism went all the way to the top. Though maintaining a cordial outward posture, Richard Nixon had double-crossed McCarthy during the Matthews affair and would join in every administration effort to cut him down. The president, conforming to a long-held principle, continued his policy of refusing to "get into the gutter with that guy." Privately, his hatred for McCarthy was explosive. One time, during a White House meeting, he wistfully expressed the desire to take out a "sudden death" insurance policy on the senator.[3]

Yet it was in January 1954 that McCarthy attained his highest rating in the Gallup poll. According to the survey, 50 percent of Americans had a "favorable" opinion of his activities, 29 percent "unfavorable," while 31 percent registered "no opinion." By contrast, the "favorable" rating was only 15 percent in August 1951 (when he was jousting with Benton) and 19 percent in April 1953 (when Cohn and Schine were "purifying" overseas libraries). But it should be taken into consideration that public opinion was far more focused on the McCarthy issue in 1954 than it had been previously. In August 1951 the "no opinion" figure was a staggering 63 percent; in April 1953 it was 59 percent.[4]

Soldiers Three

McCarthy's next headline-dominating controversy was closely linked to the fortunes of three dissimilar men who wore the uniform of the United States Army. One was a private, one a major, and one a brigadier general.

The private was G. David Schine, friend and protégé of Roy Cohn. Schine's military service was mainly the gift of Drew Pearson. The columnist had for some time been publicizing the irony of a fiery young anticommunist doing everything possible to avoid participation in a shooting war against communism. Though Schine never had to serve in Korea, pressure from Pearson caused his draft board to classify him 1-A in September 1953. This move caused Cohn to throw himself into a maximum effort to make sure that Schine's tour of duty would not be onerous. Unsuccessfully, he attempted to obtain commissions for him in the Army, Navy, and Air Force. Then a reluctant McCarthy was dragged into the controversy. Privately, McCarthy considered Schine a pest and told a Senate colleague that he wished the young playboy would be shipped to Siberia.[5] But he was so anxious to oblige Cohn that he requested that Schine be assigned to New York and given "the task of analyzing West Point textbooks for left-wing bias...."[6] Though this petition was refused, Schine was allowed two weeks temporary duty with the committee after his induction.

When Schine reported to Fort Dix for active service, Cohn really went into action. Thanks to his intervention, Schine was excused from K. P. and guard duty. While other soldiers were out on the rifle range, he would chat with officers in a heated communications hut. Schine also wore special non-regulation gloves and would hire another GI to clean his rifle.[7] As Cohn continued his efforts to make life easier for Schine, Pearson and Jack Anderson did what they could to make it more difficult. Accounts of Schine's goldbricking appeared regularly in the Pearson column, moving McCarthy to deny charges of improper pressure and call Pearson a liar.[8]

Schine's cause was also taken up by Pearson's inimical colleague at the *Mirror*. On February 1, Winchell wrote that "Pvt. David Schine must be wondering why a Red-fighter becomes a private while out-and-out Communists become majors and colonels."[9]

Winchell's reference to higher ranks introduces the second actor in this drama. Major Irving Peress, U.S. Army Dental Corps, had been called up under the Doctors Draft Law of 1950, providing that a doctor or dentist can be assigned to military service at a rank roughly equivalent to his position in civilian life. Commissioned a captain, Peress went on active service in January 1953 and was promoted to major on October 23 of that year.

There is no doubt that Peress had a left-wing background. He had been a member of the Marxist-leaning American Labor Party and, in response to loyalty/security questions on his Army form 98, he had written "federal constitutional privilege."[10]

Years later even Cohn would admit that a dentist, no matter how radical his views, was not in a position to imperil national security.[11] Far from being a menace, Peress was in fact a godsend to McCarthy and Cohn. In the person of the "pink dentist" (as Peress came to be known), they had a club to beat the Army over its lax security procedures and ensure continuing courtesies to Private Schine.

On January 31, the day before Winchell's bouquet to Schine, a page 6 story in the *Journal-American* was headlined MCCARTHY SAYS MAJOR RAN RED CELL. Peress was as yet unidentified but McCarthy described him as a "longtime Communist who attempted to recruit soldiers into Red cells at Camp Kilmer, New Jersey." On the same page was a picture of McCarthy receiving an Americanism award from the Catholic War Veterans.[12]

How had McCarthy and Cohn learned of Peress's suspect background? In an irony that would seldom be equaled, the informant was Brigadier General Ralph W. Zwicker, commandant at Camp Kilmer, where the major was stationed. Zwicker, a West Pointer and decorated veteran of the European Theater, was disturbed by Peress's file and angered because the Army was dragging its feet about getting rid of him.[13] Zwicker is the third of our military trio who would have such an effect on McCarthy's fortunes.

On January 30 Peress had endured a gruelling closed session before McCarthy's subcommittee. On return to Camp Kilmer, he requested immediate separation from the Army. This was granted, with Peress being discharged the following day under the Army's Involuntary Release Program. The alternative would have been to court-martial him, a step the Army didn't consider possible. While in service, Peress had committed no infractions against military law.

MAJOR HONORABLY DISCHARGED was the headline of a page 2 *Journal-American* story on February 2. It quoted McCarthy as saying that "I cannot believe that the Army would give an honorable discharge to someone who refused to answer questions about Communist affiliation."[14] The promotion and honorable discharge of Major Peress set the stage for one of McCarthy's most reckless and self-destructive acts.

On February 18 General Zwicker testified before McCarthy's subcommittee in closed session. Previously cooperative, the general was now evasive, in obedience to government security directives. When he hedged on whether he would recommend removal of an officer responsible for giving a Communist an honorable discharge, McCarthy exploded. "Then, general," he snarled, "you should be removed from any command." In an ensuing tirade, he told Zwicker that his actions were a "disgrace to the Army" and that he was "not fit to wear the uniform."[15]

The *Mirror's* initial response to this intemperate outburst was a blanketing article. Under the page 1 headline LADY COP NAMES EX-MAJOR AS RED, the story described how Ruth Eagle, an undercover agent on the New York Police Department's "Red Squad," had attended Communist meetings with Peress. On page 3, in a piece of heroic understatement, was an item that McCarthy was "far from satisfied" with the testimony of Brigadier General Ralph W. Zwicker.[16]

Three days later, reticence was thrown aside. Frank Conniff, that eternal trend setter, delivered the strongest attack on McCarthy that had yet appeared in a Hearst publication. "Joe McCarthy is playing dirty pool with his blanket blast at the Army," he wrote. "I hope Joe has the decency to apologize to (General) Matthew Ridgway, and other combat officers he has maligned." In a particularly nasty dig from one who shared McCarthy's Catholic antecedents, he accused McCarthy of "taking up with oil-rich, anti-Catholic Texas millionaires."[17]

On March 7 William Randolph Hearst Jr. published a front-page editorial in praise of statements made by Eisenhower at a March 3 press conference. In a rebuke to McCarthy, Ike had lauded General Zwicker and attacked the "disregard of standards of fair play in investigations."[18] As usual, he did not mention McCarthy by name. Hearst wrote that "President Eisenhower sounded just the right note" and that "he had done a great job." As for McCarthy, he should "come up with a conciliatory gesture of his own to match the President's." (Eisenhower admitted that the Peress case had been handled badly.) Hearst also criticized "Joe's explosion that the general (Zwicker) was unfit to wear the uniform."[19]

That wasn't the end of McCarthy's problems. In an *et tu, Brute* scenario, even the faithful Fulton Lewis joined the list of his critics. Lewis advised McCarthy to apologize to Zwicker and "walk away" from his controversy with the Army.[20]

The Zwicker affair triggered the greatest Hearst in-house revolt against McCarthy to date. Nor was right-wing disaffection limited to the Hearst chain. Responding to a telegram from fellow World War I veteran Robert Stevens, Bertie McCormick also denounced McCarthy's treatment of Zwicker.[21]

It was a disastrous chain reaction. To aid Private Schine, McCarthy had aggressively involved himself in the case of Major Peress. In his rage over Peress's promotion and honorable discharge, he alienated a large segment of conservative support by humiliating General Zwicker.

Seeing It Now

Of all the media, television had been the most timorous about taking on McCarthy. And of the major networks, CBS had a reputation as the one least inclined to become involved in political controversy. Stefan Kanfer writes that "CBS, despite... the anti-McCarthy journalism of Edward R. Murrow, was the most easily intimidated of all networks." For performers who were trying to get off the blacklist, "an appearance on a CBS program constituted a visa to the white list."[22]

Murrow has emerged as broadcast journalism's greatest hero in the fight against McCarthy. There are those who thought he came late to the struggle. One was William L. Shirer, who had been eased out of CBS by Murrow and board chairman William S. Paley after a sponsor found him politically controversial. Though embittered by the experience, Shirer never denied the effectiveness of Murrow's presentation. "But better late than never," he wrote. "No network, then or later, allowed one of its commentators to take on McCarthy. The broadcast of Murrow on his *See It Now* program devastated the Red-baiting senator from Wisconsin, and he never recovered from it."[23]

There was apprehension among some of Murrow's colleagues that the McCarthy program might be his last. Joseph Wershba, then one of Murrow's reporters, records this conversation with Fred W. Friendly, Murrow's co-producer. "Friendly and I lived in the same housing development. As we shared a taxi home that night... suddenly he burst out with, 'Well, even if Ed winds up without a job Tuesday night, we'll make him president of the United States yet.'"[24]

That Tuesday was March 9, 1954. The half hour program was aired on Channel 2. Consisting of a series of film clips, it denigrated McCarthy personally as well as politically. Along with terrorizing witnesses, he was shown belching, picking his nose, and giggling fatuously as he delivered his "Alger – I mean Adlai" quip. Murrow, offering McCarthy equal time, ended the program in the noble-Roman style to which he was so inclined. Explaining that McCarthy had exploited rather than created the climate of fear then prevalent, he signed off with these words: "Cassius was right. 'The fault, dear Brutus, is not in our stars but in ourselves.' Good night and good luck."[25]

Initial reaction to the broadcast was overwhelmingly pro-Murrow. The telephone call ratio was 10-1; for letters and phone calls it was 9-2. The latter had been placed in huge, equal-size cartons – eighteen marked 'favorable' and four 'unfavorable.'"[26]

McCarthy reaped one benefit from Murrow's attack: the *Journal-American* and *Mirror* writers solidly closed ranks behind him. Quelled was the rebellion that had erupted following McCarthy's savaging of General Zwicker. Zwicker was a decorated officer with no known suspect political opinions; Murrow was a pillar of the liberal establishment and Hearst press's natural enemy.

Since the controversy involved television, Jack O'Brian was selected to lead the counterattack. His March 10 column was headed AN ANALYSIS OF MURROW'S PORTSIDED POLITICAL PITCHING. O'Brian's review was mainly an attempt to drive a wedge between Murrow and his bosses. The columnist claimed that "CBS board chairman Bill Paley personally ordered the pompous portsider to take a more middle ground" but that "Murrow refused." Although CBS was in a "clean-house-of-lefties mood," Murrow led a "charmed existence" because of "his Svengali-like influence on the top officers of the corporation." In a grimly ironic aside, O'Brian wrote that the program had been followed by "a newscast featuring Murrow's protégé, (Don) Hollenbeck." In an "obviously gloating mood, Hollenbeck hoped that viewers had witnessed his patron's triumph." (On June 22, 1954 the "gloating" Hollenbeck, ill and depressed by the witch hunt, committed suicide.) O'Brian concluded, with some justification, that Murrow "is a great hand at digging into the classics, citing the words of Twain, Lincoln, Diogenes, Holmes, and other dead thinkers on subjects... about which none of these demised celebrities could be expected to have any precise retroactive opinions."[27]

McCarthy's reply to Murrow was a two-part effort. On March 11 he appeared on Fulton Lewis's radio program, ostensibly to respond to a speech by Adlai Stevenson in which he charged that the Republican party was now "half McCarthy and half Eisenhower."[28] (Though Lewis had chided McCarthy over Zwicker, he backed him to the hilt against Murrow.) In the question-and-answer session with Lewis, he devoted more time to Murrow than he did to Stevenson. Characterizing the newscaster as one of the "extreme left-wing bleeding-heart elements of television and radio," he said that Murrow had lied when he denied the American Civil Liberties Union was a Communist-front organization.[29] (Though ACLU was never on the Attorney General's list of subversive groups, it had been described by a state committee in California as a "transmission belt" doing the work of the Communist Party.)[30] McCarthy also charged that Murrow, in 1935, had been an adviser to a proposed summer school program in the Soviet Union – a program canceled by the Russians before it began.[31]

Pegler took aim at Murrow six days later. In his March 17 column he scorned him as "a radio and television propagandist... who has been attacking Senator McCarthy, Roy Cohn and others because they attacked Communists."[32]

McCarthy's official response to Murrow came on April 6. On television he reiterated his charge about the summer school and called Murrow "the leader and the cleverest of the jackal pack which is always found at the throat of anyone who dares to expose Communists and traitors."[33]

McCarthy's speech got good marks from Jack O'Brian. In a claim of dubious authenticity, he wrote that "Joe McCarthy more than doubled Murrow's 'See It Now' rating in his rebuttal."[34]

Though the Hearst writers had drawn the wagons around McCarthy in the Murrow controversy, criticism of him continued to surface on other issues. At the same time, the diehards remained loyal. If anything, their loyalty intensified as they now knew that the Hearst press no longer spoke with one voice about McCarthy.

The March 10 *Journal-American* contained an interesting illustration of this fissure. E. F. Tompkins, truest of the true, angrily decried insinuations that McCarthy was damaging the Republican party. Not only was he a "great asset," but the "most effective Republican spokesman...."[35] More effective, presumably, than the occupant of 1600 Pennsylvania Avenue.

By contrast, general topics writer Bob Considine took a poor view of McCarthy's November 24 speech, which the senator had advertised as a rebuttal to Truman's address of the 16th. Considine caustically observed that "when McCarthy demanded time to answer Truman, he spent twenty minutes batting Truman around and devoted the rest of the time to a blast against the Eisenhower administration."[36] Though Considine waited almost four months before commenting on the November controversy, from then on he was never again in the McCarthy camp.

Sokolsky remained loyal – to McCarthy and also to Cohn and Schine, two youths whom many McCarthy adherents found difficult to stomach. Hearing that Schine had had his privileges revoked and been sent to perform straight duty at Camp Gordon, Georgia, Sokolsky wrote that Schine "was a hostage to keep McCarthy in line."[37]

Another unshakable loyalist was Pegler. Next to labor unions and the Roosevelt family, nothing infuriated him more than hearing someone praise the Anderson-May "biography" of McCarthy. This time the offender was *New York Times* staffer John B. Oakes. Wrote Pegler: "Oakes did a plug... for a book by a legman for Drew Pearson after McCarthy had used Pearson for a punching dummy."[38]

William Randolph Hearst Jr. viewed the growing dissension in his ranks with anguish – though he had contributed to it with his own reproaches to McCarthy. Forlornly, he nursed the hope that McCarthy would yet become a "team player" and things would return to the way they had been in the splendid summer of 1952. Like the Italian opera singer who proclaims his loves, hates, and frustrations on stage at the top of his voice, Hearst would regularly emote via the front page editorial.

On April 18, eve of McCarthy's confrontation with the Army, Hearst granted that there were many impeccable anti-communists who did not feel comfortable with McCarthy. "As for those who cannot stand his mannerisms and methods," he wrote, "let them unite in demanding a nonpartisan exposé of Communists in government."[39]

The Hearings Open

On March 16 the subcommittee announced that it would be holding full-dress hearings on the Army-McCarthy controversy. To avoid improprieties, McCarthy stepped down as chairman in favor of the second-ranking Republican, Karl Mundt of South Dakota. Since Cohn was also involved in the dispute, a special counsel would have to be appointed. First choice was Samuel P. Sears, a Boston attorney who denied having any strong feelings for or against McCarthy. This was untrue; Sears was a rabid McCarthyite who had been recommended by Jean McCarthy to present her husband's point of view in a Boston debate.[40] Forced to step down, Sears was replaced by Ray H. Jenkins, a successful criminal lawyer from Knoxville, Tennessee. Though he was a Taft Republican, Jenkins's claim to neutrality about McCarthy was more genuine than that of Sears.

The Army's chief counsel was a sixty-three-year-old Iowa-born Bostonian named Joseph N. Welch. Dorothy Kilgallen wrote that "the Army's counsel, Mr. Welch, behaves in the manner of a man determined to play the role of an Irvin S. Cobb character."[41] "Dickens character" would have been just as good a description. With a courtly manner and a penchant for dated colloquialisms ("sic 'em," "hurt like the dickens"), Welch at first seemed outmatched by such as Jenkins and McCarthy. But behind the folksy façade was a first-rate legal mind and an uncanny knack for spotting an opponent's weakness. Cohn, repeatedly pinked by Welch during the hearings, came to have a professional's reluctant admiration for his deceptively gentle opponent.

The hearings opened on April 22. A belligerent McCarthy, raising one of his famous points of order, challenged the right of Secretary Stevens and John G. Adams, an opposing attorney, to represent the Army. Stevens and Adams, he claimed, were "civilians who are trying to hold up an investigation of Communists" and they had no right to "label themselves the Department of the Army."[42]

McCarthy also aimed a low blow at one of the Army witnesses, Major General Miles Reber. Reber denounced Cohn for putting pressure on him to obtain a commission for Schine. McCarthy shot back that Reber's brother, the former acting High Commissioner in Germany, had been forced to resign from the foreign service as a bad security risk. This had nothing to do with Communist sympathy. Cohn – of all people – had blackmailed the brother, Samuel P. Reber, into resigning by threatening to make public a homosexual relationship that dated back to his undergraduate days at Harvard.[43] So General Reber's reluctance to help Schine obtain a commission is understandable. Stevens, countering McCarthy's charges, labeled the Schine case a "perversion of power" and told of Cohn throwing a temper tantrum when he was refused entry into a special laboratory at Fort Monmouth.[44]

Bob Considine's column that day was an interesting mix of outrage and wistful yearning. Under the heading SOMEBODY IS LYING, Considine wrote that "if it turns out to be McCarthy and his aides, McCarthy may have been dealt a blow from which he will never recover."[45] A possibility, one can assume, that did not excessively sadden the columnist.

All that week there were fresh disclosures of extraordinary pressure applied by Cohn and extraordinary privileges extended to Schine. On April 29 Considine attacked the pampered private in the harshest terms ever used against a McCarthy staffer in a Hearst publication. Among other transgressions, Schine had "ducked KP duty" and "hired fellow GIs to clean his rifle." Touching on the larger issue of America's prestige in the Cold War, Considine ruefully concluded that "if there is belly laughter in the circus, it must be confined to our enemies overseas."[46]

A May 1 editorial in the *Journal-American* tried to tread the thin line between remaining on friendly terms with the administration and backing aspects of the McCarthy investigation that the Hearst press considered valid. While not questioning "the patriotism of Mr. Stevens... who is as deeply committed against Communist subversion as any good American," the editorial wanted to know why Major General Kirke Lawton, the pro-McCarthy commandant at Fort Monmouth, was ordered to withdraw security risk suspensions at his base and whether his relief was being considered.[47] Concern here was legitimate. The Army would shortly respond to this problem by ordering Lawton to Walter Reed Hospital for a medical examination and later giving him a disability discharge. The Army's handling of the Lawton case was frankly suspect. In one bizarre episode, he was given "sick leave" while a patient at Walter Reed. "Sick leave from a hospital!!!!"[48] That was Winchell's comment on this strange decision.

Considine's May 3 column demonstrates that he considered McCarthy less culpable than he did Cohn and Schine. That day he discussed two recently published works on McCarthy – a special issue of *The Progressive* titled "McCarthy: A Documented Record" and *McCarthy and His Enemies,* a book by William F. Buckley and his brother-in-law Brent Bozell. Though generally in favor of the senator, the Buckley-Bozell book did contain criticism of his tactics and methods. Considine: "When you finish both pros and cons on Joe, you'll be bewildered."[49]

The Defection of J. Edgar Hoover

In the first week of May, McCarthy was scoring points in the hearings. The bumbling Robert Stevens, under cross-examination by Ray Jenkins, had denied that he ever gave special privileges to David Schine in an effort to get McCarthy to call off the Fort Monmouth investigation. To Stevens's assertion that he treated all Army privates alike, Jenkins derisively pointed out that Stevens had been to dinner at Schine's Waldorf Towers apartment, that he had ridden the streets of Manhattan in a Schine limousine, and that he had called Allen Dulles about a position for Schine in the CIA.[50]

On May 4 McCarthy was doing the questioning, badgering Stevens about his poor performance in getting Communists out of Fort Monmouth. Suddenly he produced a "carbon copy" of a letter allegedly written by J. Edgar Hoover to the Army on January 26, 1951. It warned of subversive activities at Fort Monmouth and contained a list of thirty-four potential security risks. Was this not proof that Stevens's department had ignored a three-year-old warning from the FBI?[51]

A skeptical Joseph Welch wanted to know if Hoover had actually written the letter. Robert Collier, a subcommittee staff member, was sent to the FBI to clarify the matter. Hoover denied writing the letter, but did say he had sent a fifteen-page memorandum to the Army on the subject of security at Fort Monmouth. When Welch suggested to Collier that McCarthy's document was a "carbon copy of precisely nothing," Collier had to agree.[52]

Richard Gid Powers makes the point that "instead of focusing on what was accurate in McCarthy's statement (that the contents were a faithful summary of the FBI memo), Hoover's reply called attention to what was fraudulent about the letter – its format. Hoover's response left the impression that McCarthy had tried to foist a forged document off on the Senate, and that he had conspired with disloyal employees to obtain classified information without proper authorization."[53] (The letter had apparently come from a member of McCarthy's "Loyal American Underground."[54]

Hoover's action was neither random nor unplanned. By spring of 1954, he *wanted* to strike at McCarthy. In the beginning, Hoover considered McCarthy a valuable asset. He admired his rough-and-ready style and the two men became personal friends. Hoover would be McCarthy's dinner guest, they regularly went to the race track together, and they periodically fraternized with Winchell at the Stork Club.

The friendship flourished when McCarthy was slashing at the hated Harry Truman and lasted through the early months of the Eisenhower administration. As late as August 1953, when Hoover and McCarthy were vacationing together near San Diego, Hoover told a newspaper reporter that "I view him as a friend and I believe he so views me." Yes, McCarthy had enemies but they were enemies one could be proud of. "Whenever you attack subversives of any kind, Communists, Fascists... the Ku Klux Klan, you are going to be the victim of the most extremely vicious criticism that can be made."[55]

By early 1954, Hoover's own enemies list had increased by one. Among his grievances against McCarthy were that McCarthy had hired away some of his top agents, that Cohn and Schine were embarrassing the director by bragging of their close personal ties with him, and that at least one senator had stopped supplying information to the FBI because it always seemed to end up in McCarthy's hands.[56] Moreover, there was no way that a master bureaucratic infighter like Hoover was going to back a losing cause. As the hearings began, McCarthy was in open revolt against the administration. Hoover had to make a choice – and he was far too astute to jeopardize his position by backing a maverick senator against a popular president.

Walter Winchell: Retroactive Resister

If J. Edgar Hoover's repudiation of McCarthy was clear and unmis-takable, the same cannot be said for Walter Winchell's. In 1975, three years after his death, a book of anecdotes and reminiscences came out that detailed some of the better-known incidents in the columnist's life.

Winchell had taken a lot of flak over his support for McCarthy. In the fifteen years between McCarthy's death and his own, he repeatedly felt called upon to set the record straight or, more accurately, to invent one. Yes, he had supported McCarthy when he thought he was fighting com-munism and exposing the Truman administration's alleged softness on subversion. But he turned against McCarthy when the senator began to attack such figures as Eisenhower, Marshall, and Zwicker. In the book, Winchell describes what he claims was a visit to McCarthy's office:

> He saw me and yelled, "Mr. Winchell! What do you think of the President (Eisenhower) now?" ...With a finger pointed at him I said: "Senator, I am devoted to the Pres – let's get that straight, okay?" He faked a smile and sourcasmed, "Every man to his own taste." His staffers gave me a glare. I never went to his office again.[57]

This seems pretty clear: a principled Winchell, angered by McCarthy's attacks on Eisenhower, stalking out of his office and never returning. Though Winchell doesn't give a date for the alleged encounter, it would have had to be after January 1953, when Eisenhower took office.

There is just one problem with Winchell's scenario. Despite his post-McCarthy era claims to the contrary, scrutiny of Winchell's columns for 1954 – the year McCarthy went down – reveals a *strong and continuing support for McCarthy*. What follows is a random compilation of 1954 entries, accompanied by brief commentary to set Winchell's remarks in the context of events:

> • March 1: "Many of the people criticizing Senator McCarthy do not enjoy G-man Hoover's war on the Reds. (File that under your that's-too-bad department.)"[58]

G-man Hoover, that great keeper of secrets, apparently never con-fided to Winchell his decision to abandon McCarthy.

> • April 19: "A group of talented Hollywood whoopsies (Winchellese for homosexuals), all anti-McCarthy, meet at an agent's house to invent McCarthy mudpies."[59]

That entry appeared three days before the hearings began. It can be seen as an effort by the homophobic Winchell to aid McCarthy by making an invidious comparison between his macho self and the "whoopsies" who opposed him.

> • June 7: "The McCarthy committee is so far ahead they can coast in."[60]

By June 7 the tide had turned against McCarthy. Hoover's betrayal was followed by a furious attack on him in the Senate by Vermont Republican Ralph Flanders. Flanders compared McCarthy to Hitler, accused him (unjustly) of anti-Semitism, and hinted broadly at a homosexual relationship between Cohn, Schine, and McCarthy.[61]

> • June 9: "Roy Cohn, the Rat and Red Catcher (27 years old), is the best answer to former Commies who claim they became Reds because 'they were too young to know better'... and more Cohnverts (are) coming in every day."[62]

"Cohnverts" to what? June 9 was the date of the most celebrated single event in the hearings: Welch's historic rebuke to McCarthy after the senator had gratuitously slandered a young member of Welch's firm. McCarthy's intemperate outburst was brought on by Welch's skillful needling of Cohn.

> • June 13: "Anti-McCarthy papers enjoy noting that 'Welch Kicked In Cohn's Teeth!' and 'The Dems belted McCarthy!' But when the latter return the compliments the same gazettes whine that 'they get too rough.'"[63]

Two days earlier Senator Flanders had introduced a resolution demanding that McCarthy be removed from chairmanship of the subcommittee if he did not answer six questions raised by the Gillette-Hennings Committee in 1952. This was the prelude to the censure resolution that would sink McCarthy. Yet Winchell wrote as if McCarthy had lost none of his influence or popularity.

> • June 21: "Big blowup in the Canadian parliament over a program ridiculing Senator McCarthy on the Canuck network. The script was authored by a Canadian deported from the US for refusing to answer queries about Red activities."[64]

The writer has heard this superb lampoon, in which McCarthy dies in a plane crash, goes to heaven, and attempts to investigate God.[64]

> • June 24: "Four of New York's seven papers report their mail 'overwhelmingly' pro-McCarthy."[65]

Whether this is true or not, McCarthy's "favorable" rating in the Gallup poll had fallen from 50 to 34 percent since January, with the "unfavorable" figure rising from 29 to 45 percent.[66]

• November 12: "Sen. McCarthy's unique position: having to fight colleagues for the unique privilege of fighting Commies."[67]

In August a censure resolution against McCarthy had been introduced in the Senate. In November, shortly before Winchell's entry, McCarthy himself had predicted that it would pass.

• November 22: Winchell recalled that Senator Robert M. La Follette of Wisconsin had ridiculed Senator Frank Kellogg of Michigan for being a hunchback. The columnist asked how "this characterization of a U.S. senator, who unfortunately was slightly deformed, compared with any of the remarks charged against Senator McCarthy. Why wasn't La Follette criticized in the Senate?... Because he didn't fight Reds?"[68]

This accolade came after McCarthy's rating in the Gallup poll had slipped to around 30 percent.[69] Moreover, McCarthy had again predicted that he would lose in the most important political battle of his career. "I think I should warn you – they're going to vote censure," he told a group from the Army and Navy Union who had given him a patriotic award.[70]

• December 1: "Too many people in Washington are trying to make a mountain out of McCarthy and a molehill out of Moscow."[71]

The next day the Senate voted to censure McCarthy. In the same month McCarthy witnessed a disturbing erosion of Catholic support. In October 1952 a campus poll at Fordham University showed McCarthy rated favorably by a 5-1 margin.[72] In December 1954 101 members of the graduating class wrote a letter to *The Ram,* Fordham's undergraduate paper, expressing shock over the notion that to be a good Catholic one must necessarily support McCarthy. The letter added that, as practicing Catholics, they opposed "this attempt to yoke our Faith to a transient political doctrine."[73]

The spurious nature of Winchell's *ex post facto* "anti-McCarthyism" is also noted by Neal Gabler, latest and most comprehensive of his biographers. Writes Gabler: "Though in later years he attempted to distance himself from McCarthy... the truth is that he had defended McCarthy to the last and would be tied to him forever."[74]

Winchell's credibility is further shaken by this complaint in the book against Richard E. Berlin:

When I opposed Reds (by name!) for full columns... Mr. Berlin thought that was Just Peachy... But when I took on a Fascist or pro-Nazi... it never got into print.[75]

This is complete fabrication. Winchell's columns were full of attacks on Nazis, Fascists, collaborators, and Ku Kluxers. Some of these have been quoted in earlier chapters of this work: his denunciations of Franco, his jibe at Upton Close, and his vendetta against the "queereographer" Serge Lifar.

Winchell can be rightly considered a retroactive resister against McCarthyism. He reminds us of the World War II French collaborator who hastily donned a Resistance armband during the Liberation – or the desk officer who invented a record for himself as a tail gunner.

The Hearings End

As the Army-McCarthy extravaganza continued, Hoover's swipe at McCarthy was followed by another disruptive development: internecine warfare in the McCarthy camp between Rushmore and Roy Cohn. Rushmore, off the subcommittee and back at the *Journal-American,* wrote on May 8 that "Joe McCarthy made a mistake" in hiring an "immature publicity seeker" like Roy Cohn.[76]

Pulling the rug out from under McCarthy in no way damaged J. Edgar Hoover's prestige within the Hearst organization. May 10 was Hoover's thirtieth anniversary as FBI director. An editorial and columns by Sokolsky and Considine vied with each other in stroking the director.

Even more obsequious was a cartoon in the form of a WANTED poster. Under a likeness of Hoover was the caption PUBLIC HERO NUMBER 1. The "public hero" was "wanted" for thirty years more service.[77] The *Journal-American's* seeming indifference to Hoover's torpedoing of McCarthy did not bode well for the senator.

But the bitter-enders remained loyal. On May 18 – three days after the president posed with Stevens for numerous pictures and pledged his full support – Pegler lauded Mr. and Mrs. Archibald Roosevelt as "staunch McCarthyites" who "stand at the center of a small band of constant patriots in New York."[78]

Historians of the McCarthy era unanimously agree that the mere length of the hearings was enormously damaging to McCarthy. As viewers were exposed to the blue-jawed countenance, the menacing manner, and the constant interruptions, he began to emerge in the national consciousness as a sleazy small-town bully rather than an earnest crusader against communism. A May 28 *Journal-American* reflected this feeling with the comment that "for sheer triviality, there is nothing in our history to compare with the time spent and wasted in the Army-McCarthy hearings."[79]

Then came the 9th of June. The clash that day between Welch and McCarthy must rank as one of the great public confrontations in American political history. What few realize today is that McCarthy was not entirely at fault in going after Welch. Cohn was testifying, and Welch, using every harassing technique he had learned in his long career, was nickel-anddiming him to death about the urgency of getting subversives out of sensitive positions. "Get them out by sundown," "get them out as fast as possible," "please hurry," were among his rhetorical entreaties.

McCarthy could stand it no longer. Interrupting the questioning, he spoke the words that would be his political obituary. In fairness, McCarthy's speech was not an unadulterated smear. He was quite justified in saying that he was getting bored by Welch's phony requests that Cohn personally root every subversive out of the government by sundown. But at that point McCarthy's talent for excess took over. He suicidally crossed the line when he violated an agreement between Cohn and Welch and launched a gratuitous attack on a young attorney in Welch's firm. (According to the pact, two taboo subjects were the Welch attorney and Cohn's draft status.)[80] The man in question, Frederick G. Fisher, had once belonged to the National Lawyers Guild, a group on the Attorney General's list of subversive organizations.

A stunned Welch confronted McCarthy. "Until this moment, Senator," he said, "I think I never really gauged your cruelty or recklessness." Then Welch struck back. Yes, Fisher had belonged to the Lawyers Guild, though he was no longer a member. When Welch learned of the association, he asked Fisher to withdraw from the staff he was recruiting for the hearings. This gave the lie to McCarthy's accusation that Welch had tried to "foist him on this committee."[81]

Continuing his emotion-charged address, Welch always emphasized the same theme. How could McCarthy be so "reckless and cruel as to do an injury to that lad?" Fisher would "always bear a scar needlessly inflicted by you." When McCarthy attempted to regain the initiative, Welch cut him off:

> Let us not assassinate this lad further, Senator... Have you no sense of decency, sir, at long last. Have you left no sense of decency?

Ordinary Americans were as one with the media in realizing that a historic turn had been reached in the McCarthy era. When Welch finished, the hearing room burst into applause. Congratulatory telegrams poured in and headlines such as HAVE YOU NO SENSE OF DECENCY? were common.[82]

Though this didn't happen to be a Hearst headline, both the *Journal-American* and the *Mirror* tilted against McCarthy. The *Journal-American's* read MCC ON STAND, with the subhead "Welch Calls Him Cruel."[83] The *Mirror's*, on June 10, read M'C ON STAND AFTER BLISTERING BY WELCH.[84]

Before the hearings ended, the high drama of June 9 was succeeded by a bit of low comedy. On page 2 of the *Mirror* was a story headed NOT ATTEMPTING TO GET JACKSON: COHN, M'C. This somewhat deceptive headline referred to a farcical incident that took place on June 11. Center of the controversy was America's most famous private, G. David Schine.

Schine, not content with defining communism, now proposed to combat the Red Menace on a global scale. To counter the intrigues of the Cominform, Schine advocated creation of a "Deminform," an organization designed to promote anti-communist infiltration of the clergy and civic, fraternal, and veterans' groups. While McCarthy faintly praised Schine's plan, Democratic Senator Henry M. ("Scoop") Jackson and minority counsel Robert Kennedy found it a knee-slapper. Amusement escalated to hilarity when Jackson envisaged a scenario in which a band of Deminformers might try to infiltrate an Elks Lodge in Pakistan. (Jackson was an Elk.) Hearing his boon companion mocked, Cohn glared. After the session he cornered Kennedy and threatened to produce a letter Jackson had allegedly written on behalf of a pro-communist job applicant. Kennedy shot back with angry words and a fist fight was narrowly averted. Later, Cohn and McCarthy denied any plan to "get" Jackson.[85]

The hearings ended June 17. On June 18 this editorial appeared in the *Journal-American:* "The Hearst papers have been battling communism for 35 years and will continue to call to task any individual who, through lack of judgment or discretion, perils this fight. Including Joe McCarthy."[86]

One of the hard-liners, George Rothwell Brown, attributed McCarthy's woes to "the attacks of Flanders and the Wisconsin crackpots of the 'Joe Must Go' movement." (A local anti-McCarthy group.) A mood of weariness and disgust was apparent in Bob Considine's comment. "Who won? Personally, I think Russia did." Howard Rushmore's valedictory to the hearings praised McCarthy but was merciless to Cohn and Schine. He insisted that "McCarthy shared along with the majority of his staff a contempt for the bumbling Schine and no one was more distressed by Cohn's intervention on Schine's behalf than McCarthy." Rushmore also alluded to Cohn and Schine's "many faults of self-seeking and publicity grabbing." The Brown, Considine, and Rushmore evaluations all appeared in the June 19 *Journal-American.*[87]

The Woltman Series

One member of the subcommittee who came to hate McCarthyism was Charles E. Potter, a conservative Republican from Michigan who lost both legs in World War II. "As the hearings ended in June 1954," he wrote, "a new atmosphere swept through the Senate building. Many senators who had lived in complete fear of Joe McCarthy... were brave again. They talked openly now, instead of in whispers... They now knew he was finished and they closed in for the kill."[88]

There was a similar feeling in the media. Murrow had done his *See It Now* broadcast, radio and TV comics were beginning to mimic McCarthy, and controversy over the senator had completely fragmented the Hearst organization.

Now came a voice from another conservative newspaper chain: the Scripps-Howard press. Frederick Woltman had long been Roy Howard's resident expert on communism. Few men in America had stronger credentials as a redbaiter. He was a friend of McCarthy and the "New York crowd," he had supported the senator in the early days, and he was regularly referred to in the *Daily Worker* as "Freddie the Fink."

On July 12 Woltman began a five-part series titled "The McCarthy Balance Sheet." His opening sentence was: "Senator Joseph R. McCarthy has become a major liability to the cause of anti-communism." In the remainder of the article Woltman pointed out that communism in 1954 was not the "Red Menace" it had been ten years earlier, when the major Communist agents who had infiltrated the government were still in place. Quoting Father John F. Cronin of the National Catholic Welfare Conference, he advocated a "sharpshooter" approach to fighting communism. As Cronin put it: "You don't need an atom bomb to kill a rat." Woltman also criticized McCarthy's tendency to label all critics as Red sympathizers.[89]

The second installment was devoted to exploding some "myths" about McCarthy: that he had stopped communism in America; that he had exposed and routed a spy nest in the State Department; that he was an able and dedicated anti-communist. Woltman pointed out that Gerhardt Eisler, Carl Aldo Marzani, William Remington, and Alger Hiss had all been fingered before McCarthy entered the Red hunt.[90]

Part 3 was an attack on McCarthy's "formula of treason," where the senator imputed traitorous motives to all his opponents.[91]

The fourth installment was mainly an account of McCarthy's unsuccessful attempt to investigate the CIA – and Ike's role in keeping him out of that sensitive agency.[92]

The final part contained recommendations for effective methods of fighting communism. Woltman favored continuing vigilance by the FBI and creation of a joint congressional watchdog committee to replace the three existing bodies: HUAC, McCarthy's subcommittee, and the Senate

Internal Security Subcommittee, once headed by Pat McCarran and now by William Jenner of Indiana.[93]

Woltman's chief critic among Hearst writers was the retroactive anti-McCarthyite Walter Winchell. On 'August 4 Winchell wrote that "Freddy (the Cleaver) Woltman was promised the Pulitzer Prize (in advance) if he'd write the McCarthy hatchet job... Meanwhile most of Fred's old friends are cutting him cold and he can't abide the slobbering eggheads and doubledomes who are now idolizing him at pink teas."[94] If Woltman was promised the Pulitzer Prize for his McCarthy series, it was a promise unkept. Woltman's only Pulitzer Prize was awarded in 1947.

On July 20 Roy Cohn resigned as McCarthy's chief counsel and returned to practice law in New York. With Senator Potter joining the Democrats in demanding a shakeup of the committee, Cohn knew that his dismissal was imminent.[95] The event was noted in a *Journal-American* editorial under COHN QUITS. From the tone, it was probably written by the fanatical E. F. Tompkins. "Add one more," read the editorial, "to the honor roll of patriotic Americans who have been or are being persecuted out of federal service for fighting the treason of communism."[96]

Eight days later a group of Cohn's friends gave him a banquet at New York's Hotel Astor. Among the 2,500 guests were such poobahs of McCarthyism as Pegler, Sokolsky, William F. Buckley, Alfed Kohlberg, Fulton Lewis, and Joe and Jean McCarthy. Also on hand was Winchell, who gave the affair a friendly plug in his column: "Rabbi Ben Schultz is toastmaster and the *pièce de résistance* – you guessed it – Joe McCarthy."[97]

Rabbi Benjamin Schultz was a fixture at McCarthy rallies. An unsavory ecclesiastical adventurer, he had been locked out of Temple Emmanu-el in Yonkers by his own congregation. The faithful were angered because Schultz, in a newspaper article, ascribed communist sympathy to the venerable Rabbi Stephen S. Wise. Wise called Schultz a "professional and probably profiteering Communist-baiter, unworthy to be a member not to say a rabbi of a Jewish congregation."[98] In 1948 Schultz founded the American Jewish League Against Communism, with Alfred Kohlberg as chairman and himself as executive director. The wealthy Kohlberg was almost his sole financial backer.[99]

Schultz, his league, and the McCarthy movement were made for each other. As Cardinal Spellman was McCarthy's chief ordained booster among Catholics, so was Rabbi Schultz among Jews. At the banquet he said that "the loss of Cohn is like the loss of twelve battleships."[100] Schultz also declared that "America is for Cohn; the people are for Cohn; he stands for McCarthyism. God bless it."[101]

Censure

On July 30 Senator Flanders introduced a resolution recommending censure of McCarthy on three counts: failure to respond to the Hennings Committee's requests that he testify before it, authorizing the Cohn-Schine trip to Europe, and his "habitual contempt for people," as shown in his treatment of General Zwicker and Dorothy Kenyon.

Following heated debate, the Senate on August 2 called for a select committee to consider the censure resolution. This motion was passed by a 75-12 vote. The committee, consisting of three Republicans and three Democrats, was chaired by Republican Senator Arthur V. Watkins of Utah. Watkins, a sixty-seven-year-old Mormon elder, had a center-right voting record and solid anti-communist credentials through service on Pat McCarran's Senate Internal Security Subcommittee, where he had congratulated Judy Holliday for hiring people to investigate her. The other members were moderate to conservative and all from the South and West, areas where McCarthyism had minimal impact.

The public sessions began August 31 in the Senate Caucus Room, scene of the Army-McCarthy hearings. McCarthy, immediately going on the attack, challenged the right of Colorado Democrat Edwin C. Johnson to serve on the committee. Johnson, he claimed, had told a *Denver Post* reporter that "there is not a man among the Democratic leaders of Congress who does not loathe Joe McCarthy."[102]

When the Watkins Committee was formed to deal with McCarthy, newsmen quipped that it was a case of throwing a lion into a den of lambs.[103] Watkins himself was compared to an elderly mouse.[104]

He turned out to be a mouse that roared. When McCarthy made his complaint against Johnson, Watkins firmly gaveled him down, saying that his differences with Johnson were irrelevant to the subject matter of the hearing. After the session, McCarthy uttered one of his historic verbal howlers, telling reporters that Watkins's action was "the most unheard of thing I ever heard of."[105]

The public hearings, nine in number, ended on September 13. As his attorney, McCarthy had hired the highly rated Edward Bennett Williams. Williams was "informed that either he or McCarthy could question a witness or raise an objection, but that once one of them spoke the other would be barred from participating.[106]

Knowing his client's tendency to shoot from the hip, Williams insisted that McCarthy remain silent except when testifying. Sokolsky saw this as an unfair gag order. "In effect," he wrote, "he was never able to put in a complete defense. Maybe his defense for using violent language was no defense at all, but he was never able to say it."[107]

"Violent language" was a reference to some of McCarthy's descriptions of other senators: Flanders as "senile," Fulbright as "halfbright," and Hendrickson as "a living miracle... without brains or guts."

The Watkins Committee's report came out on September 27. Three days earlier the *Journal-American* editorialized that "Joe McCarthy has a right to speedy termination of this trumped-up case against him, so he can get on with the business of ferreting... Red conspirators out of the government woodwork."[108] This was obviously written by Tompkins or one of the other hard-liners. It contrasts sharply with the *Journal-American* editorial of the 28th, the day after the Watkins Committee issued its report. It read: "He might (after attacking Zwicker) have been well advised to modify his position but he did not."[109]

The Watkins Committee report recommended censure of McCarthy on two counts: contempt for Senator Hendrickson and the Gillette-Hennings Committee and his treatment of General Zwicker. Offenses discussed but not included were the "purloined letter" from J. Edgar Hoover, McCarthy's description of Senator Flanders as "senile" (provoked by Flanders comparing him to Hitler and hinting at homosexuality), and calling on government employees to feed him classified information.

Fulton Lewis saw the Watkins Committee's activities as part of an attempt to silence McCarthy during the coming mid-term election. Under the column heading THEY SILENCED JOE, he wrote that "pink-tinged presidential advisers" have "partially accomplished their primary mission of silencing McCarthy's voice during the campaign." He added that "the victory is pyrrhic, it may be at the cost of the election."[110]

In an attempt to patch up the disintegrating alliance, the *Journal-American* fired Howard Rushmore in late October. Though the ostensible motive for Rushmore's dismissal was "economy," few believed that economy was the real reason, least of all Rushmore. Said he: "My criticism of Cohn played a major part in my discharge."[111]

A week before Rushmore's firing, he and Frederick Woltman had journeyed to Sayville, Long Island, to debate the issue of McCarthy. Though Rushmore took McCarthy's side, he repeatedly attacked Cohn and even defended his opponent, Woltman, when spectators began to heckle him over his anti-McCarthy series. "You'll be fired for this," Woltman told Rushmore on the way back to New York.[112]

The dismissal of Rushmore did nothing to suppress the anti-McCarthy faction within the Hearst organization. More often than not these days, Bill Hearst himself sympathized with that faction. Besides, Rushmore was considered a marginal figure. An ex-Communist with a history of mental disorders, he perished in 1958 in a grisly murder-suicide. Leaping into a taxi with his estranged wife, he shot her and then himself.[113]

On October 24 Bill Hearst commented in a signed front-page editorial that "in 1952 Joe McCarthy was a tremendous Democratic problem. In 1954 Joe is a tremendous Republican problem."[114] Five days later he relented to the extent of praising McCarthy's endorsement of all Republicans but one in the coming election. Under JOE'S BIG DEED, he wrote that McCarthy's act demonstrated "moderation and unselfishness in his attitude."[115] An eternal optimist, Hearst clung to the slender hope that McCarthy would put rebellion behind him and become a "team player" with the administration.

The one Republican senator McCarthy refused to back was the New Jersey liberal Clifford Case. Case was running against a Democratic liberal, Charles R. Howell. The Howell-Case contest produced a comment from Frank Conniff which demonstrates how far into anti-McCarthyism he had progressed. In a statement that two years before would have been inconceivable, Conniff denounced Americans for Democratic Action for *helping* McCarthy. So attractive were their records that ADA had endorsed both Howell and Case. Conniff deplored this decision. In not giving its sole support to Howell – "a liberal with a fine record" – ADA demonstrated its "disruptive influence" by jeopardizing the Democrats' chances of recapturing the Senate and ending McCarthy's chairmanship at Government Operations.[116]

After a recess, Congress reconvened on November 8 to debate McCarthy's censure. Two days later, McCarthy destroyed whatever chances he might have had for avoiding censure with a reckless and abusive speech. Predicting that the vote would go against him, he described the Watkins Committee as an "unwitting handmaiden," and "involuntary agent," and "attorneys in fact" of the Communist party.

He also charged that the committee had "imitated Communist methods."[117] Earlier, in a November 4 statement to the press, McCarthy called the committee a "lynch party."[118] On November 7, in a television interview, he used the term "lynch bee."[119]

Sokolsky, fighting a rear guard action, tried to present McCarthy as more sinned against than sinning. Conceding that "there is little doubt that he will be censured," he added that "never did (McCarthy) treat a witness as cavalierly as Senator Watkins and his committee treat McCarthy and his counsel."[120]

McCarthy, stubborn and inflexible, refused to tone down his statements. On November 13 a page 2 story in the *Mirror* was headed M'C WON'T RETREAT ON 'HANDMAIDENS.' The text, unslanted, stated that "the Wisconsin Redhunter stuck to his charges that his critics were 'unwitting handmaidens' of the Communists."[121]

On November 17 McCarthy entered Bethesda Naval Hospital for treatment of chronic bursitis. The Senate voted to adjourn till the 29th, scheduled date of McCarthy's return.

In the meantime, the McCarthy legions put on a fevered burst of last moment activity. On December 1 an anti-censure petition containing 1,000,816 signatures was delivered to the Capitol by armored truck. This was the work of Ten Million Americans Mobilizing for Justice, a pro-McCarthy group organized by Admiral Crommelin and others.[122] Two nights earlier, the same organization had sponsored a pro-McCarthy rally at Madison Square Garden that was attended by 13,000 of the faithful. It was an ugly demonstration of fanaticism, with one speaker calling the proud Ralph Zwicker a "crybaby general."

McCarthy, just out of Bethesda, was unable to attend. Roy Cohn assured the crowd that "Joe McCarthy and I would rather have American people of this type than all the politicians in the world."[123] 13,000 HAIL COHN AND SENATOR'S WIFE was the headline of a page 4 story in the November 30 *Journal-American*. Quoting Cohn: "If the Senate moves to censure, it will be committing the blackest act in our history."[124]

Two weeks earlier, a *Journal-American* editorial had informed "readers who wish to join the efforts of Ten Million Americans Mobilizing for Justice" that they could obtain petitions at the Roosevelt Hotel.[125] Despite disillusionment with McCarthy, there was little enthusiasm within the Hearst organization for a measure as strong as censure.

McCarthy was censured on December 2, by a 67-22 vote. In the final resolution, the count on McCarthy's abuse of Zwicker was dropped but one on the insult to the Watkins Committee was added. (Joe McCarthy paid dearly for his "handmaidens" remark.) All the Democrats supported censure, with the Republicans split down the middle.

McCarthy voted "present," four senators were paired, and the absent and not announced legislators were Wiley of Wisconsin and Kennedy of Massachusetts. Passions ran high in Wisconsin and Wiley, refusing to take a stand, got himself sent on a government mission to Brazil. Kennedy, ill in the hospital, had written a speech in favor of censure.[126]

On December 3 the *Journal-American's* editorial was headed JOE'S CENSURE. Probably written by Bill Hearst, it was a resigned, melancholy admission that McCarthy "spoke in terms too strident for the Senate" and "failed to show a proper respect" for "the most exclusive club in the world."[127]

The *Mirror's* editorial that day was coldly objective – and not comforting to diehard McCarthy partisans: "The immediate effect of the McCarthy censure is that it splits the Republican party right down the middle... This split cannot be healed by 1956, as it is too fundamental."[128]

The Ship Sinks

The final break between McCarthy and Eisenhower came on December 4. It was initiated by the president. That day he invited Senator Watkins to the White House for a forty-five minute talk. The meeting was reported in a page 1 *Journal-American story,* headed PRES HAILS JOB BY WATKINS. The text mentioned that the president "adopted a hands-off policy throughout the censure proceedings" but was now congratulating Watkins on having done "a very splendid job."[129] There was no column or editorial comment.

This was a direct slap in the face. Indeed, the possibility cannot be excluded that it was an act calculated to psych McCarthy into a savagely disproportionate reaction. If this was the White House strategy, it succeeded brilliantly. M'C ASSAILS IKE FOR PRAISING WATKINS was the headline of a page 1 story in the December 7 *Journal-American.* In a volley of billingsgate that might have been directed at the "Red Dean," McCarthy accused Eisenhower of a "shrinking show of weakness" in the face of communism. On the meeting with Watkins, he shrilled that Ike "sees fit to congratulate those who hold up the exposure of Communists and... urges tolerance and niceties to those who are torturing our uniformed men." McCarthy concluded with an "apology to the American people" for ever having supported Eisenhower.[130]

Though column and editorial comment would not come until later, there was a negative story on page 11 of the same issue, under M'CARTHY RALLY DISAPPOINTING. This function, which took place in Queens, was sponsored by the Veterans of Foreign Wars and the Catholic War Veterans. Among the bitter-end McCarthyites in attendance were William F. Buckley, J. B. Matthews, Pegler, Admiral Crommelin, and Fordham Political Science Professor Godfrey Schmidt. Pegler was the first to admit that the rally had been a failure: "We've been laying some terrible eggs lately," he wrote. "We're a minority, I don't know why we can't turn out a good crowd." Pegler added that McCarthy's failure to appear, allegedly on doctor's orders, was a "cruel disappointment."[131]

The first editorial attack on McCarthy came on December 9 in the *Journal-American.* "Senator McCarthy has done nothing to close the breach within the Republican party by accusing President Eisenhower of being soft on Communism." The editorial added that McCarthy "has confused his recent troubles with the issues of war and peace, a field in which Ike continues to operate with poise and determination."[132]

A page 2 story in the same issue was headed WARNED M'C NOT TO BLAST IKE. The "warner" was Senator Karl Mundt, a longtime McCarthy ally who voted against censure. Said Mundt: "Everybody knows that Ike is not for Communism."[133]

The next day the *Mirror* carried an even stronger anti-McCarthy editorial: "Senator McCarthy should realize that the American people are not going to be sold a bill of goods that President Ike is 'soft' on Communism." The editorial ended with the dismissive comment that "as far as Joe's fevered blast goes toward making Ike unpopular, Joe should have stood in bed."[134]

The blows were coming thick and fast. On December 11 a page 1 story in the *Journal-American* covered a repudiation of McCarthy by an influential former supporter. General James Van Fleet, ex-commander of the Eighth Army in Korea, had been on the staff of Ten Million Americans Mobilizing for Justice. Hearing of McCarthy's attack on Eisenhower, he sent off an angry telegram:

> I AM SHOCKED BY YOUR BITTER ATTACK AGAINST THE
> PRESIDENT OF THE UNITED STATES... IN THE PAST I HAVE
> SUPPORTED YOU IN YOUR FIGHT AGAINST INTERNA-
> TIONAL COMMUNISM BUT I HAVE NEVER AGREED WITH
> YOUR METHODS... THIS LATEST ATTACK ON OUR GREAT
> PRESIDENT CAUSES ME TO WITHDRAW ALL SUPPORT.[135]

The next day Winchell wrote that "*Newsweek* revealed the public is thoroughly bored with the McCarthy controversy."[136] Winchell would make only two more references to McCarthy: a friendly one (about his diet) in 1956 and a favorable one at the time of his death. Though he still liked McCarthy – despite later disclaimers – he was too much of a professional to continue writing about a figure who was now causing vast public apathy.

A profound change had taken place at the *Journal-American* and *Mirror* during the past twenty-one months. Between March 1950 and March 1953 the New York Hearst papers functioned as a pro-McCarthy monolith; in 1953 the façade cracked; in 1954 it fragmented. By late 1954 the *Journal-American/Mirror* umbrella covered true believers like Pegler and Tompkins, occasionally critical McCarthyites like Sokolsky and Fulton Lewis, more-in-sorrow-than-anger anti-McCarthyites like Bill Hearst, moderate anti-McCarthyites like Bob Considine, strong anti-

McCarthyites like Frank Conniff, and, until his dismissal in October, anti-Cohn McCarthyites like Howard Rushmore.

David Oshinsky writes that McCarthy's December 7 attack on Eisenhower (a Pearl Harbor in reverse) was "the last front-page McCarthy story (except for his death in 1957)...."[137] Though Oshinsky was talking about the press in general, he could as easily have been referring to the Hearst press alone. A new policy on McCarthy coverage was coming – a policy that would be implemented as vigorously by journals that once supported McCarthy as by those which once opposed him. Nineteen fifty-five ushered in what Joe McCarthy hated and feared most: the reign of silence.

8. 1955-57: The Reign of Silence

When we speak of a reign of silence covering press coverage on McCarthy in his last years, this should not be interpreted as meaning a total blackout. A better term would be "brownout." News articles appeared from time to time – but these were usually brief and well away from the front pages.

If a blackout existed, it was in area of comment. The news writers played McCarthy down but the editorialists and columnists played him *out*. This policy was multi-partisan; McCarthy's utterances and actions were as much ignored on the right as on the center and left. It was often said of McCarthy that he wanted to be liked but would rather be hated than ignored. Now his worst nightmare had come true. Nothing he said, nothing he did, could gain either praise from the right-wing opinion writers or denunciation from their liberal *confrères*.

Why, almost without exception, did McCarthy's remaining partisans among Hearst writers join in the conspiracy of silence? Simply, because they were professionals and McCarthy was no longer news. In the past, the Peglers and Sokolskys had never scrupled at outraging readers by championing McCarthy's worst excesses. Hatred, after all, indicates interest. But now they were facing a blank wall of boredom. So they turned to more provocative subjects.

McCarthy was further damaged by the Democratic victory in November. He no longer had his committee chairmanship, having been replaced by John McClellan of Arkansas. McClellan was a conservative, a segregationist, and had exemplary anti-communist credentials. With such a man at the head of Government Operations, the Hearst press saw no need to be nostalgic about McCarthy. On January 11 a *Journal-American* editorial hailed as "bipartisanship" the fact that McClellan and another Democratic colleague on the committee, Henry M. ("Scoop") Jackson of Washington, had vigorously criticized the way the Army handled the Peress case.[1] Though Jackson was a domestic liberal (we recall his capework with poor David Schine), he was also a defense-minded hawk and arch-foe of Soviet expansionism.

At first, McCarthy didn't seem to grasp that he had been targeted for oblivion. On January 8 the *Journal-American's* headline read SENATE SEEN REOPENING PERESS CASE. Seeing a profile-raising opportunity, McCarthy called for a new investigation that would include Robert Stevens, General Zwicker, Army counsel John G. Adams, and Lieutenant General Walter L. Werble, the Army's deputy chief of staff. The probe would focus on a report prepared by Adams and Werble that Peress had been honorably discharged because he had engaged in no subversive activity during his tour of duty in the Army. Though McCarthy's demand was mentioned in the news story, there was no editorial or column comment.[2] In view of the sensational nature of McCarthy's charge, that silence in the opinion pages represented a definite break with tradition.

Five days later there was a column comment on the revived Peress case. But it wasn't calculated to bring solace to McCarthy. In a bored and reductive summary, Sokolsky dismissed the case as a "hardly important... paper snafu" and proof that "men do not like to admit errors if they can cover them up."[3]

On January 18 a *Journal-American* editorial did praise the committee's renewed interest in the Peress case – but in a manner that excluded McCarthy. By now the Hearst hero was McClellan, a "highly-respected investigator" who "intends to find out definitely who promoted and protected Major Peress."[4]

On that same day there appeared one of the rare favorable column references to McCarthy. His benefactor was that most loyal and uncompromising of the hard-liners: E. F. Tompkins. Tompkins, noting that McCarthy still had four years to serve in the Senate, expressed the wistful hope that he would "continue to be a figure of political importance."[5]

During the honeymoon years of the alliance, any personal affront to McCarthy would have been greeted by Hearst writers with howls of outrage. On January 21st he suffered a social indignity so spiteful that even such anti-McCarthy commentators as Rovere, Reeves, and Oshinsky remarked on its pettiness.[6] Mary Jane McCaffree, social secretary to Mrs. Eisenhower, announced that henceforth McCarthy would be the only senator not invited to White House dinners. Predictably, the sole expression of protest in a New York Hearst paper came from Pegler. "Now I want to say," he wrote, "that I would not accept an invitation to anything from Eisenhower because I consider him my social, moral, and ethical inferior."[7]

But the news accounts were cold and unsympathetic. A page 2 story in the *Journal-American* was headed MCCARTHYS NOT ASKED TO IKE DINNERS. It quoted McCaffree as saying that the deliberate snub was a "decision on the part of the President and Mrs. Eisenhower." The article also noted that McCarthy had assailed Ike for "a shrinking show of weakness toward communism" on December 7, 1954 – leaving the impression that McCarthy was rather getting what he deserved.[8]

A page 6 *Mirror* story on the same day appeared under M'C NOT ASKED TO IKE DINNERS. The article claimed that McCarthy had "laughed over the phone" when asked his reaction to the Eisenhower snub.[9] Though McCarthy feigned amusement, he was in fact deeply hurt by the Eisenhowers' cavalier gesture.[10]

Mr. Hearst Goes to Moscow

If ever a man was in the right place at the right time, it was the amiable Bill Hearst in January-February 1955. In December of the previous year, more as a joke than anything else, he had applied for a visa to the Soviet Union. Fully expecting to be turned down, he was astounded when his application was approved immediately. Wary, conscious of his limitations, Hearst did not want to make the trip without two of his top aides. He requested visas for them and they too were granted on the spot. The aides in question were Frank Conniff, now serving as editorial assistant and part-time ghost writer for Hearst, and J. Kingsbury Smith, European general manager of INS, the Hearst wire service.

Things could not have gone better for the Hearst team. Among the Soviet dignitaries they interviewed were Secretary of the Communist Party Nikita Khrushchev, Marshal Gyorgy Zhukov, who led the Russian armies into Berlin, and Foreign Minister Vyacheslav Molotov. Then came an unexpected dividend. The one figure they had not interviewed, Premier Gyorgy Malenkov, was deposed in a bloodless coup on February 8 and replaced by Marshal Nikolai Bulganin. Bulganin immediately agreed to see the Hearst correspondents. Not only did they interview the Soviet Union's leading statesmen but were on hand to witness a dramatic change in leadership.

All the high-level interviewees had the same message for their American guests: the Soviets were interested in peaceful coexistence with the West. On his return to America, Bill Hearst was invited to the White

House. There he told the president that he endorsed the principle of peaceful coexistence – while "keeping our guard up and maintaining a strong retaliatory force in readiness."[11] In 1956, the Hearst team jointly received the Pulitzer Prize for international reporting. The White House meeting represented an epic change in Hearst policy toward the Soviets. Where the Hearst papers continued to be wary of Soviet intentions and tough on domestic subversion, gone was the milleniary attitude of the late forties and early fifties, when Hearst writers seemed to be preparing their readers for atomic Armageddon.

I have been unable, from research, correspondence, and interviews, to uncover any criticism by McCarthy of the Hearst team's mission to Moscow. Thomas A. Bolan, Roy Cohn's former law partner, informed the writer that he had no recollection of McCarthy ever commenting on the trip.[12]

This is strange, especially if we consider some of the things that McCarthy had said, and would be saying, about the administration's "shrinking show of weakness" toward the Soviets. Perhaps reticence was induced by his longtime friendship with Bill Hearst; also, McCarthy may have been reluctant to break irrevocably with a newspaper chain where he still had supporters.

If McCarthy withheld criticism of Hearst's relations with Moscow, the administration enjoyed no such exemption. On February 13 the headline of á page 12 *Journal-American story* was IKE ACCUSED BY MCC OF GIVING LANDS TO REDS. McCarthy charged that "the Eisenhower administration had reneged on its campaign promises and surrendered territory piecemeal through so-called coexistence."[13] In what was becoming an increasingly familiar pattern, McCarthy's blast elicited no column or editorial comment in either the *Journal-American* or *Mirror*.

The Hearst strategy was clearly one of undermining McCarthy by indirection. Instead of attacking him frontally – which would have violated the "brownout" principle – the New York Hearst papers speeded McCarthy's decline by praising his rivals and enemies.

On March 16 George Rothwell Brown got in some kind words for a new Hearst favorite. "Mr. McClellan," he wrote, "has informed that his inquiry into the Peress case will be thorough and sweeping."[14]

Brown's praise of McClellan came on the heels of a McCarthy charge that John Foster Dulles "had set a hundred and fifty men to censoring the Yalta papers."[15] There was no mention of the accusation in either the *Journal-American* or *Mirror*. Instead, the former carried a front page editorial by Bill Hearst lauding Eisenhower in a manner reminiscent of those obligatory tributes to Stalin or Mao. "Eisenhower has been a great president," he gushed, "and the country is prosperous under an administration which has returned to American principles."[16]

On March 19 a strongly pro-Zwicker article appeared on page 9 of the *Journal-American.* Headed ZWICKER TRIED TO OUST PERESS, it called attention to a 1953 memorandum prepared by the general. The memo stated that "retention of Captain Peress is clearly not consistent with the interests of national security. It is requested that immediate steps be taken to effect his relief from active duty."[17] Though Zwicker, for security reasons, had not told McCarthy of the memo during their February 18, 1954 confrontation, the article emphasized that he did send a copy to Lieutenant General W. A. Burress, commanding general of the First Army.[18]

In June came the worst defeat of McCarthy's career, even more humiliating than the censure resolution. Eisenhower was then preparing to meet Khrushchev at the Geneva summit. The president had pleased all the Democrats and almost all the Republicans by assuring them that he had no intention of giving anything away at Geneva. "Geneva," he said, "is not going to be another Yalta."[19]

Still, McCarthy saw the opportunity to make trouble. By now he would do anything to embarrass the administration and make Ike and his advisers appear soft on the Soviets. On June 21 he introduced a resolution that the summit agenda should include the status of the Eastern European nations that had been saddled with pro-Soviet regimes.

The proposal was absurd. Moscow's overriding obsession was to have "friendly" states on its borders and Khrushchev was not going to Geneva to put his country's military security on the bargaining table.

McCarthy's resolution was defeated by a 77-4 margin, with only Jenner, George W. ("Molly") Malone of Nevada, and the North Dakota liberal isolationist William L. Langer supporting McCarthy. Backing the administration were such erstwhile McCarthy stalwarts as Welker of Idaho, Styles Bridges of New Hampshire, Mundt, Dirksen of Illinois, Hugh Butler of Nebraska, and minority leader William Knowland of California.

McCarthy, probably impaired by advancing alcoholism, appears to have taken leave of his senses. After blasting the Democrats' tendency to "whine and whimper" in the face of Communist aggression, he launched an attack on Knowland, a hard-liner so enamored of Chiang Kai-shek and his cause that he was known as "the senator from Formosa." In a page 1 story on June 22, McCarthy was quoted as being "surprised, shocked, and disappointed" by Knowland's vote against his resolution. McCarthy reminded Knowland that "it is not the role of the Republican party to backtrack, to appease, to whine, to whimper." A furious Knowland shot back that "I'll lay my record of opposition to communism against that of the senator from Wisconsin."[20]

This rebuff made McCarthy even more of a pariah in the Senate. During the 1952 campaign he was considered a major Republican asset and was continually in demand as a speaker. Now he was deemed an embarrassment even by the GOP right-wingers. Commenting on the dazzling rapidity of McCarthy's decline, David Oshinsky points out that "in February 1954 the Senate voted to fund his committee by an 85-1 margin, in December the censure vote was 67-22, and in June 1955 his resolution was squashed by a 77-4 total."[21]

McCarthy's personal conduct also played a part in his deterioration. Noting his increasing irrationality and dependence on alcohol, colleagues would pointedly shun him. Still, there were bizarre incidents. McCarthy had conceived a special hatred for Arthur Watkins. When they encountered each other, McCarthy would whisper, "How is the little coward from Utah?" Ralph Flanders, himself high on McCarthy's hate list, wrote that "the Wisconsin senator never forgave (Watkins). McCarthy's seat was directly behind that of the Utah senator, and he took advantage of his location to murmur jibes and insults into the ear of the man who had brought him to judgment before his peers. Watkins finally asked to be moved to a new location so he could be free of daily annoyance."[22]

For the time that was left to him, Joe McCarthy existed in the Senate as a sort of political zombie. He was biologically alive, he had his seniority and committee assignments, but he was totally without influence, without respect, and – increasingly – without friends.

McCarthyism Without McCarthy

If McCarthy was "dead" in those last twenty-nine months between his censure and medical death, McCarthyism was alive and well. Despite the Wisconsin senator's political and personal troubles, 1955 was the blacklisters' best year.[23]

As McCarthy faded, a new figure was coming into prominence as America's most feared guardian of political conformity. Vincent Hartnett was an unpleasant combination of puritan and blackmailer. A graduate of Notre Dame University and World War II Navy Intelligence officer, he began his postwar career by writing radio scripts for $60 a week.[24] In 1952, Hartnett teamed up with a blacklister named Paul Milton and founded Aware Inc. This was an organization "which published, listed, and cleared names for pay."[25]

Hartnett made no bones about his "greed-is-good" philosophy. As he expressed it: "I think I would be a complete ass if I did it for nothing."[26] Hartnett had a sliding scale of fees: $5 for a report on any person's political background; $2 for additional checking; $20 for a compilation of letterheads, petitions, etc. For $500 any qualified person could inspect his files – a "qualified person" being one with $500.[27] At the same time, Hartnett had none of the joviality that characterized such other celebrated scoundrels as Gaston B. Means. A humorless prig, he withdrew his patronage from a drugstore because he was displeased by calendars of "scantily-clad" women above the candy counter.[28]

Yet this Pecksniff became the most ruthless blacklister of the decade.[28] The only reason he wasn't more dangerous is that he pretty much confined himself to the entertainment industry. What Hartnett had going for him was energy. Along with blacklisting and blackmailing, he was a tireless writer and lecturer on subversion. In June 1953 he published an article in the *American Mercury* called "The Great Red Way." It began: "As the purge of Communist and notable Communist-fronters continues in Hollywood, Broadway is fast emerging as the last stronghold of show business Marxists."[30] These included Leonard Bernstein, James Thurber, Oscar Hammerstein, Melvyn Douglas, Lillian Hellman, and Moss Hart.[31] Hartnett was also offended by Broadway's moral tone, even when there was no discernible Red connection. In this context he singled out producer Cheryl Crawford, an "Algonquin oddity" with a "mannish bob."[32] Hartnett even voiced suspicions about Elia Kazan, a man who had recanted, informed, and been denounced by the *Daily Worker* in the most sulphurous terms. Why Kazan? Hartnett was disturbed because Kazan had produced Tennessee Williams's *Camino Real*. Williams, according to Hartnett, had been "conducting a flirtation with the Communist-front movement for years." "When," he signed off, "will he theater-going public get wise to the con game being operated on New York's Great Red Way?"[33]

With this background, Hartnett was well suited to play an important role in the era of post-McCarthy McCarthyism. Hartnett's industry and innovative style breathed new life into such as Jack O'Brian, the *Journal-American's* telecommunications ferret who no longer had McCarthy to praise.

Armed with tidbits from one of the blacklisting groups, O'Brian went into a frenzy of denunciation in his column of July 13, 1955. Pointing a finger at the proprietors of the off-Broadway Phoenix Theater, he bashed them for "providing employment for all sorts of lefties." Among them were Waldo Salt ("a 5th amendment character named eleven times as a

Red member"), Howard De Sylva ("named as a Commie member"), and Howard Bay ("another 5th amendment Red dauber"). Significantly, the same column contained a plug for the "savage elegance" of Lena Horne. Horne – for a fee – had recently been cleared by American Business Consultants, the blacklist group that supported *Red Channels*.[34]

Three weeks earlier O'Brian had gone after a figure who needed no identification from Vincent Hartnett or anyone else. Tex McCrary, co-host of the "Tex and Jinx" radio interview show, had invited the recently released Alger Hiss to appear as a guest. O'Brian expressed pleasure over news that McCrary had bowed to pressure and withdrawn the invitation.[35]

In the meantime, Hartnett continued on his merry way. In May 1955 he received a letter of congratulation from J. Edgar Hoover – who was no longer speaking to McCarthy – for the help he had rendered FBI agents. Hartnett was also adept at helping himself. In one article, under a pseudonym in a Catholic magazine, he lauded Vincent Hartnett for his "firsthand knowledge of certain Communist activities in program production."[36] Under his own name, he wrote an article for the *American Legion Magazine* criticizing the Borden Milk Corporation for its laxness in permitting subversives to act in Borden-sponsored programs. With touching solicitude, Hartnett informed Borden executives of the forthcoming story – and immediately found himself hired as a security consultant at $10,000 a year. The article still appeared, but as one of commendation for Borden's vigilance in *not* sponsoring subversives.

Happily, this story has an ending that would do credit to a medieval morality play. Hartnett and an ally, a Syracuse supermarket proprietor named Laurence Johnson, were sued by one of their victims. He was John Henry Faulk, the Texas humorist mentioned in Chapter 2. In his suit, Faulk was represented by Louis Nizer. At the trial, an advertising agent named Jack Wren said of Hartnett that "I had to treat with him as a merchant treats with a racketeer who sells him protection."[38] In 1962 the jury handed down a $3.5 million judgment against Hartnett, Aware Inc., and the estate of the recently deceased Laurence Johnson. The award was cut to $350,000 by the Appellate Division in 1963; that figure was upheld by the New York State Court of Appeals in 1964.[39]

With the Faulk case, the era of post-McCarthy McCarthyism came to end. The blacklist was broken and the blacklisters were out of business.

The ignominious failure of his satellite nations resolution did not deter McCarthy from continuing his attacks on the administration. At the same time, he began making efforts to ingratiate himself with powerful figures who had been allies and supporters in the past.

One of these was Douglas MacArthur. On September 13, 1955, a page 4 *Journal-American* article was headed M'C PROPOSES IKE NAME MAC HIS ADVISER IN EAST. In suggesting that such an appointment would "lighten" the president's "work load and worries," McCarthy was attempting to exploit underlying friction that undoubtedly existed between Eisenhower and MacArthur.[40] (Eisenhower had been MacArthur's aide, MacArthur had had presidential ambitions, and now Ike was in the White House.)

Nothing came of this ill-fated venture. Though a Chicago eccentric named Lar Daly (who campaigned in an Uncle Sam suit) once proposed a MacArthur-McCarthy ticket, there is no evidence that they were ever more than temporary allies. While McCarthy followed the Hearst line and supported MacArthur in 1952, MacArthur must have remembered McCarthy's vicious campaign against him in 1948. In support of Stassen, McCarthy "accused MacArthur of railroading (General) Billy Mitchell, dredged up details of his divorce... and charged that the General was Stalin's agent."[41]

In the meantime, the Hearst-Eisenhower love feast continued. In a 1956 New Year's Day editorial, printed on the front page of the *Journal-American,* Bill Hearst expressed delight over reports that the president's health was good and on his decision to run for a second term. He concluded that "this editorial will close with sincere wishes to... Ike and Dick for a Healthy, Happy, and Prosperous New Year."[42]

Two days later McCarthy struck at an old enemy – the bibulous Tom Hennings of Missouri. M'CARTHY SEEKS TO END TWO PROBES OF SECURITY PROGRAM was the headline of a page 19 story in the *Mirror.* He proposed to cut funds to two committees that had been critical of the government's loyalty/security program. These were the Senate Judiciary Committee, headed by Hennings, and the Senate Civil Service Committee, under Olin Johnston of South Carolina. Johnston was one of the Southern conservatives who had voted for censure. McCarthy charged that the committees were "wrecking the security program, what there is of it." He reminded his colleagues that in 1955 the Democratic-controlled Senate passed a resolution calling for a continuing investigation of communism. "Instead," he said, "we have two committees doing everything they can to make it hard on a person fighting communism."[43]

On January 27 a picture of McCarthy appeared on the front page of the *Journal-American.* The photograph – showing a grossly fat McCarthy – could only have been taken with malice aforethought. McCarthy's grotesque appearance was directly related to his drinking problem. He would go on the wagon (which for him meant substituting beer for bourbon), "run alarmingly to fat, and then he would grow gaunt" as he resumed heavy drinking and eating next to nothing.[44] The accompanying story needed no slanting to reflect McCarthy's paranoid state of mind. Speaking of the censure, he described it as "a conspiracy to do a good smear job on me."[45]

With his many sources, and with McCarthy's alcoholism now Washington's worst-kept secret, it is inconceivable that Winchell could have been unaware of it. Yet he was moved to render his old friend one more service. On April 16 he wrote that "Senator Joe McCarthy lost 29 lbs. in 6 weeks with this diet – no bread, potatoes, sugar, or salt. His breakfast: one poached egg."[46] This portrayal of the senator as a health-conscious dieter was the last Winchell column mention in McCarthy's lifetime.

In July McCarthy made another futile attempt to bring down an enemy. Of all the liberal Republican businessmen who supported Eisenhower, there was none McCarthy detested more than Paul Hoffman, board chairman of Studebaker. During the censure fight Hoffman had raised $12,000 against McCarthy. He also joined a group of prominent Americans, including theologian Reinhold Niebuhr, Hollywood's Sam Goldwyn, and labor leader Walter Reuther, in sending a public telegram that urged bipartisan support for the censure motion.[47]

Learning that Eisenhower was planning to appoint Hoffman U.S. representative to the UN General Assembly, McCarthy furiously denounced him on a television program. Among other inelegant characterizations, he called Hoffman "a throwback on the human race."[48]

On July 13 the *Journal-American* took note of the controversy in "Latest News," a column feature of press bulletins. Under the heading IKE ANSWERS MCC – NAMES HOFFMAN ENVOY TO UN, the text noted that "President Eisenhower accepted a challenge by Senator Joseph McCarthy to name Paul Hoffman as U.S. representative to the UN General Assembly."[49] The "challenge" referred to McCarthy daring Eisenhower to appoint Hoffman, whom he described as "a huckster of one of the major themes of the Communist Party line," that the fight against communism is destroying civil liberties.[50]

If McCarthy had given up on Eisenhower, he apparently nursed the forlorn (and completely unrealistic) hope that he could patch things up with Nixon. With the 1956 Republican convention coming up, Harold Stassen was leading a drive to get Nixon off the ticket and replace him with Massachusetts governor Christian Herter. Though he never attended the convention, McCarthy leaped into the controversy and attacked the man he had once supported for president. (Relations between McCarthy and Stassen had been frigid since their clash over the Greek shipowners.) On August 6 a page 5 story in the *Journal-American* quoted McCarthy as saying that Stassen was "trying to ingratiate himself with the (Republican) left-wingers so he could be nominated for president in 1960."[51]

The following day the *Mirror* carried a more explicit story. On page 6, under M'CARTHY SAYS STASSEN WANTS TO BE IKE HEIR, McCarthy accused Stassen of launching a "dump Nixon" campaign in an effort to become "heir-apparent to President Eisenhower as leader of the left wing of the GOP." McCarthy also described Stassen as "one of the most contemptible politicians of our era."[52]

Gratitude was not one of Richard Nixon's defining characteristics, as McCarthy would learn from a humiliating experience during the campaign. That fall, having turned back Stassen's effort to get him off the ticket, Nixon was campaigning in Wisconsin. One night there was a dinner for him at Milwaukee's Schroeder Hotel. Though McCarthy had not been invited, he showed up anyway. He may have believed, in his alcohol-fogged mind, that Nixon would remember his assistance against Stassen. This was not to be. As a frozen-faced vice-president looked on, one of the banquet dignitaries asked McCarthy to leave, which he did. Later, a reporter encountered him sitting in an alley and weeping uncontrollably.[53]

Of all the defections McCarthy had to endure in his last years, none hurt him more than that of J. Edgar Hoover. Despite the damage Hoover had done him during the Army-McCarthy hearings, McCarthy never turned on the FBI director. Instead, his behavior resembled that of an unrequited lover who refuses to acknowledge rejection. In and out of the Senate, he mentioned his friendship with Hoover in "speech after speech, giving the impression that they remained bosom buddies in the fight against the subversive menace."[54] This was pathetic wishful thinking. When McCarthy called FBI headquarters, Hoover was either "in conference" or "out of town." Even Lou Nichols, the FBI's publicity director, referred McCarthy's calls to an assistant. Desperately, McCarthy launched a "Hoover for President" boomlet in 1956. Hoover neither acknowledged the effort nor thanked him. Even the accomplishments of McCarthy's heyday were denigrated. In *The FBI Story,* a Bureau-approved book by Don Whitehead, McCarthy's name is not mentioned in the index.[55]

In early 1957 the *Journal-American* supported a White House appointee opposed by McCarthy. William J. Brennan, a Democratic New Jersey judge, was named by Eisenhower to the Supreme Court. Testifying before the Senate, Brennan avowed his strong support for congressional committees investigating subversion. Brennan's testimony was reported on page 2 of the February 26 *Journal-American,* under BRENNAN SEES POWER TO QUIZ REDS AS VITAL. Casting the lone dissenting vote against Brennan's confirmation, McCarthy said that the nominee "demonstrated an underlying hostility to Congressional attempts to expose the Communist conspiracy."[56]

In fairness, McCarthy was partly right. In a Paris-is-worth-a-mass gesture, Brennan got himself approved by talking like a tough, hard-line foe of domestic subversion who would not be too squeamish about civil liberties. Once on the Court, he became one of its most liberal members.

On April 1, a month before his death, McCarthy made yet another futile attempt to scuttle an adversary. The Senate was considering the promotion of Ralph W. Zwicker to temporary major general and permanent brigadier general. Zwicker breezed in with only two dissenting votes – those of McCarthy and George W. ("Molly") Malone of Nevada.

Though there was no editorial or column comment, both the *Journal-American* and *Mirror* ran stories with an anti-McCarthy tilt. The *Journal-American's* story, on page 2, stated that "in a speech before today's vote, McCarthy contended that Zwicker had lied under oath... Senator Russell (D.-Ga.), chairman of the Armed Forces Committee... retorted that he had no evidence that... Zwicker had lied. Both Russell and Sen. Stennis (D.-Miss.)... praised Zwicker as an outstanding officer."[57] The *Mirror* story appeared on p. 7, under the highly slanted headline SENATE IGNORES M'CARTHY, OKS GEN. ZWICKER. The story noted that both McCarthy and Zwicker had lied under oath when they denied giving investigators security information about Major Peress.[58]

Joe McCarthy died on May 2, at 5:02 p.m. in the Bethesda Naval Hospital. He had been admitted on April 28, his ever-protective wife explaining that he was being treated for a knee injury. Though cause of death was given as acute hepatic failure, it was an open secret that McCarthy really died of cirrhosis of the liver.

McCarthy's physical decline was surely accelerated by a financial disaster he suffered in early 1957. In January a brief ray of sunshine had come into his life. Through the influence of Cardinal Spellman, the McCarthys adopted a baby girl from New York's Catholic Foundling Hospital. His spirits revived by the adoption, McCarthy talked of quitting politics, buying a ranch in Arizona, and practicing law for a few of his friends. Then came chilling news: a uranium company in which he was heavily invested had gone belly up. His partner, a Green Bay man, was a fugitive in South America.[59] With this reverse, "he fell off the wagon in a heap and never did get on again."[60]

Final commentary on McCarthy reflected the broad spectrum of opinion among Hearst writers. On May 3, the *Mirror's* headline read M'C DIES IN HOSPITAL. The article's emphasis was slightly anti-McCarthy. "The Wisconsin senator," it read, "had been one of the most controversial men in American public life. He was a key figure in the investigations of communism which roused high feelings in the early 50s, but he faded to relative obscurity after the Senate voted condemnation of some of his conduct in 1954."[61]

More sympathetic was a page 2 editorial in the same issue, probably written by Bill Hearst. Under A WARRIOR IS LOST, it described "Senator Joe McCarthy as a young giant of our times... he struck hard when powerhouse punching was needed. Some times (sic) the swings were wild. We criticized him for his means, never for his ends."[62]

This for-all-his-faults-we-love-him-still tone was conspicuously absent from a story that appeared that same day on page 1 of the *Journal-American*. Under MCCARTHY SERVICES IN SENATE TODAY, the article began with the information that "this was the first such rite since the death of (Idaho Republican) Senator (William E.) Borah." While the article's presentation was balanced, it demonstrated not the slightest friendliness toward McCarthy. "The Wisconsin senator with the grindstone voice was admired by some as an anti-Communist patriot, but denounced by others as a witch hunter... His end closed out a brawling chapter in American history."[63]

On page 4 of the same issue was a human interest story about Jean McCarthy by INS special correspondent Ruth Montgomery. The headline – TOOK COURAGE TO WED JOE – AND JEAN HAD IT – must have struck readers as ambiguous. Though the story turned out to be a puff piece about the McCarthys' supposedly idyllic domestic life, the headline might incline one to think that it was about the difficulty of living with McCarthy.[64]

That issue also contained a signed editorial by Bill Hearst. Headed VALIANT WARRIOR, it mourned the passing of an old pal who had gone astray. Recalling that their friendship dated back to 1947, Hearst went on to encapsulate McCarthy's career. He was "a saber-slashing warrior... whose one motive was to smash the Communist conspiracy." Yet "there were times when his saber swings were misdirected." He was "reckless and overzealous" and "did not have positive proof that many of those he suspected were actual card-holding Communists." Hearst concluded that "we on this paper have lost a friend."[65]

On May 6 came Sokolsky's tribute; the column heading was JOE'S

ONLY INTEREST WAS HIS COUNTRY. Though affectionate, Sokolsky's final homage paints the picture of a man who is not overly bright. "He never understood the Army's fight against him, because he thought it was the Army's first duty to protect the country from traitors." There was definitely a high-level cabal out to get McCarthy, "though Bob Stevens had little to do with the effort to destroy (him)." The conspiracy was headed by individuals who "acted as if they were his close political friends" but who "knew his weaknesses" and were determined to "kill his influence."[66] Though Sokolsky was no stranger to the paranoid style of reporting, this assessment is essentially correct. As validation of his point, one has only to consider the deviousness of Nixon, Rogers *et al.*

Sokolsky next turned to the 1958 campaign. "Though McCarthy believed he could win in 1958, he knew he would have to take on the entire Republican administration." On the touchy subject of McCarthy's alcoholism, Sokolsky took refuge behind euphemisms. "McCarthy appeared physically powerful, but he was not a strong man and he faced a terrific fight while his health was ebbing away." In the end, "he was hounded to death by those who would not forget and could not forgive." Sokolsky wound up the column with this undoubtedly sincere tribute: "Joe McCarthy was my friend and I have never encountered an opponent of his who equaled him in patriotism and courage. God rest his soul and forgive those who sent him to his death."[67]

Walter Winchell's farewell came on the same day: "One thing about Senator McCarthy's leaving. At least there aren't as many Commies to rejoice."[68] This from the man who supposedly broke with McCarthy over his attacks on Eisenhower!

In the May 7 *Mirror* it was Victor Riesel's turn to salute the fallen hero. His approach was to treat readers to some interesting, if little-known, McCarthyiana. Under the column heading THE REAL ISSUE LEFT BY M'CARTHY, Riesel claimed that early in his career McCarthy advocated "a national commission to sift all that was known about communism." This body would be headed by labor leader David Dubinsky, Bernard Baruch, and Judge Harold Medina, who presided over the trials of the twelve Communist leaders. Nothing came of the idea and it wasn't mentioned again for years. But one day Riesel brought up the subject. McCarthy grinned and said, "Don't print that, you'll only embarrass your friends." This was clearly a reference to Dubinsky, the liberal but militantly anti-communist president of the International Ladies Garment Workers Union. Riesel added that "there was in his jest the recognition that he was feared by many crusading anti-communists."

Analyzing McCarthy's methodology, Riesel said that his tactic was "to fight Stalin as Stalin would have fought Stalin – no holds barred, no attack too rough, no stratagem too relentless." Riesel concluded that McCarthy "focused attention on the Communist issue as no man did in the decades that ran turbulently between the days of the Russian Revolution and his days in the Senate."[69]

How much did the press "brownout" of 1955-57 contribute to McCarthy's spectacular collapse and early death? This is a question that should be considered in the context of McCarthy's dominating compulsion. No serious student of the McCarthy era has ever suggested that he had the ruthless fixation on power that characterized a Hitler or a Stalin. Though some detected fascism in McCarthy's style, there is nothing in his words or actions to indicate that he dreamed of becoming an American Führer.

Richard Rovere and Edward Bennett Williams wrote that McCarthy possessed not a power drive but a glory drive. He had in him little of the dictator and much of the demagogue – but a demagogue who seeks tumult, headlines, and public attention more than he does control. (One could never see McCarthy in the role of a powerful, though little known, *éminence grise.*)

Given these priorities, McCarthy was particularly vulnerable to the sort of damage that a reign of silence could inflict. A serious revolutionary would have taken advantage of a press brownout to build up a clandestine organization; Joe McCarthy got drunk and gave way to despair.

If there is a metaphor for the extent to which McCarthy was discredited in those last twenty-nine months, it is an incident that took place in July 1956. John Cogley, editor of the liberal Catholic periodical *Commonweal,* had published his two-volume *Report On Blacklisting,* sponsored by the Fund for the Republic. The *Report* had sufficient impact to trigger an investigation by HUAC, which worked hand-in-glove with the blacklisters.[70] Along with detailing the activities of Hartnett, Aware Inc. *et al.,* Cogley related instances of the menacing pressure that the blacklisters could exert. By 1955, for example, they had intimidated so many members of the Writers Guild that that body came within three votes of constitutionally barring from membership any writer who had taken the Fifth Amendment before a congressional committee.[71] Stung by Cogley's charges, Hartnett, the master blacklister, turned on his tormentor and accused him of – McCarthyism![72]

Epilogue:
McCarthy as Redbaiter – An Inquiry

Though this is primarily a study of the relationship between Joe McCarthy and New York's Hearst press, it is nevertheless appropriate to call in the larger question of his anti-communism. What was its essence? Was there something about it that would account for such puzzling behavior as McCarthy's indifference to the great Hearst crusades of the late forties? Or, for that matter, his wild post-censure attacks on the Eisenhower administration while the *Journal-American* and *Mirror* were trumpeting Ike's praises? Where opinion is unanimous that McCarthy was a redbaiter, it is sharply divided over exactly what kind of redbaiter he was.

There are two competing schools of thought about McCarthy's anti-communism. One contends that it was intrinsically phony, that McCarthy was very much a latecomer to the anti-communist fight, and that he redbaited with the instinct of a speculator. He needed an issue to get reelected in 1952 and, had either served his purpose, he would as eagerly have embraced ecology or Free Silver.

This view is challenged by more recent historians. They insist that McCarthy was sincere in his anti-communism and – by citing instances from the past – they reject notions that he was a redbaiter by instant conversion in late 1949 or early 1950.

Among leading proponents of the first view were investigative reporter Fred J. Cook, *New York Post* editor James Wechsler, and author-essayist Richard Rovere. Cook defined the 1945-50 period as a time when communist influence in government and the labor unions was being effectively nullified. Citing Walter Reuther's success in ousting Communist officials from the United Automobile Workers, Cook described that five-year period as "a span during which McCarthy expressed no great awareness of the (Communist) menace."[1]

Wechsler recalled McCarthy's attitude toward him when the editor was subpoenaed to appear before his committee. At no time did Wechsler detect a trace of ideological fervor. "I had the feeling," he wrote, "that he really wanted me to understand his point of view. He seemed to be saying, 'Look, bud, you've got your racket and I've got mine, and this is it. There's no need for you to be such a wet blanket.'"[2]

Rovere was the true godfather of the McCarthy-as-political-speculator family. In his book, published a year before Wechsler's and twelve years before Cook's, he returns to this theme again and again. McCarthy "was the leader of a fanatical movement, and he gave his name to a fanatical doctrine, but he was no kind of fanatic himself."[3] He was a "prince of hatred" and "the haters rallied round him... But this most successful and menacing of all our apostles of hatred was himself as incapable of true rancor, spite, and animosity as a eunuch is of marriage... He faked it all and could not understand anyone who didn't."[4]

Rovere was often amusing in recounting episodes that demonstrated McCarthy's cynicism. On one occasion, at a Washington party, McCarthy met "a former drinking companion, a man he had publicly betrayed and ruined. He went up to this man and within the hearing of astonished guests asked why they had not seen each other in months. 'Jeanie was talking about you the other night... how come we never see you? What the hell are you trying to do – avoid us?'"[5] Rovere concluded from this, and other incidents, that McCarthy was "numb to the sensations he produced in others. He could not comprehend true outrage, true indignation, true anything."[6]

Arthur Schlesinger, Rovere's collaborator in another work, was so impressed by his book that he wrote this effusive appraisal: "Senator Joe McCarthy is a brilliant essay in contemporary history, overflowing with wit and perception, and informed by an acute understanding of American politics. It is a memorable book."[7] Schlesinger fully endorsed Rovere's view of McCarthy as a manipulative opportunist who lacked firm anticommunist convictions. Both were convinced that McCarthy was very much a late hitter in tackling subversion. Rovere wrote that at "the start of 1950, (McCarthy) was a jackstraw in Washington. Then he discovered Communism – almost by inadvertence, as Columbus discovered America."[8]

Schlesinger relates that in 1952 McCarthy falsely accused him of advocating that Communists "should be allowed to teach your children." Schlesinger retorted that he was tired of "Joe-come-latelies" in the fight against communism. "At the time some of us were alerting the American people to the dangers of communism, McCarthy was accepting Communist support in his fight against Bob La Follette."[9]

In promoting the view that McCarthy won the 1946 Wisconsin primary with Communist support, Rovere is more guarded than Schlesinger. He notes that the Communists despised La Follette as a "liberal who regarded communism as totalitarian."[10] But he adds that "there is no evidence that the Communists instructed their following to enter the Republican primaries or give McCarthy any assistance beyond generalized attacks on La Follette."[11] He does, however, attribute to McCarthy the quote that "Communists have the same right to vote as anyone else."[12]

Curiously, a supporter of the Joe-come-lately position was Roy Cohn. In his book defending McCarthy, Cohn disputed a widely accepted theory that the senator first discovered communism during a 1950 dinner meeting with three fellow Roman Catholics. They were William A. Roberts, a liberal lawyer, Charles H. Kraus, professor of political science at Georgetown, and Father Edmund A. Walsh, regent of Georgetown's School of Foreign Service. According to this account, Roberts suggested that McCarthy's chances for reelection in 1952 would be enhanced if he came forward as a champion of the St. Lawrence Seaway. McCarthy rejected the issue as lacking sex appeal but responded eagerly to Father Walsh's suggestion that he focus on the power of communism to subvert American institutions. Though McCarthy promised Walsh, Kraus, and Roberts that he would never adopt an irresponsible approach to the fight against communism, "within a matter of months, all three of his companions felt called on to repudiate him."[13]

Cohn's own version revealed a penchant for melodrama. While he admitted that the dinner meeting took place, he insisted that "McCarthy had already bought the package a month or two earlier."[14] The "package" was McCarthy's decision to make communism his main issue; the "salesmen" were three men who visited his office just before Thanksgiving 1949. They were Pentagon officials, and what they brought him was a hundred-page report prepared in 1947 by the FBI about Communist espionage in the United States. Though the report had been circulated to several government agencies, including the Department of State, no action of any kind had ever been taken. Then McCarthy was shown the report and, if Cohn can be believed, the rest was history.

This cloak-and-dagger tale should not detract attention from a more important point: Cohn's conviction that McCarthy came late to the anti-communist struggle. "Joe McCarthy," he wrote, "bought Communism in much the same way as other people purchase a new automobile... (he) kicked the tires, sat at the wheel... asked some questions, and bought. It was just as cold as that." Cohn added that while McCarthy "reacted in quite the same reflexive manner as most Americans to foreign 'isms,'" he had "no special interest in Communism prior to the late fall of 1949."[15] Cohn represents a deviation from the norm set by Rovere, Wechsler, *et al.* While he agreed with them that McCarthy was tardy in embracing anti-communism, he believed, as they did not, that he was sincere.

It is wondrously ironic that Cohn, McCarthy's *fidus Achates,* saw him as a late-blooming Red hunter while later historians, all anti-McCarthy, insist that his anti-communism long preceded the November 1949 meeting with the Pentagon trio or the January 1950 meeting with the Catholic trio.

Thomas Reeves is particularly critical of Rovere, charging that his book was "more rhetorical than factual" and did not display "a serious commitment to historical research."[16] The nearest Rovere ever came to conceding that McCarthy recognized the existence of communism before 1950 was his admission that he had "trifled a bit with the Communist issue."[17] In the 1946 general election McCarthy had referred to his opponent as a candidate of the "Communist-controlled" CIO Political Action Committee and claimed that Communists favored public housing.[18] Rovere dismissed this as the "cant of the day," adding that McCarthy was just "playing with nonce words" and that "his voting record on the Cold War was that of a man who has not yet conceded its existence."[19]

Reeves rejects these attempts at trivialization. In the 1946 general election McCarthy's opponent was Howard J. McMurray, former congressman and lecturer in political science at the University of Wisconsin. McMurray, an anti-communist New Deal liberal, was dealt a low blow when he received a kiss-of-death endorsement from Fred Blau, chairman of the Wisconsin Communist party. Even worse, it came in the form of an open letter to the *Daily Worker.*

Though McMurray promptly disavowed the endorsement, McCarthy described him as "comunistically inclined."[20] Reeves concludes that "Joe had quickly learned how useful Red scare rhetoric can be."[21] Since McCarthy made redbaiting his major weapon in an election for the United States Senate, it is difficult to accept Rovere's assertion that McCarthy had just "trifled a bit with the Communist issue."

When did McCarthy become a True Believer? "If McCarthy ever had faith in a holy cause," wrote Rovere, "he lost it early (or acquired it very late, too late to do him any good), and he reposed all trust in himself."[22] Reeves, on the other hand, is very specific on this point, dating "the transformation (to zealotry) very soon after McCarthy's return to Washington in mid-February" of 1950. His one-time "frank cynicism... was soon replaced by an intense, almost fanatical interest in the Reds who lurked in high places... It was ironic that while critics railed at McCarthy for being wholly cynical... those closest to him knew that he had become a zealot."[23] An incident that convincingly buttresses this view was a meeting McCarthy had with Jack Anderson. The two were in McCarthy's office and "Joe began to lecture about the Communist conspiracy in Washington." Anderson thought it was all an act and asked McCarthy to "save it for the Senate floor." "No, no, no," he replied, "this is the real thing, Jack. This is the real thing."[24] Reeves states that "Anderson was shocked to learn that McCarthy was sincere."[25]

David Oshinsky is another leading proponent of the revisionist position. He insists that "contrary to popular opinion, the Senator did not 'discover' the Communist issue in February 1950."[26] Oshinsky cites McCarthy's redbaiting campaign against McMurray and shows McCarthy making use of anti-communism on both a "superficial" and "more serious" level. Superficial were his charges that "supporters of public housing were Reds" and that "fur imports from Communist-bloc nations were subsidizing Russian spy operations in America"; more serious his advocacy of bills to register subversive organizations and efforts to force the Communist Party off the ballot.[27]

Though abstract thought was not McCarthy's strong suit, Oshinsky also shows him attacking communism at the philosophical level. In 1947, on the popular "Town Meeting of the Air" radio show, McCarthy echoed the Catholic denunciation of communism's view that "human life is valueless, that there is no human soul."[28] Then, drawing on a probably spurious war experience, he evoked the figure of a Navy chaplain who said that fighting men at sea could have no finer grave than the " vast, moon-swept, wind-tossed Pacific."[29]

Michael O'Brien also dissents from the view that McCarthy was first alerted to communism by Father Walsh and that his anti-Red crusade began at Wheeling. O'Brien's principal contribution to revisionist historiography is his account, discussed in Chapter 3, of McCarthy's 1949 vendetta against the *Madison Capital Times* reporter Cedric Parker.

It is difficult to quarrel with the arguments advanced by the later historians. The evidence they have put forth militates strongly in favor of views that redbaiting was a major feature of McCarthy's campaign against McMurray and that his anti-communist crusade began not at Wheeling but in November 1949, when he distributed the mimeographed document on Cedric Parker.

Yet – conceding all this – there are three core questions that remain unanswered. Why did McCarthy ignore such emotionally charged issues of the late forties as the Hiss case and the Mindszenty trial? And – by contrast – whatever possessed him to ascribe appeasement and weakness in the face of communism to such unlikely figures as William Knowland and Dwight Eisenhower? Also, why was he so harsh toward some anti-communist adversaries while showing surprising leniency toward others with demonstrable records of pro-Soviet sympathy?

These questions penetrate to the very essence of McCarthy's thinking. In the search for enlightenment, two conclusions emerge: 1) McCarthy's anti-communism passed through three phases: parochial, opportunistic, and self-centered before Wheeling; ideologically committed and true believing during his alliance with the Hearst press; irrational and paranoid between censure and death, this state exacerbated by McCarthy's advancing alcoholism and psychological deterioration; 2) McCarthy's anti-communism was strongly tinged with ethnic prejudice – a prejudice directed far more against privileged WASPs than against minorities.

The insular nature of McCarthy's anti-communism before Wheeling has been covered in Chapter 3. As Hiss confronted Chambers and endured two sensational trials, as a drugged Cardinal Mindszenty made his wooden confession, as the *Journal-American* blazoned Cardinal Spellman's lurid pronouncements about the "red god," McCarthy's attention was pre-empted by potential subversion in public housing projects and a gadfly reporter in Wisconsin.

McCarthy's actions between Wheeling and the censure vote demonstrate how closely he embraced the Hearstian *Weltanschauung* on communism. Totally abandoning his 1946-49 priorities, he reversed himself on MacArthur at the 1952 convention, focused on the previously ignored Alger Hiss as a symbol of treachery, and yielded to no one in howling about traitors and appeasers in the State Department.

The delusional nature of McCarthy's anti-communism after censure was as striking as its opportunism before Wheeling. As alcoholism took its toll, he was afflicted with *delirium tremens* (once shrieking that snakes were coming at him) and later telling friends that he was "being persecuted constantly by Communists over the telephone."[30]

The second point requires more ample comment. Joe McCarthy was arguably the least ethnically bigoted of America's great demagogues. Where Father Coughlin attacked Jews and Rankin interchangeably reviled blacks, Jews, and Catholics, McCarthy shared none of these prejudices.

This was conceded by his sternest critics. Richard Rovere, commenting on how organized hate groups fell into his lap after Wheeling, readily admitted that he "did not cater to all their manias and phobias; he was not anti-Semitic."[31] Rovere, whose sense of humor never deserted him, described how one of the more virulent anti-Semites, "a Washington oddity named Mrs. Agnes Waters," denounced McCarthy as a "crypto Jew" and claimed that "McCarthy" was a pseudonym.[32]

Though a great majority of the Jewish community opposed McCarthy, some of his strongest and most effective backers derived from the minority that supported him. This faction included Walter Winchell, George Sokolsky, Victor Riesel, Alfred Kohlberg, Roy Cohn, and Steve Miller, his campaign manager in Wisconsin. McCarthy resisted all efforts to draw him into any actions that might be construed as anti-Semitic. He consistently supported Israel, denounced Soviet persecution of Jews, expunged Upton Close's material from the Congressional Record, and repudiated Gerald L. K. Smith and Benjamin Freedman. When asked to explain his attitude, he said, "I have many friends who are Jewish."[33]

McCarthy's attitude toward blacks is somewhat more difficult to define. It is difficult because he interacted with them so little in his life and career. To him, the African American was truly an "invisible man." Probably the best description of McCarthy's attitude toward blacks is that it was one of benign neglect. The three best-known African Americans interrogated by his subcommittee were Annie Lee Moss, Langston Hughes, and Eslanda Robeson. One was an unlettered low-level Signal Corps employee, one a distinguished poet, and one the educated, politically active wife of an international celebrity.

The story of Annie Lee Moss is well-known to students of the McCarthy era. Relying on the testimony of a beautician-turned-FBI-informant, McCarthy and Cohn believed Moss was an important "Red link" to the Army.[34] Moss testified on March 11, 1954 and the result was disaster for the McCarthy forces. The sinister "Red link" turned out to be a shabbily dressed woman who delivered her testimony in a frightened whisper. Barely literate, she revealed under questioning that she had never heard of Karl Marx. A bored McCarthy, demonstrating neglect if not benignity, left the hearing to confer with Fulton Lewis. Since Lewis was helping him prepare his rebuttal to Edward R. Murrow's *See It Now* attack, McCarthy had more pressing concerns than the fate of Annie Lee Moss.[35]

Left to carry on, Cohn did his best to retrieve the situation. Insinuatingly, he asked Moss if she had ever received copies of the *Daily Worker* from the Communist leader Rob Hall. Moss recalled that a "colored man" had left some copies at her house and that his name could have been Rob Hall. This brought a rejoinder from Robert Kennedy, acting as minority counsel, that the Communist Rob Hall was white.[36] The farcical affair ended with Democratic Senator Stuart Symington expressing confidence that Moss was telling the truth and offering to find her a job if she was dismissed by the Signal Corps.[37]

McCarthy's lack of hostility toward blacks may have contributed to the double standard that was applied during the witch hunt. Harry Belafonte, who sang for Henry Wallace and opposed the Rosenberg death sentence, was visited by HUAC representatives but never pressured to name names.[38] William Marshall, who played "de Lawd" in Green Pastures, said the double standard explained "why they caused white men like (Larry) Parks and (Elia) Kazan to lay themselves bare in public but not blacks. They wanted to use blacks, not humiliate them."[39]

The little evidence that exists shows that McCarthy enjoyed a good rapport with Native Americans. In 1938 he was campaigning for circuit judge against a sixty-six-year-old incumbent named Edgar V. Werner. McCarthy emphasized his youth (he was then twenty-nine) and, for good measure, added seven years to Werner's age. During an all-out, door-to-door campaign, McCarthy took special pains to cultivate the local Menominee Indian leaders, asking for their support against "that feeble fellow" serving as judge.[40] He also established friendly relations with a tribe near Lake Winnebago.[41] Years later, during the Army-McCarthy hearings, McCarthy revealed that inspiration for his brass-knuckle political style derived partly from a boyhood mentor he identified only as "Indian Charlie." Charlie, a no-quarter type, instructed his protégé "to go straight for an adversary's groin whenever he was in serious trouble."[42]

McCarthy, then, had little or no animus against minorities. This does not mean that he was free of prejudice. Rovere was on target when he wrote that "McCarthy was not anti-Semitic but in his demonology... a supposedly decadent Eastern aristocracy played the accomplice role that Hitler assigned to the Jews."[43]

It was unquestionably these sons and daughters of privilege who aroused McCarthy's special antipathy. One can understand how this distaste for allegedly subversive members of the WASP élite would engender populist support, especially among Catholic ethnics. Here was a poor Irish farm boy from Wisconsin taking on a despicable band of silver spoon renegades who faddishly embraced communism and betrayed their country. This reasoning would have been valid only if McCarthy's targets had been American equivalents of Britain's upper-class Cambridge traitors. But to compare Acheson, Jessup, and Kenyon to Burgess, Maclean, and Blunt is an exercise in fantasy. While McCarthy was fulminating against Jessup and the "Red Dean," the most dangerous Cambridge spy of them all, Kim Philby, was in Washington as liaison between the two British intelligence services (MI5 and MI6) and the FBI and CIA.[44]

A notable example of McCarthy's particular brand of ethnic prejudice was his attack on a fellow Wisconsinite named Nathan M. Pusey. Pusey, president of Lawrence College in Appleton, was named president of Harvard in 1953. McCarthy greeted the announcement by saying, "I don't think Pusey is or has been a member of the Communist Party, but he is a rabid anti-anti-Communist."[45] McCarthy added that "he appears to hide a combination of bigotry and intolerance behind a cloak of phony, hypocritical liberalism."[46] (In McCarthy's lexicon, "bigotry" and "intolerance" were code words for WASP snobbery toward the Irish.)

Why did McCarthy attack Pusey so recklessly? Pusey was completely free of communist taint, and a Republican to boot. An explanation is ventured by Edwin Bayley. Pusey came from Appleton's First Ward and McCarthy was born in the adjoining farm village of Grand Chute. The First, known as the "silk stocking ward," was "populated by Anglo-Saxons, Protestants, professional people and business executives."[47] The Second Ward was the heart of downtown and most of the inhabitants were transients. Though McCarthy usually stayed at the Appleton Hotel, in the Second, most of his support derived from the Third Ward. This entity, known as "the bloody Third," was overwhelmingly Irish. "There was one grade school in each ward, and athletic contests between schools often produced fist fights... this hostility among children was a reflection of similar, more restrained, attitudes among the elders. When McCarthy attacked Nathan Pusey... he did so with a degree of ferocity that was more than political; it was the Third Ward against the First."[48]

At no time were McCarthy's prejudices more evident than when he was questioning witnesses. An interesting microcosm is offered us between March and June 1953, when McCarthy interrogated four witnesses of three differing ethnic backgrounds: one WASP, one Jewish, and two black.

Reed Harris

At the time of his appearance before McCarthy's subcommittee, Reed Harris was serving as Acting Administrator of the State Department's International Information Administration. This was the agency that supervised the Voice of America. Harris headed IIA during the interregnum between the departure of Dr. Wilson Compton and the accession of his successor, Dr. Robert L. Johnson, president of Temple University.

Apart from wartime duty in the Army Air Force, Harris had been in government since 1934. His record was excellent and he had no background of communist sympathy. If anything, Harris was something of a premature anti-communist. In 1937, that Popular Front year when redbaiting was unfashionable, Harris broke with Henry G. Alsberg, head of the Federal Writers Project, over Alsberg's leniency toward Communist-controlled unions. To McCarthy's subcommittee, Harris produced a November 12, 1937 memorandum to Alsberg in which he wrote that Communist domination of the projects in New York, Chicago, and St. Louis "is scandalous and should be stopped."[49]

This cut little ice with McCarthy. Harris's transgression was not pro-communism but his past record as an irreverent campus rebel. At Columbia Harris was editor of *The Spectator,* the university daily. On April 1, 1932 he was suspended from classes because some of the paper's editorials were considered in bad taste. Harris was later reinstated but then voluntarily resigned from Columbia. Following his suspension, Harris took three weeks to produce a book called *King Football.*

Impertinent and immature, *King Football* mocked conventional marriage, the DAR, and the American Legion as well as decrying overemphasis on football. The book also defended the right of Communists to teach.

That was all McCarthy needed. As a WASP, Ivy Leaguer, and graduate of a fashionable military school, Harris represented everything that McCarthy detested. His two-day, four-session grilling of Harris was so brutal that Edward R. Murrow selected segments of it for the *See It Now* program.[50]

McCarthy lost no time in going after Harris's throat, immediately steering the subject to his difficulties at Columbia. In his appeal against suspension, Harris had been represented by the American Civil Liberties Union:

> The Chairman: The question is: did the Civil Liberties Union supply you with an attorney?...
> Mr. Harris: They did supply me with an attorney.
> The Chairman: You know the Civil Liberties Union has been listed as doing the work of the Communist party?
> Mr. Harris: Mr. Chairman, this was in 1932.
> The Chairman: I know this was 1932. Do you know they have since been listed as doing the work of the Communist Party?[51]

With this, McCarthy defined his strategy against Harris. In a reckless, go-for-broke attack, he would use the flimsiest evidence in an effort to discredit his witness.

Edward R. Murrow noted McCarthy's accusation against Harris on his television program. Murrow denied ACLU was a Communist front, saying that it had never been so listed by the attorney general's office, the FBI, or any government agency.[52] McCarthy, in an interview with Fulton Lewis, shot back that Murrow "was not telling the truth" and that ACLU had been listed as a "transmission belt" doing the work of the Communist Party by the California Un-American Activities Committee.

In the narrowest technical sense, McCarthy was correct. When he made his original charge that ACLU had been listed as a Communist front, he didn't specify whether the accuser was a state or federal body.

As the grilling continued, Harris attempted to address broader issues. Recalling the political climate that prevailed in the early thirties, he reminded the subcommittee that "the attitudes of students, the attitudes of the general public, were considerably different than they are at this moment... there was no awareness to the degree that there is today, of the way the Communist Party works." McCarthy rudely cut him off. "When I ask for a background, you can give it," he snapped.

Then McCarthy wrung an embarrassing admission out of Harris. As an illustration of constraints on academic freedom, Harris wrote in *King Football* of a Princeton professor "with whom I am intimately acquainted" who "told a class of freshmen that... the (Soviet) form of government was ideal at least in theory." After the freshman wrote home to his mother, "Mama wrote to Princeton" and "the head of my friend's department... suggested that he keep his thoughts on things political to himself unless he desired to discontinue teaching."[54]

> The Chairman: Well, who was this Communist friend? You were intimately acquainted with this Communist at Princeton... Do you know who that Communist was, or do you not?
> Mr. Harris: Mr. Chairman, as I testified in executive session, I used what was called author's license...
> The Chairman: In other words, when you said you had an intimate friend at Princeton who was a Communist... you were not telling the truth, then?
> Mr. Harris: I was not telling the truth... no, I was not.[55]

The questions were of course rhetorical. From the executive session testimony, McCarthy already knew that the Princeton professor was a fictional creation. Yet he couldn't resist the temptation to publicly brand Harris a liar.

Nor did McCarthy scruple at demeaning Harris personally. The hard-pressed witness mentioned that he and Senator Barry Goldwater had been fellow cadets at Staunton Military Academy. When Senator Symington asked if Goldwater would appear as a character witness, McCarthy saw a fresh opportunity to denigrate Harris.

> Mr. Harris: He (Goldwater) could only testify as to my character at the time I was there. I have had practically no contact with him since.
> The Chairman: He just went to the same college you were at...
> Mr. Harris: He... knew a great deal about my conduct at the academy.
> The Chairman: But he was no particular friend of yours... I understand you do not know Goldwater, that he was no special friend of yours. Have you seen him over the past ten or fifteen years?[56]

Harris of course had not. In this particularly degrading exchange, McCarthy made Harris look like a namedropper who is desperately trying to establish innocence by association. The battered Harris retrieved a measure of dignity with this statement to the subcommittee at the final session of the hearings:

"The worst part of this situation is the improper questions, the questions that are so loaded with implications that are false, improper. They are constantly used. They are quoted in the press. They are not actually definite charges, but they imply all sorts of things about whoever happens to be sitting in this very hot seat."[57]

As we know, Harris's tenure in this "very hot seat" was soon to end.

William Marx Mandell

William Marx Mandell testified before the McCarthy subcommittee on March 24, 1953. A former research fellow at Stanford, the author of four books, Mandell was employed as an advertising copywriter at the time of his testimony.[58]

Nobody could ever accuse Mandell of being intimidated by a McCarthy investigation. His testimony had two salient characteristics: belligerence and constant references to his Jewishness. Toward McCarthy he was combative and toward Cohn contemptuous. The tenor of the hearing was set by the opening exchange.

> Mr. Mandell: My name is William Marx Mandell... I would like to make clear that I am a Jew.
> Mr. Cohn: That you are a what?
> Mr. Mandell: That I am a Jew.
> Mr. Cohn: So am I, and I don't see that this is an issue here.
> Mr. Mandell: Well, a Jew who works for McCarthy is thought of very ill by most of the Jewish people in this country.

Mandell apparently believed that McCarthy was some sort of closet Father Coughlin. If he challenged and baited McCarthy enough, if he kept emphasizing his Jewishness, McCarthy would eventually blow up and be goaded into anti-Semitic utterances in the nationally televised hearings.

If this was Mandell's strategy, it backfired. Showing a restraint that would have served him well when he interrogated General Zwicker a year later, McCarthy took all Mandell's best shots. In one particularly unpleasant exchange, Mandell said "that you, Senator McCarthy, murdered Maj. Raymond Kaplan by... driving him to the point where he jumped under a truck."[60] (Raymond Kaplan was a VOA engineer deeply disturbed by allegations that he had deliberately misplaced a transmitter section so that it would not function effectively.) Even in the face of such a provocation, McCarthy kept his cool.

> The Chairman: May I say for the benefit of other members of the committee... Mr. Kaplan would have been a friendly witness insofar as this committee is concerned... He had no fear of this committee whatsoever... We went through his files and found that apparently there was no wrongdoing on his part....[61]

McCarthy went on to suggest that Kaplan's death was no suicide, adding that his co-workers had expressed doubts in sworn testimony that the engineer took his own life.[62] Such a theory is not consistent with a note Kaplan left to his wife, explaining that he was a "patsy" and that "once the dogs are set upon you, everything you have done from the beginning of time is suspect."[63]

Later in the interrogation, McCarthy addressed himself to Mandell's constant playing of the Jewish card.

> The Chairman: I think the Jewish race is a great race of people. I do not think you represent them... Every race has its renegades,
> Mr. Mandell: It certainly does. (looking directly at Cohn)
> The Chairman: Every race has its traitors.
> Mr. Mandell: It certainly does. (again looking at Cohn)
> The Chairman: And, as a whole, we have gotten as much if not more help from outstanding Jewish people in this fight against communism than from any other race. Let us have that clear.[64]

McCarthy also told Mandell that "you were not asked what your race was. You came up and volunteered it belligerently. I do not care what race you belong to."[65]

Within the Jewish community, Mandell was viewed as a disaster. Morton Clurman, an official of the American Jewish Committee, wrote in an internal memo that Mandell was "an extremely unpleasant, evasive, unctuous character who reinforces every stereotype of the Communist Jewish intellectual." Clurman also lamented that, thanks to Mandell raising the Jewish issue, "McCarthy... came out looking like Abraham Lincoln and Thomas Jefferson compared with the witness."[66]

During the hearing, McCarthy handled Mandell roughly several times. On one occasion he told him to be quiet[67] and on another he openly called him a Communist.[68] But – thanks to Mandell's obtuseness and arrogance – these were never viewed as expressions of anti-Semitism.

Langston Highes

A far different atmosphere prevailed when Langston Hughes took the stand on March 25. If Reed Harris was an injured innocent and William Marx Mandell a pugnacious McCarthy-Cohn baiter, Hughes was a fondly welcomed prodigal son.

McCarthy played a secondary role in the interrogation, with Cohn asking the more important questions. Also participating in the questioning was the conservative Arkansas Democrat John McClellan.

Hughes's testimony validates William Marshall's thesis that McCarthy wanted to use blacks rather than humiliate and destroy them. The only reason Hughes was called in the first place was because some overseas information centers contained books he had written when he was a communist sympathizer. But the committee had no wish to banish all his writings from overseas libraries. Instead, their aim was to enlist the poet as a guide on how to expunge the works of "subversive" Hughes and replace them with those of "patriotic" Hughes.

As the hearing opened, Cohn was mainly interested in learning when Hughes stopped sympathizing with communism.

> Mr. Hughes: There was no abrupt ending, but... roughly the beginnings of my sympathy with the Soviet ideology were coincident with the Scottsboro case, the American depression, and that they ran... further, because we were allies... with the Soviet Union during the war.[69]

When Cohn asked him when he "completely broke with the Soviet ideology," Hughes said that "reorientation of my thinking and emotional feeling occurred roughly four or five years ago."[70]

For the first time, Cohn expressed skepticism, recalling that in 1949 Hughes had made "a statement in defense of the Communist leaders who were on trial, which was published in the *Daily Worker*."[71] Hughes adroitly parried the thrust, saying that his statement had been made "in a spirit of wishing to preserve our civil liberties for everyone." He added that he had found the Nazi-Soviet pact "disillusioning" and that in 1932-33, when he visited Russia, he was disturbed by "the lack of freedom of expression in the Soviet Union for writers."[72]

McCarthy entered the interrogation when Cohn brought up a Hughes poem titled "Put Another 'S' In the USA and Make It Soviet." When McClellan asked if the poem was currently in any information center, Cohn replied that it was not and McCarthy commented that the subject had been brought up "to show the type of thinking on the part (of Hughes) at the time he wrote those books."[73])

Cohn next referred to *Simple Speaks His Mind,* a book of short stories that Hughes published in 1950. One of these sketches, "When A Man Sees Red," was a lampoon on HUAC. Again, Hughes was equal to the occasion. He had written the satire, he replied, because a member of the committee had "called a Negro witness a very ugly name."[74] Not wishing to be placed in the position of hounding Hughes for protesting racial bigotry, McCarthy and Cohn quickly dropped the subject.

In the end it was McClellan, the Southern segregationist, who proved to be Hughes's strongest supporter.

> Senator McClellan: Do I understand that since you came to the conclusion that you were wrong about communism, and subsequent to the time you wrote these books... you have written other works that repudiate the philosophy that you expressed in these writings that we now find in the (overseas) libraries?
> Mr. Hughes: I would say that they certainly contradict the philosophy, and that they certainly express my pro-democratic beliefs....[75]

As examples of his "pro-democratic" writings, Hughes cited the poems "Freedom's Plow" and "Mystery," a short story titled "One Friday Morning," and an excerpt from his last book declaring that "our country has many problems still to solve, but America is young, big, strong, and beautiful, and we are trying very hard to be... one Nation, indivisible, with liberty and justice for all."[76]

> Senator McClellan: I certainly commend you for that authorship of those remarks. I think they indicate that you have had a change in your beliefs and convictions about this country, and I wish the books that are in the libraries, your earlier publications, might be replaced with some of your later works.[77]

McCarthy asked Cohn if the information program had bought any of "Mr. Hughes's books after his reversal, when he quit supporting the Soviet system, and started to support ours?" Cohn said he wasn't sure but would check with the State Department.[78]

As Hughes's testimony drew to a close, McCarthy gave another example of how little animus he had against his witness.

The Chairman: I have been asked to put in the record a poem written by Mr. Hughes while he was... following the Communist party line... I do not believe it is necessary to read it. We will merely insert it in the record.[79]

The unread poem, "Goodbye Christ," was an inflammatory piece of pro-communist, anti-religious propaganda. It reads in part:

> Goodbye
> Christ Jesus Lord God Jehova
> Beat it on away from here now.
> Make way for a new guy with no religion
> at all–
> A real guy named
> Marx Communist Lenin Peasant Stalin
> Worker ME–[80]

One can imagine McCarthy's reaction if he had been able to attribute authorship to an Acheson, a Lattimore, or a Reed Harris.

The hearing ended with this exchange between Hughes and McCarthy.

Mr. Hughes: Am I excused now, sir?

The Chairman: Yes. May I ask you one question first? We have had so much screaming by certain elements of the press that witnesses have been misused... Do you feel that you were in any way mistreated by the staff (McCarthy's) or by the committee?

Mr. Hughes: I must say that I was agreeably surprised at the courtesy and friendliness with which I was received.[81]

Eslanda Robeson

Eslanda Cardozo Goode Robeson, the wife of Paul Robeson, testified before McCarthy's committee on July 7, 1953. An attractive, light-skinned black woman of part-Sephardic Jewish ancestry, she was every bit as articulate and committed to left-wing causes as her husband. Mrs. Robeson had written several books, including two that were purchased for the overseas libraries. One was a biography of her husband and the other, *African Journey,* contained material that the committee found objectionable. Particularly displeasing was this excerpt:

> And the one hopeful light on the horizon
> – the exciting and encouraging conditions
> in Soviet Russia, where for the first time
> in history our race problem has been squarely
> faced and solved; where for the first time
> the words of the poets, philosophers, and
> well-meaning politicians have been made a
> living reality; Robert Burns's "a man's a

> man for a' that"; France's Liberté, Egalité,
> Fraternité; America's "all men are created
> equal"... All these grand ideas and statements
> have been hauled down from the dusty reference
> shelves at the backs of men's minds and have
> been put into active, vigorous, and successful
> practice by the Russians....[82]

Robeson was certainly aware that the number of blacks in the Soviet Union was negligible; her script might have undergone revision if she had been around when African students in Moscow and other university cities began to experience Russian "friendliness" at first hand.

As a witness, Robeson was charming, spirited, and infuriatingly evasive. Evasiveness was a quality that McCarthy would later ascribe to General Ralph W. Zwicker, using it as a pretext for the insults he heaped on him. The general was a model of forthrightness compared to Eslanda Robeson. The clearest statement she made all day was her opening affirmation that she was "very proud" to be the wife of Paul Robeson.[83]

Aiding McCarthy and Cohn in the interrogation were J. B. Matthews, David Schine, and Democratic Senator Stuart Symington of Missouri. When Matthews asked her if she was a member of the Communist party, she took both the Fifth and Fifteenth amendments, the latter stipulating that the right to vote shall not be abridged "on account of race, or previous condition of servitude."

Senator McCarthy: By the Fifteenth Amendment?

Mrs. Robeson: Yes, the Fifth and Fifteenth. I claim the Fifteenth as a Negro.

Senator McCarthy: Let us see if the Fifteenth Amendment could possibly apply. Let me read it to you. (Reads the amendment)... Before this committee, we do not have Negroes and whites. We do not have Catholics, Protestants, and Jews. We have American citizens... We care about your rights. The Fifteenth Amendment has nothing to do with this... I may say, Mrs. Robeson, if you or your husband were in Russia, and you were asked over there whether you were committing espionage, you would have no privilege under the Fifth Amendment. Now you will answer the question, unless you feel the question might tend to incriminate you.

Mrs. Robeson: I don't quite understand your statement that we are all American citizens. I have been fighting for this all my fifty-six years. I am a second-class citizen now, as a Negro. That is the reason I always claim (the Fifteenth Amendment). I would be very happy if we didn't have to discuss race, and I hope we will at some point get to a place where we don't have to. But in the meantime you are white and I am Negro, and this is a very white committee, and I feel I must sort of protect myself. I am sorry it is necessary.[84]

Robeson simply refused to be pinned down on anything. When she was queried about her book, the interrogation was conducted by McCarthy's leading dialectician and expert on Marxism.

Mr. Matthews: Mrs. Robeson, in your book... did you say that the one hopeful light on the horizon is the exciting and encouraging condition in Soviet Russia?
Mrs. Robeson: You would have to read it to me. It was written over a period of ten years and published in 1945, and this is 1953.[85]

Even when he quoted chapter and verse, Matthews found the going rough. When Robeson asked him to read the sentence before the controversial passage, he did so. Then he returned to his main point.

Mr. Matthews: Was that your feeling?
Mrs. Robeson: If I wrote it in the book, that was definitely my feeling. I have never written anything that I did not feel, never.[86]

Along with the declaration of loyalty to her husband, that was the closest the committee came to getting a candid answer that day. As the hearing continued, Robeson gave answers that would have made McCarthy explode with rage if delivered by other witnesses. When Matthews asked her if she had ever said she wanted her son educated in the Soviet Union, she replied that "I would have to think of this in context."[87] Symington, playing the good cop, suggested that her refusal to answer questions about her Communist affiliation might have come from a belief that she was being treated like a second-class citizen because of her race. Robeson responded briskly that "my opinions are my private personal affair, and I really do not think anybody has the right to ask me.[88]

When McCarthy resumed the questioning, Robeson became even more elusive.

Senator McCarthy: Have you attended Communist cell meetings at which there was discussed espionage or sabotage?
Mrs. Robeson: Well, I don't know, sir, what a Communist cell is. Would you explain that to me?[89]

McCarthy tried a new tack.

Senator McCarthy: Let me use the word "unit" instead of "cell." Do you belong to a Communist unit?
Mrs. Robeson: I don't know what a unit is. These are technical questions I don't understand.[90]

Whatever tension existed at the Robeson hearing had been dispelled in an earlier humorous exchange between the witness, McCarthy, and Matthews. Robeson told Matthews that a few weeks earlier she had given a speech on McCarthyism to a Detroit meeting of the Civil Rights Congress, a group on the attorney general's list of subversive organizations. Grinning broadly, McCarthy pretended not to have heard what Robeson said to Matthews.

> Senator McCarthy: I missed the witness's answer. She made a speech on what?
>
> Mr. Matthews: She made a speech on McCarthyism in Detroit under the auspices of the Civil Rights Congress. She did not say whether she was for it or against it.
>
> Mrs. Robeson: I will give you two guesses.[91]

After eliciting an admission from the witness that the committee had not discriminated against her racially, McCarthy made a polite closing statement in which he described Robeson as "a very charming woman," and an "intelligent lady." He even defended her right to advocate communism because "I do not propose to argue with a lady."[92] The witness returned the compliment.

> Mrs. Robeson: Well, I think this is very nice of you, Senator McCarthy, but I must say that I am a very, very loyal American, and I really have fought most of my life... for the Constitution and the Bill of Rights, which I think are marvelous.[93]

After the hearing, Robeson wrote a friend that her encounter with McCarthy's committee had been "all sweetness and light, very clear, respectful and reasonable."[94] "McCarthy really let her off easy," was David Oshinsky's comment on the Robeson hearing.[95]

Of the four witnesses I have discussed, it was Harris and Robeson who placed McCarthy's ethnic prejudice into the sharpest focus. His sadistic savaging of the premature anti-communist Reed Harris plays interesting counterpoint to his amiability toward Eslanda Robeson, a woman who – for all her evasions – made little secret of her continuing sympathy for the Soviet experiment.

How does Joe McCarthy's anti-communism compare with that of the *Journal-American* and *Mirror?* The dominant characteristic of Hearstian anti-communism was consistency. Rigid and icy, it took shape in the thirties, when William Randolph Hearst divested himself of the last traces of youthful progressivism. This rigidity was particularly apparent during World War II, with the refusal of the Hearst papers to join other conservative organs in blessing the Soviet-American honeymoon. It also manifested itself in the late forties, with its messianic zeal in support of Cardinal Mindszenty and against the high-level domestic subversion symbolized by Alger Hiss. It continued during the peak period of the McCarthy alliance, when the *Journal-American* and *Mirror* gave him maximum support in his attacks on the "Truman-Acheson regime." It relaxed, but not too much, with the Hearst team's Moscow mission and cautious advocacy of coexistence – with the caveat that America keep up her military guard and continue to hang tough against home-gown members of suspect groups. The growth of an anti-McCarthy faction among New York's Hearst writers in no way implied a softening toward communism. On the contrary, Frank Conniff and such non-Hearstian Red hunters as Frederick Woltman turned against McCarthy because they thought he had become a *liability* to the anti-communist cause.

If the operative term for Hearstian redbaiting is consistency, for Joe McCarthy's it is volatility. In phase #1, the pre-Wheeling years, he completely ignored issues of maximum concern to such as Matthews, Pegler, and Sokolsky; in phase #2, between Wheeling and the 1954 fragmentation, he served these ideologues as a powerful and philosophically committed ally; in phase #3, between censure and death, he caused the Hearst organization acute embarrassment as he babbled alcoholic accusations of appeasement at Republican right-wingers.

Joe McCarthy was truly a loose cannon. Extending the metaphor, the Hearst organization was for a time able to seize the cannon and use it with great effectiveness. Then it got away and resumed its destructive course. At that point it had to be dumped overboard.

Notes to Chapters

1. The Cold War Within the Hot War: Hearst as Pioneer

1. W. A. Swanberg, *Citizen Hearst,* p. 49
2. Ibid, p. 50
3. Ibid, p. 73
4. Ibid, p. 105
5. Ibid, p. 114
6. Ibid, p. 209
7. Ibid, p. 209
8. Ibid, p. 234
9. Ibid, p. 237
10. Ibid, p. 295
11. Ibid, p. 370
12. Ibid, p. 371
13. Ibid, p. 382
14. Ibid, p. 443
15. Ibid, p. 474
16. Ibid, p. 476
17. Ibid, pp. 488-89
18. Lindsay Chaney and Michael Cieply, *The Hearsts: Family and Empire —The Later Years,* p. 44
19. William Manchester, *American Caesar,* p. 248; Richard Fried, *Nightmare In Red,* p. 14
20. James L. Baughman, *Henry R. Luce and the Rise of the American News Media,* p. 138
21. John Cooney, *The American Pope: The Life and Times of Francis Cardinal Spellman,* p. 135
22. Ibid, p. 143
23. Baughman, p. 138
24. Joseph E. Davies, *Mission to Moscow,* p. 470
25. Ibid, p. 471
26. Swanberg, p. 506; *New York Journal-American,* 2/29/1944
27. *Journal-American,* 10/31/1945
28. Stanley J. Kurnitz and Howard Haycraft (ed.), *Twentieth Century Authors,* p. 359
29. Ibid, p. 360
30. Brendan Gill, *Here at the New Yorker,* p. 284
31. Arthur and Barbara Gelb, *O'Neill,* p. 642
32. Ibid, p. 640
33. Ibid, p. 783
34. many columns
35. *Journal-American,* 1/15/1942
36. Ibid, 1/24/1942
37. Ibid, 2/6/1942
38. Ibid, 2/14/1942
39. Ibid, 2/18/1942

40. Ibid, 3/3/1942
41. Ibid, 3/16/1942
42. Ibid, 4/1/1942
43. Ibid, 4/3/1942
44. Ibid, 4/21/1942
45. Swanberg, p. 506
46. *Journal-American,* 7/22/1942
47. Ibid, 7/19/42
48. Ibid, 2/4/1942
49. Baughman, p. 138
50. *Journal-American,* 7/16/1943
51. Ibid, 11/2/1943
52. *New York Daily Mirror,* 6/22/1944
53. Thomas Reeves, *The Life and Times of Joe McCarthy,* p. 491
54. Mirror, 11/9/1944
55. Fried, p. 15
56. Frederick V. Field, *From Right to Left,* p. 179
57. *Mirror,* 11/9/1944
58. Baughman, pp. 144-45
59. Ibid, p. 145
60. *Mirror,* 2/8/1945
61. Ibid, 3/13/1945
62. Ibid, 8/22/1945
63. Ibid, 9/28/1945
64. Ibid, 10/24/1945
65. Ibid, 11/2/1945
66. Ibid, 12/7/1945
67. Chaney and Cieply, p. 144
68. Ibid, p. 144
69. Jack Anderson and Ronald May,

McCarthy: The Man, The Senator, the "Ism", p. 292
70. Herman Klurfeld, *Winchell: His Life and Times,* p. 157
71. Chaney and Cieply, p. 144
72. Oliver Pilat, *Pegler: Angry Man of the Press,* p. 190
73. Ibid, p. 190
74. Ibid, p. 190
75. *Journal-American,* 1/19/1950
76. Victor Navasky, *Naming Names,* p. 152
77. Chaney and Cieply, p. 144
78. *Journal-American,* 11/1/1944
79. Ibid, 11/10/1944
80. Ibid, 1/26/1945
81. Ibid, 2/14/1945
82. Ibid, 4/22/1945
83. Ibid, 5/10/1945
84. Ralph Martin, *Cissy,* p. 434
85. Margaret Truman, *Harry S. Truman,* p. 235
86. Ibid, pp. 279-80
87. Walter Trohan, *Political Animals,* p. 222
88. Reeves, p. 372
89. Reeves, p. 372
90. Richard Rovere, *Senator Joe McCarthy,* p. 133
91. Ibid, p. 265
92. David Oshinsky, *A Conspiracy So Immense,* p. 96

2. Pre-McCarthy McCarthyism: The Hearst Press and Parnell Thomas

1. *Journal-American,* 9/14/1946
2. *Biographical Dictionary of the American Congress, 1774-1961,* p. 1704
3. David Caute, *The Great Fear: The Anti-Communist Purge Under Truman and Eisenhower,* p. 97
4. Oshinsky, p. 98
5. Walter Goodman, *The Committee: The Extraordinary Career of the*

House Committee on Un-American Activities, p. 197
6. Ibid, p. 222
7. Ibid, pp. 190-1
8. Ibid, p. 196
9. Ibid, p. 195
10. Ibid, p. 196
11. *Journal-American,* 5/15/1947
12. Goodman, p. 263

13. *Journal-American,* 5/15/1947
14. *Mirror,* 5/15/1947
15. Ibid, 5/19/1947
16. Klurfeld, p. 66
17. John Roy Carlson, *The Plotters,* p. 365
18. Bob Thomas, *Winchell,* p. 175
19. Richard Gid Powers, *Secrecy and Power: The Life of J. Edgar Hoover,* p. 180
20. *Mirror,* 1/5/1947
21. Klurfeld, p. 69
22. Powers, p. 281
23. Ibid, p. 286
24. Goodman, p. 197; Powers, p. 286
25. Klurfeld, p. 125
26. Ibid, p. 125
27. Bob Thomas, p. 220
28. Ibid, p. 221
29. Ibid, pp. 222-23
30. Powers, p. 286
31. Ibid, p. 287
32. Joseph C. Goulden, *The Best Years,* p. 395
33. Chaney and Cieply, p. 129
34. Ibid, p. 134
35. Cedric Belfrage, *The American Inquisition,* p. 40
36. Chaney and Cieply, pp. 130-1
37. Goodman, p. 207
38. *Mirror,* 10/27/1947
39. Goodman, p. 202
40. *Journal-American,* 10/20/1947
41. Goodman, p. 216
42. Navasky, p. 81
43. Ibid, p. 207
44. Ibid, p. 208
45. *Mirror,* 10/21/1947
46. Chaney and Cieply, pp. 125-26
47. *Journal-American,* 10/22/1947
48. *Mirror,* 10/22/1947
49. Goodman, p. 208
50. *Journal-American,* 10/24/1947
51. Goodman, p. 208
52. *Journal-American,* 10/27/1927
53. Ibid
54. Carlson, p. 154
55. Ibid, p. 137
56. Ibid, p. 137
57. Michael O'Brien, *McCarthy and McCarthyism in Wisconsin,* p. 119
58. *Journal-American,* 10/27/1947
59. Navasky, p. 399-400
60. Ibid, p. 399
61. Goodman, p. 211
62. *Journal-American,* 11/1/1947
63. Goodman, p. 211
64. Ibid, pp. 211-1
65. Ibid, p. 212
66. Navasky, p. 153
67. *Mirror,* 12/16/1947; Navasky, p. 154
68. *Mirror,* 10/6/1947
69. Nicholas von Hoffman, *Citizen Cohn,* p. 107
70. Goodman, p. 213
71. Field, p. 179
72. Goodman, pp. 213-14
73. Ibid, pp. 213-14
74. Ibid, p. 220
75. Ibid, p. 217
76. Ibid, p. 220
77. *Journal-American,* 11/3/1947
78. Ibid, 11/5/1947
79. Ibid
80. Ibid, 11/3/1947
81. Goodman, p. 218
82. Ibid, p. 217
83. Navasky, p. 83
84. Ibid, p. 327
85. Allen Weinstein, *Perjury: The Hiss-Chambers Case,* p. 4
86. Goodman, p. 244
87. Belfrage, p. 19
88. Ibid, p. 46; Goodman, pp. 245-46
89. *FACTS ON FILE* (1948), p. 274
90. Ibid, 301
91. Ibid, p. 308
92. Oliver Pilat, *Drew Pearson,* p. 209
93. *Journal-American,* 10/23/1948

94. *Mirror,* 10/23/1948
95. *Journal-American,* 10/27/1948
96. Ibid, 10/22/1948
97. *Mirror,* 11/5/1948
98. *Journal-American,* 11/9/1948
99. *FACTS ON FILE* (1948), p. 365
100. *Journal-American,* 12/1/1948
101. *Mirror,* 12/1/1948

102. Belfrage, pp. 68-69; Fried, p. 97
103. Goodman, p. 270; Reeves, p. 604
104. Jack Anderson, *Confessions of a Muckraker,* p. 115; *Biographical Dictionary...,* p. 1705
105. Caute, p. 97
106. Goodman, p. 233
107. Ibid, p. 221

3. The Hiss Case and the Mindszenty Trial

1. Field, p. 147
2. Caute, p. 502
3. Jack Lait and Lee Mortimer, *USA Confidential,* p. 231
4. Ibid, p. 57
5. Lee Israel, *Kilgallen,* p. 225
6. Ibid, p. 225
7. Ibid, p. 220
8. Igor Cassini, *I'd Do It All Over Again,* p. 59
9. Ibid, p. 10
10. Ibid, p. 112
11. Ibid, p. 113
12. Weinstein, p. 15; Richard Nixon, *Six Crises,* p. 9
13. Ralph de Toledano and Victor Lasky, *Seeds of Treason,* p. 152
14. Weinstein, p. 15
15. Ibid, pp. 7-8
16. Ibid, p. 16
17. *Journal-American,* 8/4/1948
18. Weinstein, p. 15
19. *Journal-American,* 8/5/1948
20. *Mirror,* 8/6/1948
21. Whittaker Chambers, *Witness,* pp. 561-65; Weinstein, p. 20
22. Weinstein, p. 20
23. Ibid, pp. 21-22
24. Chambers, p. 600
25. Weinstein, p. 34
26. *Mirror,* 8/17/1948
27. *Journal-American,* 8/18/1948; Weinstein, pp. 146-47
28. *Journal-American,* 8/24/1948
29. Weinstein, pp. 42-43

30. Ibid, pp. 43-44
31. *Journal-American,* 8/24/1948
32. Chambers, p. 654
33. Weinstein, p. 49
34. *Journal-American,* 2/26/1948
35. Weinstein, p. 57
36. Chambers, pp. 613-14
37. Ibid, p. 711
38. Ibid, pp. 736-37
39. *Journal-American,* 8/28/1948
40. Ibid, 12/16/1948
41. Ibid, 12/1/1948
42. Herbert R. Lottman, *The Purge: The Purification of French Collaborators After World War II,* pp. 260-61
43. *Mirror,* 10/17/1948
44. Ibid, 12/8/1948
45. Ibid, 12/16/1948
46. Ibid, 12/29/1948
47. Ibid, 12/31/1948
48. Joszef Kosi-Horvath, *Cardinal Mindszenty: Confessor and Martyr of Our Time,* p. 13
49. Joseph Vecsey, *Mindszenty the Man,* p. 46
50. Cooney, p. 166
51. *FACTS ON FILE* (1948), p. 379
52. *Journal-American,* 12/17/1948
53. Swanberg, p. 425
54. *Mirror,* 12/28/1948
55. *Journal-American,* 12/29/1948
56. Ibid
57. *Mirror,* 12/29/1948
58. *Journal-American,* 12/30/1948

59. Ibid
60. *Journal-American,* 12/31/1948
61. Ibid, 2/3/1949
62. Vecsey, pp. 105-7
63. *Journal-American,* 2/4/1949
64. Ibid, 2/6/1949; *Mirror,* 2/6/1949
65. *Journal-American,* 2/5/49
66. Ibid
67. Ibid
68. Ibid
69. Donald F. Crosby, *God, Church, and Flag: Senator Joseph R. McCarthy and the Catholic Church,* 1950-57, p. 12
70. *FACTS ON FILE* (1949), p. 45
71. *Journal-American,* 2/8/1949
72. *Mirror,* 2/8/1949
73. FACTS ON FILE (1949), p. 55
74. Weinstein, p. 413
75. *Journal-American,* 6/1/1949
76. Ibid
77. Weinstein, p. 414
78. Ibid, p. 415
79. *Journal-American,* 6/6/1949
80. Weinstein, p. 156
81. Ibid, p. 432
82. *Journal-American,* 6/6/1949
83. Ibid, 6/7/1949
84. Weinstein, p. 512
85. *Journal-American,* 6/14/1949
86. Ibid, 6/21/1949
87. Ibid, 6/27/1949
88. Ibid
89. *Journal-American,* 7/7/1949
90. Ibid, 7/9/1949
91. Ibid
92. Caute, p. 61
93. Weinstein, p. 10
94. Ibid, p. 470

95. Ibid, p. 10
96. *Mirror,* 11/22/1949
97. Rovere, p. 201
98. *Journal-American,* 12/9/1949
99. Ibid, 12/12/1949
100. Weinstein, p. 487
101. *Journal-American,* 1/11/1950
102. Weinstein, p. 489
103. *Journal-American,* 1/13/1950
104. *Mirror,* 1/19/1950
105. *Journal-American,* 1/18/1950
106. Ibid, 1/25/1950
107. Ibid
108. *Mirror,* 1/26/1950
109. Ibid, 1/30/1950
110. *Journal-American,* 2/1/1950
111. Ibid
112. Swanberg, p. 312
113. Reeves, p. 149
114. Ibid, p. 134
115. Ibid, p. 153
116. Oshinsky interview with author, 12/12/1990
117. Reeves letter to author, 7/19/1991
118. O'Brien letter to author, 7/23/1991
119. Fried letter to author, 4/13/1992
120. Bolan letter to author, 1/22/1991; interview 1/9/1992
121. O'Brien, p. 86
122. Ibid, p. 87
123. Reeves, p. 179
124. O'Brien, p. 92
125. Ibid, p. 93
126. Ibid, p. 9
127. Ibid, p. 196
128. *FACTS ON FILE* (1949), p. 328
129. Ibid, p. 373
130. Ibid, p. 373
131. Rovere, p. 235

4. 1950: The Alliance Forms

1. Edwin R. Bayley, *Joe McCarthy and the Press,* p. 17
2. Rovere, p. 126
3. Reeves, p. 23

4. Bayley, p. 18
5. *Journal-American,* 2/16/1950
6. Ibid, 2/21/1950
7. Ibid

8. Reeves, p. 241; Bayley, pp. 42-43
9. *Mirror,* 2/25/1950
10. Reeves, p. 241
11. Bayley, pp. 42-43
12. Reeves, p. 347
13. *Journal-American,* 2/25/1950
14. Ibid
15. *Mirror,* 2/26/1950
16. Ibid, 2/27/1950
17. *Journal-American,* 2/28/1950
18. *Mirror,* 3/19/50
19. Rovere, p. 147
20. Ibid, p. 256
21. *Journal-American,* 3/9/1950
22. Ibid, 3/12/1950
23. Ibid
24. *Mirror,* 3/14/1950
25. *Journal-American,* 3/14/1950
26. Ibid
27. *Mirror,* 3/15/1950
28. *Journal-American,* 3/14/1950
29. Ibid, 3/15/1950
30. *Mirror,* 3/16/1950
31. Chaney and Cieply, p. 133
32. Bayley, p. 3
33. Ibid, p. 3
34. *Mirror,* 2/19/1950
35. Bayley, p. 49
36. Goulden, p. 395
37. Chaney and Cieply, p. 127
38. Ibid, p. 128
39. Ibid, p. 128
40. Ibid, p. 12
41. Ibid, p. 129
42. Rovere, p. 141
43. Ibid, p. 52
44. Chaney and Cieply, p. 128
45. Rovere, p. 135
46. Reeves, p. 249
47. Chaney and Cieply, p. 130; Robert Griffith, *The Politics of Fear: Joseph R. McCarthy and the Senate,* p. 63
48. Oshinsky, p. 117; Athan Theoharis, *The Boss: J. Edgar Hoover and the Great American Inquisition,* p. 283
49. Joseph Keeley, *The China Lobby Man,* p. 13
50. *Journal-American,* 3/16/1950
51. Ibid, 3/19/1950
52. *Mirror,* 3/18/1950
53. *Journal-American,* 3/21/1950
54. Oshinsky, p. 136
55. *Journal-American,* 3/21/1950
56. *Mirror,* 3/21/1950
57. Ibid, 3/27/1950
58. *Journal-American,* 3/26/1950
59. *Mirror,* 3/29/1950
60. Oshinsky, p. 145; Rovere, p. 153
61. Oshinsky, p. 145
62. *Journal-American,* 3/31/1950
63. Oshinsky, pp. 149-50
64. *Journal-American,* 4/1/1950
65. Ibid, 4/4/1950
66. Ibid, 4/6/1950
67. Oshinsky, p. 150
68. *Mirror,* 4/2/1950
69. *Journal-American,* 4/21/1950
70. Ibid, 5/10/1950
71. *Mirror,* 4/22/1950
72. *Journal-American,* 4/17/1950
73. Crosby, p. 61
74. Ibid, p. 66
75. Chaney and Cieply, p. 137
76. *Mirror,* 2/27/1950
77. Ibid, 5/1/1950
78. Ibid, 5/12/1950
79. Ibid, 5/18/1950
80. Bob Thomas, pp. 226-27
81. Klurfeld, p. 143
82. Joe McCarthy, *McCarthyism: The Fight for America,* p. 1
83. Oshinsky, p. 167
84. Ibid, p. 167
85. *Journal-American,* 7/16/1950
86. Oshinsky, pp. 168-69
87. Ibid, p. 170
88. *Mirror,* 7/18/1950
89. *Journal-American,* 7/18/1950

90. Ibid, 7/19/1950
91. Ibid, 7/20/1950
92. Ibid, 7/21/1950
93. Ibid, 7/22/1950
94. *Mirror,* 7/24/1950
95. Oshinsky, p. 175
96. Ibid, p. 175
97. Ibid, p. 175
98. Reeves, pp. 344-45
99. *Journal-American,* 11/8/1950
100. Ibid, 11/11/50
101. Ibid, 10/19/1950
102. Ibid, 10/21/1950
103. Klurfeld, p. 140
104. Pilat, *Drew Pearson,* p. 238
105. *Mirror,* 6/5/1950
106. Ibid, 7/1/1950
107. Ibid, 7/2/1950
108. Ibid, 9/18/1950
109. Ibid, 10/29/1950
110. Ibid, 12/22/1950
111. Pilat, *Drew Pearson,* pp. 29-31
112. *Journal-American,* 12/14/1950
113. Reeves, p. 349
114. Oshinsky, p. 182
115. *Journal-American,* 12/20/1950
116. Klurfeld, p. 145
117. Bob Thomas, p. 246
118. Bob Thomas, p. 246; Klurfeld, p. 146
119. Reeves, p. 357
120. July 1957 report prepared by the Anti-Defamation League
121. Arnold Heidenheimer, "Case History of a Smear," *The New Republic,* 12/25/1950
122. Reeves, p. 361
123. Moshe Decter and James Rorty, *McCarthy and the Communists,* p. 121

5. 1951-52: The Alliance at High Noon

1. Decter and Rorty, p. 151
2. Ibid, p. 152
3. *Journal-American,* 2/2/1951
4. Reeves, p. 340
5. Ibid, p. 340
6. *Mirror,* 2/12/1951
7. O'Brien, p. 119
8. Manchester, p. 638
9. Ibid, p. 638
10. Ibid, p. 639
11. Oshinsky, p. 194
12. Reeves, pp. 145-47
13. *Journal-American,* 4/11/1951
14. Ibid
15. *Mirror,* 4/12/1951
16. Ibid
17. *Journal-American,* 4/12/1951
18. *Mirror,* 4/13/1951
19. *Journal-American,* 4/27/1951
20. Rovere, p. 172
21. Ibid, p. 175
22. Ibid, p. 177
23. Oshinsky, p. 200
24. Ibid, p. 201
25. *Journal-American,* 6/14/1951
26. *Mirror,* 6/15/1951
27. Reeves, pp. 374-75
28. *Journal-American,* 8/8/1951
29. Ibid, 8/9/1951
30. Reeves, pp. 365-66
31. Ibid, p. 366
32. Oshinsky, p. 222
33. Ibid, p. 224
34. Ibid, p. 248
35. *Journal-American,* 4/10/1951
36. Anderson, *Confessions...,* pp. 238-39
37. *Journal-American,* 2/3/1952
38. Reeves, p. 455
40. Bob Thomas, p. 236
41. Klurfeld, p. 163
42. Neal Gabler, *Winchell: Gossip, Power and the Culture of Celebrity,* pp. 442-43.
43. Rovere, pp. 8-9
44. Ibid, p. 9
45. *Journal-American,* 2/2/1951

46. Ibid, 2/5/1951
47. Ibid, 4/15/1951
48. *Mirror,* 6/23/1951
49. Bob Thomas, p. 252
50. Stefan Kanfer, *A Journal of the Plague Years,* pp. 186-187
51. Ibid, p. 187
52. *Journal-American,* 8/7/1952
53. *Journal-American,* 8/12/1952
54. American Business Consultants, *Red Channels,* p. 93
55. *Journal-American,* 9/5/1952
56. Ibid, 10/19/1952
57. *Mirror,* 10/23/1952
58. Donald R. McCoy, *The Presidency of Harry S. Truman,* p. 300-1
59. Truman, pp. 532-33
60. *Mirror,* 3/31/1952
61. *Journal-American,* 3/31/1952
62. Truman, p. 533
63. McCoy, p. 301
64. Ibid, p. 302
65. Ibid, p. 302
66. Ibid, p. 303
67. Ibid. p. 303
68. Ibid. p. 303
69. Truman, p. 283; David McCullough, *Truman,* p. 904
70. Trohan, p. 293
71. Ibid, p. 283
72. Manchester, p. 686
73. *Journal-American,* 7/9/1952
74. Ibid
75. Reeves, p. 425; Rovere, p. 180
76. *Journal-American,* 7/9/1952
77. Ibid
78. *Mirror,* 7/10/1952
79. Klurfeld, p. 169
80. Bob Thomas, p. 241
81. Ibid, p. 242
82. *Mirror,* 7/10/1952
83. *Journal-American,* 7/10/1952
84. Reeves, p. 428
85. Ibid, p. 429
86. *Journal-American,* 9/2/1952
87. Ibid, 9/3/1952
88. Ibid, 9/4/1952
89. Ibid, 9/4/1952
90. Reeves, p. 445
91. *Journal-American,* 9/8/1952
92. Reeves, p. 420
93. *Journal-American,* 9/10/1952
94. Ibid
95. *Journal-American,* 10/1/1952
96. Ibid, 10/16/1952
97. Ibid, 10/24/1952
98. *Mirror,* 10/27/1952
99. *Journal-American,* 10/28/1952
100. Ibid, 11/2/1952
101. Anderson, p. 254
102. Anderson and May, p. 103
103. Oshinsky, p. 47n
104. Reeves, p. 449
105. *Journal-American,* 11/23/1952
106. Oshinsky, p. 183
107. *Journal-American,* 11/6/1952
108. *Mirror,* 12/11/1952
109. *Journal-American,* 12/17/1952
110. Harvey Matusow, *False Witness,* p. 136

6. 1953: The Alliance Cracks

1. Oshinsky, p. 31
2. Anderson, *Confessions...,* p. 241; Rovere, p. 54
3. Anderson, *Confessions...,* p. 241
4. Oshinsky, p. 32; Anderson, *Confessions...,* p. 243
5. Anderson, Confessions..., p. 246
6. *Mirror,* 1/1/1953
7. Oshinsky, p. 224
8. Ibid, p. 224
9. Anderson, *Confessions...,* pp. 258-59
10. Reeves, p. 410
11. Reeves, p. 414; Oshinsky, p. 250
12. Reeves, p. 413
13. *Journal-American,* 1/4/1953

14. Reeves, p. 459
15. *Journal-American*, 1/5/1953
16. Arthur Schlesinger, *Robert Kennedy and His Times*, p. 107
17. *Journal-American*, 1/14/1953
18. von Hoffman, p. 182
19. Howard Rushmore, "Young Mr. Cohn," *American Mercury*, February 1953
20. Rovere, p. 194
21. Ibid, p. 206
22. *Mirror*, 3/2/1953
23. William F. Buckley and L. Brent Bozell, *McCarthy and His Enemies*, p. 137
24. *Journal-American*, 3/2/1953
25. Ibid, 3/3/1953
26. Ibid
27. Ibid
28. Ibid, March 4 and 5, 1953
29. U.S. Senate, Committee on Government Operations, Permanent Subcommittee on Investigations. State Department Information Program - Voice of America, 3/3/1953, p. 394
30. Ibid, p. 398
31. *Journal-American*, 3/8/1953
32. Oshinsky, p. 276
33. *Journal-American*, 3/16/1953
34. Ibid, 3/23/1953
35. Oshinsky, p. 290
36. *Journal-America*, 3/23/1953
37. *Mirror*, 3/14/1953
38. Oshinsky, p. 289
39. *Mirror*, 3/24/1953
40. Oshinsky, p. 289
41. *Mirror*, 3/14/1953
42. Oshinsky, p. 288n; von Hoffman, pp. 169-70
43. *Journal-American*, 3/24/1953
44. Ibid, 3/25/1953
45. Ibid, 3/26/1953
46. Ibid, 3/27/1953
47. Ibid, 3/30/1953
48. Ibid, 4/1/1953
49. Ibid, 4/6/1953
50. *Mirror*, 4/2/1953
51. Navasky, p. 62
52. *Mirror*, 4/29/1953
53. Oshinsky, p. 283
54. *Journal-American*, 4/6/1953
55. Ibid, 4/7/1953
56. Ibid, 4/22/1953
57. Emmett J. Hughes, *The Ordeal of Power*, p. 92
58. *Mirror*, 3/21/1953
59. Oshinsky, p. 287
60. Ibid
61. Ibid
62. Rovere, p. 200
63. von Hoffman, p. 173
64. Oshinsky, p. 318
65. Schlesinger, p. 11
66. J.B. Matthews, "Reds in Our Churches," *American Mercury*, July 1953, p.3
67. Cohn, p. 61
68. Oshinsky, p. 319
69. Cohn, p. 61
70. Fred J. Cook, *The Nightmare Decade*, p. 431
71. Hughes, p. 96
72. Cook, p. 452
73. Cook, 7/5/1953
74. Oshinsky, p. 329
75. *Mirror*, 7/8/1953
76. Ibid, 7/9/1953
77. *Journal-American*, 7/9/1953
78. *Mirror*, 7/10/1953
79. William Wright, *Lillian Hellman: The Image, the Woman*, p. 218
80. *Journal-American*, 7/11/1953
81. Oshinsky, pp. 326-27
82. Reeves, p. 506
83. Oshinsky, pp. 325-26
84. Cohn, p. 94
85. Oshinsky p. 337
86. Ibid, p. 337
87. Ibid, p. 332

88. Reeves, 516-17
89. Oshinsky, p. 332
90. *Mirror,* 10/16/1953
91. Reeves, p. 591
92. *Journal-American,* 10/17/1953
93. Ibid, 10/23/1953
94. Oshinsky, p. 336
95. *Mirror,* 11/3/1953
96. Ibid, 11/12/1953
97. Reeves, p. 523
98. *Journal-American,* 10/24/1953
99. *Mirror,* 10/24/1953
100. Cooney, pp. 226-27
101. Ibid, p. 268
102. *Mirror,* 11/17/1953
103. Curt Gentry, *J. Edgar Hoover: The Man and the Secrets,* p. 429
104. *Mirror,* 11/18/1953
105. Reeves, p. 529; Oshinsky, pp. 348-49
106. *Mirror,* 11/25/1953
107. Reeves, p. 530; Oshinsky, p. 350
108. *Mirror,* 11/26/1953
109. Reeves, p. 531

7. 1954: Fragmentation

1. Oshinsky, p. 351; Sherman Adams, *Firsthand Report,* p. 135
2. Oshinsky, p. 358
3. Ibid, p. 358
4. Michael P. Rogin, *The Intellectuals and McCarthy,* p. 232
5. von Hoffman, p. 145
6. Anderson, *Confessions...,* 263
7. von Hoffman, p. 214
8. Anderson, Confessions..., 264
9. *Mirror,* 2/1/54
10. von Hoffman, 194; Cohn, p. 97
11. von Hoffman, p. 194
12. *Journal-American,* 1/21/1954
13. Oshinsky, p. 368; William B. Ewald, *Who Killed Joe Mc-Carthy?,* pp. 194-55
14. *Journal-American,* 2/2/1954
15. Oshinsky, p. 377; Reeves, p. 544
16. *Mirror,* 2/19/1954
17. *Journal-American,* 2/21/1954
18. Ibid, 3/3/1954
19. Ibid, 3/7/1954
20. Booton Herndon, *Praised and Damned: The Life of Fulton Lewis Jr.,* pp. 112-13
21. Ibid, p. 111
22. Kanfer, p. 232
23. William L. Shirer, *Twentieth Century Journey,* vol. 3, p. 116
24. Joseph Wershba, "Murrow and McCarthy: See It Now," *New York Times Magazine,* 3/4/1954
25. Ibid
26. Oshinsky, p. 399
27. *Journal-American,* 3/10/1954
28. Reeves, p. 562
29. "Radio Re-Runs" cassette, Edward R. Murrow *See It Now,* 3/9/1954
30. Ibid
31. Reeves, p. 569
32. *Journal-American,* 3/17/1954
33. Reeves, p. 589
34. *Journal-American,* 4/23/1954
35. Ibid, 3/10/1954
36. Ibid
37. Ibid, 3/11/1954
38. Ibid, 3/12/1954
39. Ibid, 4/18/1954
40. Reeves, p. 588
41. *Journal-American,* 5/6/1954
42. Reeves, p. 597
43. von Hoffman, pp. 148 and 184
44. Reeves, p. 589
45. *Journal-American,* 4/21/1954
46. Ibid, 4/29/1954
47. Ibid, 5/2/1954
48. *Mirror,* 5/24/1954
49. *Journal-American,* 5/3/1954
50. Oshinsky, p. 423
51. Ibid, p. 429

52. Ibid, p. 430
53. Powers, p. 322
54. Reeves, p. 610
55. Powers, p. 321
56. Gentry, p. 435; Theoharis, p. 296
57. Walter Winchell, *Walter Winchell Exclusive,* p. 265
58. *Mirror,* 3/1/1954
59. Ibid, 4/19/1954
60. Ibid, 6/7/1954
61. Reeves, p. 626
62. *Mirror,* 6/9/1954
63. *Mirror,* 6/13/1954
64. Ibid, 6/21/1954
65. Ibid, 6/24/1954
66. Rogin, p. 232
67. *Mirror,* 11/12/1954
68. Ibid, 11/22/1954
69. Oshinsky, p. 465
70. Reeves, p. 660
71. *Mirror,* 12/1/1954
72. Crosby, p. 219
73. Ibid, p. 218
74. Gabler, p. 476
75. Winchell, p. 255
76. *Journal-American,* 5/8/1954
77. Ibid, 5/10/1954
78. Ibid, 5/18/1954
79. Ibid, 5/28/1954
80. Cohn, pp. 200-3
81. Reeves, p. 629
82. Ibid, p. 621
83. *Journal-American,* 6/9/1954
84. Ibid, 6/10/1954
85. *Mirror,* 6/13/1954
86. *Journal-American,* 6/18/1954
87. Ibid, 6/19/1954
88. Charles E. Potter, *Days of Shame,* p. 285
89. *New York World-Telegram,* 7/12/1954
90. Ibid, 7/13/1954
91. Ibid, 7/14/1954
92. Ibid, 7/15/1954
93. Ibid, 7/16/1954
94. *Mirror,* 8/4/1954
95. Reeves, p. 642; Oshinsky, p. 473
96. *Journal-American,* 7/21/1954
97. *Mirror,* 7/21/1954
98. Merle Miller, *The Judges and the Judged,* p. 153
99. Ibid, p. 153
100. *Mirror,* 7/29/1954
101. Reeves, p. 692
102. Ibid, p. 649
103. Reeves, p. 647
104. Ibid, p. 647
105. Rovere, p. 227
106. Reeves, p. 648
107. *Journal-American,* 9/20/1954
108. Ibid, 9/24/1954
109. Ibid, 9/28/1954
110. Ibid, 10/15/1954
111. *Time,* 11/1/1954
112. Ibid
113. Rovere, p. 262n
114. *Journal-American,* 10/24/1954
115. Ibid, 10/29/1954
116. Ibid, 11/4/1954
117. Rovere, p. 230
118. Ibid, p. 230
119. Ibid, p. 230
120. *Journal-American,* 11/6/1954
121. *Mirror,* 11/13/1954
122. Rovere, p. 235
123. Ibid, p. 235-36
124. *Journal-American,* 11/30/1954
125. Ibid, 11/12/1954
126. Schlesinger, p. 122
127. *Journal-American,* 12/3/1954
128. *Mirror,* 12/3/1954
129. *Journal-American,* 12/4/1954
130. Ibid, 12/7/1954
131. Ibid
132. *Journal-American,* 12/9/1954
133. Ibid
134. *Mirror,* 12/10/1954
135. *Journal-American,* 12/10/1954; Lately Thomas, *When Even Angels Wept,* p. 626

135. *Mirror,* 12/12/1954

136. Oshinsky, p. 493

8. 1955-57: The Reign of Silence

1. *Journal-American,* 1/11/1955
2. Ibid, 1/8/1955
3. Ibid, 1/13/1955
4. Ibid, 1/18/1955
5. Ibid
6. Rovere, p. 238; Oshinsky, p. 496; Reeves, p. 667
7. Reeves, p. 667
8. *Journal-American,* 1/21/1955
9. *Mirror,* 1/21/1955
10. Oshinsky, p. 407; Reeves, p. 667
11. Chaney and Cieply, p. 186
12. Bolan letter to author, 1/12/1991
13. *Journal-American,* 2/13/1955
14. Ibid, 3/16/1955
15. Rovere, p. 239
16. *Journal-American,* 3/16/1955
17. Oshinsky, p. 501
18. *Journal-American,* 2/19/1955
19. Oshinsky, pp. 498-99
20. *Journal-American,* 6/22/1955
21. Oshinsky, p. 495
22. Ralph Flanders, *Senator from Vermont,* p. 238
23. Kanfer, p. 260
24. Caute, p. 534
25. Navasky, p. 85
26. Kanfer, p. 216
27. Ibid, p. 163
28. Ibid, p. 162
29. Caute, p. 524
30. Vincent Hartnett, "The Great Red Way," *American Mercury,* June 1953, p. 66
31. Ibid, p. 68
32. Ibid, p. 69
33. Ibid, p. 69
34. *Journal-American,* 7/13/1955
35. Ibid, 6/22/1955
36. Caute, p. 534
37. Ibid, p. 524
38. Ibid, p. 524
39. Ibid, p. 535
40. *Journal-American,* 9/13/1955
41. Manchester, p. 524
42. *Journal-American,* 1/1/1956
43. *Mirror,* 1/3/1956
44. Rovere, pp. 244-45
45. *Journal-American,* 1/27/1956
46. *Mirror,* 4/16/1956
47. Reeves, p. 641
48. Rovere, p. 290
49. *Journal-American,* 7/13/1956
50. *Mirror,* 7/14/1956
51. *Journal-American,* 8/6/1956
52. *Mirror,* 8/7/1956
53. Anderson, *Confessions...,* p. 271; Oshinsky, p. 503
54. Gentry, p. 437
55. Ibid, p. 427
56. *Journal-American,* 2/26/1957
57. Ibid, 4/1/1957
58. *Mirror,* 4/2/1957
59. Oshinsky, pp. 404-5
60. Rovere, 345-46
61. *Mirror,* 5/3/1957
62. Ibid
63. *Journal-American,* 5/3/1957
64. Ibid
65. Ibid
66. *Journal-American,* 5/6/1957
67. Ibid
68. *Mirror,* 5/6/1957
69. Ibid, 5/7/1957
70. Caute, p. 527
71. John Cogley, *Report on Blacklisting,* vol. 1, p. 11
72. Caute, p. 527

Epilogue: McCarthy as Redbaiter – An Inquiry

1. Cook, p. 145

2. Rovere, pp. 57-58

3. Ibid, p. 58
4. Ibid, p. 59
5. Ibid, p. 58
6. Ibid, p. 60
7. Ibid, read cover
8. Ibid, p. 2
9. Clifton Brock, *Americans for Democratic Action,* p. 152
10. Rovere, pp. 103-4
11. Ibid, pp. 10-11
12. Ibid, p. 123
13. Ibid, p. 123
14. Cohn, p. 11
15. Ibid, p. 8
16. Reeves, p. 81
17. Rovere, p. 119
18. Ibid, p. 119
19. Ibid, pp. 119-20
20. Reeves, p. 103
21. Ibid, p. 103
22. Rovere, p. 254
23. Reeves, p. 287
24. Ibid, p. 288
25. Ibid, p. 288; Anderson, *Confessions...,* p. 194
26. Oshinsky, p. 81
27. Ibid, pp. 81-82
28. Ibid, p. 82
29. Ibid, p. 82
30. Reeves, pp. 669 and 671
31. Rovere, p. 141
32. Ibid, 141n
33. Oshinsky, p. 205
34. Ibid, p. 381
35. Reeves, p. 568
36. Oshinsky, p. 401
37. Ibid, pp. 402-3
38. Navasky, p. 192
39. Ibid, p. 193
40. Reeves, p. 29
41. Oshinsky, p. 23
42. Rovere, p. 49
43. Ibid, p. 19
44. Gentry, p. 375
45. Oshinsky, p. 322

46. Reeves, pp. 507-8
47. Bayley, p. 9
48. Ibid, p. 10
49. State Department Information Program – Voice of America, 3/3/1953, p. 331
50. Oshinsky, p. 399
51. State Department... Voice of America, 3/3/1953, p. 333
52. "Radio Re-Runs," See It Now, 3/9/1954
53. State Department... Voice of America, 3/3/1954, p. 334
54. Ibid, p. 339
55. Ibid, p. 430
56. Ibid, p. 363
57. Ibid, 3/4/1953, p. 501
58. State Department Information Program – Information Centers, pp. 26-27, 30
59. Ibid, p. 25
60. Ibid, p. 27
61. Ibid, p. 27
62. Ibid, p. 27
63. Cook, p. 403
64. State Department... Information Centers, 3/24/1953, p. 37
65. Ibid, p. 37
66. Navasky, pp. 118-19
67. State Department... Information Centers, 3/24/1953, p. 37
68. Ibid, p. 38
69. State Department... Information Centers, 3/25/1953, p. 74
70. Ibid, p. 74
71. Ibid, p. 74
72. Ibid, p. 7
73. State Department... Information Centers, 3/25/1953, p. 74
74. Ibid, p. 78
75. Ibid, p. 80
76. Ibid, p. 81
77. Ibid, p. 81
78. Ibid, p. 81
79. Ibid, p. 81

80. Ibid, pp. 81-82
81. Ibid, pp. 82-83
82. Eslanda C.G. Robeson, *African Journey,* p. 47
83. State Department... Information Centers, 7/7/1953, p. 374
84. Ibid, pp. 473-74
85. Ibid, p. 475
86. Ibid, p. 475
87. Ibid, p. 476
88. Ibid, p. 478
89. Ibid, p. 479
90. Ibid, p. 479
91. Ibid. p. 477
92. Ibid, p. 481
93. Ibid, p. 481
94. Martin Duberman, *Paul Robeson,* p. 423
95. David Oshinsky to author, 12/16/91

Bibliography

Archive Material and Government Documents

Anti-Defamation League. July 1975 report on Benjamin H. Freedman.

U.S. Senate, Committee on Government Operations, Permanent Subcommittee on Investigations. State Department Information Program – Voice of America, 1953.
- Testimony of Reed Harris, March 3-4, 1953

State Department Information Program – Information Centers, 1953.
- Testimony of William Marx Mandell, March 24, 1953
- Testimony of Langston Hughes, March 25, 1953
- Testimony of Eslanda C. G. Robeson, July 7, 1953

Microfilm Collections and Audio Material

American Mercury (February and June 1953)
New York Daily Mirror (1942-1957)
New York Journal-American (1942-1957)
New York Times Magazine (March 4, 1979)
New York World-Telegram (July 12-16, 1954)
"Radio Re-Runs." Cassette with Edward R. Murrow commenting on his controversy with Senator McCarthy. Taken from March 12, 1954 *See It Now* program
Time (November 1, 1954)

Other Sources

Adams, Sherman. *Firsthand Report*. New York: Harper and Row, 1961.

American Business Consultants. *Red Channels*. New York: 1950.

Anderson, Jack and Ronald May. *McCarthy: The Man, the Senator, the "Ism"*. Boston: Beacon Press, 1954.

– and James Boyd. *Confession of a Muckraker*. New York: Random House, 1979.

Baughman, James L. *Henry R. Luce and the Rise of the American News Media*. Boston: Twayne Publishers, 1987.

Bayley, Edwin R. *Joe McCarthy and the Press*. Madison: University of Wisconsin Press, 1981.

Belfrage, Cedric. *The American Inquisition*. Indianapolis and New York: Bobbs Merrill, 1973.

Biographical Dictionary of the American Congress, 1774-1961. Washington, DC: U.S. Government Printing Office, 1961.

Brock, Clifton. *Americans for Democratic Action*. Washington, DC: Public Affairs Press, 1962.

Buckley, William F. and L. Brent Bozell. *McCarthy and His Enemies*. Chicago: Regnery, 1954.

Carlson, John Roy. *The Plotters*. New York: E. F. Dutton, 1946.

Cassini, Igor with Jeanne Molli. *I'd Do It All Over Again*. New York: Putnam, 1977.

Caute, David. *The Great Fear: The Anti-Communist Purge Under Truman and Eisenhower*. New York: Simon and Schuster, 1978.

Chambers, Whittaker. *Witness*. New York: Random House, 1952.

Chaney, Lindsay and Michael Cieply. *The Hearsts: Family and Empire - The Later Years*. New York: Simon and Schuster, 1981.

Cogley, John. *Report On Blacklisting*, 2 vols. New York: Fund for the Republic, 1956.

Cook, Fred J. *The Nightmare Decade*. New York: Random House, 1971.

Cooney, John. *The American Pope: The Life and Times of Francis Cardinal Spellman*. New York: New York Times Books, 1984.

Crosby, Donald F. *God, Church, and the Flag: Senator Joseph R. McCarthy and the Catholic Church,* 1950-57. Chapel Hill: University of North Carolina Press, 1978.

Davies, Joseph E. *Mission to Moscow*. New York: Pocket Books, 1943.

Decter, Moshe and James Rorty. *McCarthy and the Communists*. Boston: Beacon Press, 1954.

De Toledano, Ralph and Victor Lasky. *Seeds of Treason*. New York: Funk and Wagnalls, 1950.

Duberman, Martin B. *Paul Robeson*. New York: Knopf, 1988.

Emanuel, James E. *Langston Hughes*. New Haven: Twayne Publishers,

1967.

Ewald, William Bragg Jr. *Who Killed Joe McCarthy?* New York: Simon and Schuster, 1984.

FACTS ON FILE. New York: Facts on File, Inc., 1948-1957.

Field, Frederick V. *From Right to Left.* Westport, CT: Lawrence Hill and Co., 1983.

Fried, Richard M. *Nightmare in Red.* New York and Oxford: Oxford University Press, 1990.

Gabler, Neal. *Winchell: Gossip, Power and the Culture of Celebrity.* New York: Alfred A. Knopf, 1994.

Gelb, Arthur and Barbara. *O'Neill.* New York: Harper and Row, 1973.

Gentry, Curt. *J. Edgar Hoover: The Man and the Secrets.* New York: Norton, 1991.

Gill, Brendan. *Here at the New Yorker.* New York: Berkeley Medallion Books, 1975.

Goodman, Walter. *The Committee: The Extraordinary Career of the House Committee on Un-American Activities.* New York: Farrar, Straus, and Giroux, 1964.

Goulden, Joseph. *The Good Years.* New York: Atheneum, 1975.

Griffith, Robert. *The Politics of Fear: Joseph R. McCarthy and the Senate.* Amherst: University of Massachusetts Press, 1987.

Hartnett, Vincent, "The Great Red Way," *American Mercury,* June 1953.

Heidenheimer, Arnold, "Case History of a Smear," *The New Republic,* 12/25/1950.

Herndon, Booton. *Praised and Damned: The Story of Fulton Lewis Jr..* New York: Duell, Sloane, and Pierce, 1954.

Hughes, Emmett J. *The Ordeal of Power.* New York: Atheneum, 1963.

Israel, Lee. *Kilgallen.* New York: Dell, 1979.

Kanfer, Stefan. *A Journal of the Plague Years.* New York: Atheneum, 1973.

Keeley, Joseph. *The China Lobby Man.* New Rochelle, NY: Arlington House, 1969.

Kempton, Murray. *America Comes of Middle Age.* Boston and Toronto: Little Brown, 1965.

Klurfeld, Herman. *Winchell: His Life and Times.* New York: Praeger, 1976.

Kosi-Horvath, Joszef. *Cardinal Mindszenty: Confessor and Martyr of Our Time.* Chulmleigh, England: Augustine Publishing Co., 1979.

Kurnitz, Stanley J. and Howard Haycraft (ed.). *Twentieth Century Authors.* New York: H. W. Wilson Co., 1973.

Lait, Jack and Lee Mortimer. *USA Confidential.* New York: Crown Publishers, 1952.

Lottman, Herbert R. *The Purge: The Purification of French Collaborators After World War II.* New York: William Morrow, 1986.

McCarthy, Joseph R. *McCarthyism: The Fight for America.* New York: Devin Adair, 1952.

McCoy, Donald R. *The Presidency of Harry S. Truman.* Lawrence, KS: University of Kansas Press, 1984.

McCullough, David. *Truman.* New York: Simon and Schuster, 1992.

Manchester, William. *American Caesar: Douglas MacArthur 1880-1964.* Boston and Toronto: Little Brown, 1978.

Martin, Ralph. *Cissy.* New York: Simon and Schuster, 1979.

Matthews, J. B. Matthews, "Reds in Our Churches," *American Mercury,* July 1953.

Matusow, Harvey. *False Witness.* New York: Cameron and Kahn, 1955.

Miller, Merle. *The Judges and the Judged.* Garden City, NY: Doubleday, 1952.

Navasky, Victor. *Naming Names.* New York: Viking, 1980.

Nixon, Richard M. *Six Crises.* Garden City, NY: Doubleday, 1952.

O'Brien, Michael. *McCarthy and McCarthyism in Wisconsin.* Columbia, MO: University of Missouri Press, 1980.

Oshinsky, David M. *A Conspiracy So Immense: The World of Joe McCarthy.* New York and London: MacMillan, 1983.

Pilat, Oliver. *Pegler: Angry Man of the Press.* Boston: Beacon Press, 1963.
- *Drew Pearson.* New York: Pocket Books, 1973.

Potter, Charles E. *Days of Shame.* New York: Coward McCann, 1965.

Powers, Richard Gid. *Secrecy and Power: The Life of J. Edgar Hoover.* New York and London: MacMillan, 1987.

Reeves, Thomas C. *The Life and Times of Joe McCarthy.* Briarcliff Manor, NY: Stein and Day, 1982.

Robeson, Eslanda C. G. *African Journey.* New York: John Day Co., 1945.

Rogin, Michael. *The Intellectuals and McCarthy.* Cambridge, MA: MIT Press, 1967.

Rovere, Richard. *Senator Joe McCarthy.* New York: Meridien Books, 1960.

Rushmore, Howard, "Young Mr. Cohn," *American Mercury,* February 1953.

Schine, G. David. *Definition of Communism.* New York and Los Angeles: G. David Schine, 1952.

Schlesinger, Arthur. *Robert Kennedy and His Times.* New York: Ballantine, 1979.

Shirer, William L. *Twentieth Century Journey,* vol. 3. Boston and Toronto:

Little Brown, 1990.

Summers, Anthony. *Official and Confidential: The Secret Life of J. Edgar Hoover.* New York: Putnam, 1993.

Swanberg, W. A. *Citizen Hearst.* New York: Scribner's, 1961.

Theoharis, Athan. *The Boss: J. Edgar Hoover and the Great American Inquisition.* Philadelphia: Temple University Press, 1988.

Thomas, Bob. *Winchell.* New York: Doubleday, 1971.

Thomas, Lately. *When Even Angels Wept: The Senator Joseph McCarthy Affair - A Story Without a Hero.* New York: Morrow, 1973.

Trohan, Walter. *Political Animals.* Garden City, NY: Doubleday, 1975.

Truman, Margaret. *Harry S. Truman.* New York: Morrow, 1973.

Vecsey, Joseph. *Mindszenty the Man.* St. Louis: Cardinal Mindszenty Foundation, 1972.

von Hoffman, Nicholas. *Citizen Cohn.* New York: Doubleday, 1988.

Watkins, Arthur V. *Enough Rope.* Englewood Cliffs, NJ: Prentice-Hall, 1979.

Wechsler, James. *Reflections of a Middle-Aged Editor.* New York: Random House, 1960.

Weinstein, Allen. *Perjury: The Hiss-Chambers Case.* New York: Knopf, 1978.

Wershba, Joseph, "Murrow and McCarthy: See It Now," *New York Times Magazine,* 3/4/1979.

Winchell, Walter. *Walter Winchell Exclusive.* Englewood Cliffs, NJ: Prentice-Hall, 1975.

Woltman, Frederick, "The McCarthy Balance Sheet," *New York World-Telegram,* July 12-16, 1954.

Wright, William. *Lillian Hellman: The Image, The Woman.* New York: Simon and Schuster, 1986.

INDEX

About the Author

Jim Tuck is a freelance writer and syndicated columnist who has been active mainly, though by no means exclusively, in the fields of historical nonfiction and travel. Among his publications are a regional analysis of Mexico's 1926-29 Cristero Rebellion and a biography of Karl Radek, leading defendant of the 1937 Stalin Purge Trial. His column of opinion, "Insight Straight," is syndicated by Continental News Service in San Diego. Another column, "Bookbrief Mexico," appears bimonthly in *Travelmex* magazine. Between 1970-83 Tuck was affiliated with the Fodor Guides, as Regional Editor in Mexico and Area Editor for Romania. His freelance travel articles have appeared in such leading journals as the *Los Angeles Times, Newsday,* and *Toronto Star,* covering destinations ranging from Morocco to China. Tuck's credit list includes over 725 published articles, book reviews and essays. As contributor to AMERICAN NATIONAL BIOGRAPHY, he prepared the sections on Benjamin De Casseres and Pancho Villa. Politically active, Tuck founded and served three terms as president of the only overseas chapter of Americans for Democratic Action. He has twice been a delegate to the ADA national convention. Tuck and his wife, the former Maria Ruiz, live in Guadalajara, Mexico. This is his fifth book.